Landscape and Urban Design for Health and Well-Being

In this book Gayle Souter-Brown explores the social, economic and environmental benefits of developing green space for health and well-being. She examines the evidence behind the positive effects of designed landscapes, and explains effective methods and approaches which can be put into practice by those seeking to reduce costs and add value through outdoor spaces.

Using principles from sensory, therapeutic and healing gardens, Souter-Brown focuses on landscape's ability to affect health, education and economic outcomes. Already valued within healthcare environments, these design guidelines for public and private spaces extend the benefits throughout our towns and cities.

Covering design from school grounds to public parks, from public housing to gardens for stressed executives, this richly illustrated text builds the case to justify inclusion of a designed outdoor area in project budgets. With case studies from the USA, the UK, Africa, Asia, Australasia and Europe, it is an international, inspirational and valuable tool for those interested in landscapes that provide real benefits to their users.

Gayle Souter-Brown is founder and director of Greenstone Design UK Ltd, saluto-genic landscape and urban design consultants. Her research interests in design for health and well-being follow years working with disabled adults and children. With twenty-five years of international experience she lectures, writes and designs from the UK and New Zealand.

Presenting green space as a human lifeline, this is an excellent and accessible read for the practitioner and students alike. Concepts of architecture, design, sustainability and well-being are blended with whole of life costing approaches to make the case for a supportive urban environment in which individuals, families, communities and business can thrive.

– *Teena Hale Pennington, CEO New Zealand Institute of Architects (NZIA)*

Landscape and Urban Design for Health and Well-Being

Using healing, sensory and therapeutic gardens

Gayle Souter-Brown

Routledge
Taylor & Francis Group

LONDON AND NEW YORK

First published 2015
by Routledge
2 Park Square, Milton Park, Abingdon, Oxon OX14 4RN

Simultaneously published in the USA and Canada
by Routledge
711 Third Avenue, New York, NY 10017

Routledge is an imprint of the Taylor & Francis Group, an informa business

British Library Cataloguing in Publication Data
A catalogue record for this book is available from the British Library

Library of Congress Cataloging in Publication Data
Souter-Brown, Gayle.
  Landscape and urban design for health and well-being : using healing, sensory, therapeutic gardens / Gayle Souter-Brown.
    pages cm
  Includes bibliographical references and index.
  1. Gardens—Philosophy. 2. Gardening—Therapeutic use. 3. Landscapes—Psychological aspects. 4. Nature—Psychological aspects. 5. Landscape design. I. Title.
  SB454.3.P45S68 2014
  615.8'515—dc23   2014000647

ISBN: 978-0-415-84351-5 (hbk)
ISBN: 978-0-415-84352-2 (pbk)
ISBN: 978-1-315-76294-4 (ebk)

Typeset in Frutiger
by Keystroke, Station Road, Codsall, Wolverhampton

To the children of Kimi Ora School and to Jane and Airini who, 45 years ago, first opened my eyes to the concept and reality of disability, the challenges and opportunities of living outside the statistical norm. And to my grandparents, who showed me how to garden with grace and humour.

Contents

Illustrations

Figures

Table

Foreword

What makes people healthy? Kaplan and Kaplan's attention restoration theory (ART), as explained in their book *The Experience of Nature: A Psychological Perspective*, describes how people concentrate better after spending time in natural environments, because watching a beautiful sunset or the nesting of birds in a tree does not demand the same level of attention that filtering a multitude of competing stimuli on a busy city street does. With recent rapid urbanisation, millions of people spend most days in, on and around city streets. Our functional ability to concentrate is just one measure of our health, but it has important implications socially and economically. If it is possible for design environments to facilitate and improve concentration, is it possible to improve other sensory and cognitive functions?

The design of healing healthcare environments has recently received increasing attention, as our knowledge of the links between the mind and the body are more widely understood. Landscape and urban design for health and well-being is of critical importance not only because healthcare systems around the world are under pressure, but also because of the broad social, economic and environmental factors at play. If the link between environment and health is evident, there is a direct implication on the focus of urban planning, health and education interventions where the population is unhealthy, dysfunctional and unproductive. How and where we live, work, play and go to school determines in large part our longevity, productivity and quality of life. Can design specifically for health and well-being be used to stimulate positive social change in and around our cities? The answer is yes, and the author of this comprehensive text explains how.

Globally a significant proportion of people live in cities today, and inevitably, urban living affects population health. Health is critical to our ability to function within society. Increasing rates of urbanisation coupled with financial and environmental challenges requires us to look for innovative solutions. It is therefore important to understand how we can adapt to this era of chronic "lifestyle" diseases. Using principles from sensory, therapeutic and healing gardens, the author focuses on landscape's ability to affect health, education and economic outcomes. Already valued within healthcare environments, these design guidelines for public and private spaces extend the benefits throughout our towns and cities. To start off, there are various perspectives on what constitutes health and its relation with landscape and green space. In society, as in building codes, disability as a physical condition is frequently afforded more attention than mental illness. The 1999 World Health

Organization definition of mental health as 'a state of well-being in which the individual realises his or her own abilities, copes with the normal stresses of life, works productively and fruitfully and makes a contribution to his or her community' does not mention illness. This positive state relies in large part on our response to the urban environment.

Research within the emerging fields of environmental and geographical psychology adds weight to the body of evidence from medical science. Internationally respected authorities such as the World Health Organization, universities and US and British medical associations suggest that a well-designed built environment with green space can positively shape the social, psychological, and behavioural patterns of society, leading to improved health and well-being.

The growing prevalence of non-communicable diseases (NCDs), or "lifestyle" diseases, is highly related to the quality of infrastructure and the design of the built environment. Suggestions about how we can reduce NCDs such as obesity are one of the primary challenges facing the designer and planner. Ageing populations and urban growth are two further huge challenges to which design can apply itself. This book shows why and how we must focus on the innovative design and planning of green, sustainable and healthy urban planning around the world. The author challenges the reader to confirm it is the task of the designer and planner to reconsider the value of landscape and health with a knowledge-driven approach to salutogenic design.

Landscape and urban design for health and well-being uses knowledge of the efficacy of healing, sensory and therapeutic garden design to reduce stress, treat depression and facilitate an active, healthy lifestyle. Urban farming, community gardens and edible sensory gardens combine to facilitate urban lifestyles that treat obesity and reduce the risk of coronary artery disease, stroke, dementias and depression.

The quality of the built environment can promote health and well-being by exposing our brain to the right balance of stimuli in a way that creates positive emotions and experiences. The author provides clear guidelines as to how to design to facilitate such responses. The design quality of the built environment is shown to be critical to our ability to manage stress. Cities with high-quality green infrastructure reflect the image and vision of governments to create a healthy society.

The aesthetic value of our surroundings communicates the values of our society; beautiful places are not only stimulating, but they have also been proven to be sources of enjoyment that make us feel less anxious and stressed. They also attract investment. A well-designed built environment can positively shape the social, psychological and behavioural patterns of our society. If we embrace nature within the built environment, for example, or fill our workplaces with greenery and access to plants, flowers and sunlight, it is possible to optimise brain performance and restore our energies.

The approach of salutogenic architecture promotes a healthy lifestyle by creating a built environment that focuses on wellness factors that promote health, thereby contributing to the realisation of a healthy society though well-integrated nature and green space.

The world needs a new paradigm and the creation of a healthy global society is a vision we should all embrace by establishing closer connections to nature and through living with nature. This book shows how, and provides cost–benefit analyses to demonstrate the economic case for enhanced green space. Exchanging knowledge to influence government policy, change commercial incentives and encourage positive changes in people's lifestyles through the design of the built environment is the path to a new future. Through an interdisciplinary approach, architects, landscape planners, designers, engineers, public health scientists, psychologists and economists could do more to alleviate the human condition by creating stimulating, enjoyable and sustainable environments that enhance the quality of health and well-being for all.

As more scientific research demonstrates the links between emotional well-being and good physical health, so it becomes even more apparent that our physical environment when endowed with high-quality green space has tremendous potential to promote positive emotions. With positive emotions comes a reduction in "lifestyle diseases" and hence improved physical health.

Gardens with therapeutic qualities have been used for decades in healthcare design. However, we need good-quality gardens and green space to restore and rehabilitate our mind everywhere that people live, work and play. Gardens and green spaces are an integral part of a salutogenic approach to the design of the built environment and infrastructure. While significant progress has been made in understanding the value of green space and access to nature, there are still inadequacies when it comes to implementation and understanding the therapeutic impact that gardens have on our life. One of the most pressing subjects is the rehabilitation of our existing cites and built environments into eco-cities that can integrate green spaces and gardens to support the creation of a healthier society.

The author explains in this very extensive book many aspects of landscape and urban design in relation to health and well-being, while she argues that landscape design for health and well-being is a new concept for many people. Designers may need to be able to educate the client and actively work with them to develop the design brief. Research-based design requires examination of what people have done before, the purpose and the outcome.

The International Academy for Design and Health acknowledges and applauds the excellent work of Gayle Souter-Brown in the development of this book and considers it to be one of the most valuable contributions to the dissemination of knowledge on nature and health. Architects, developers, medical practitioners and educators will find value in how access to nature could improve our health and well-being. I strongly recommend this very enjoyable book to anyone who would like to find out about this important topic.

Stockholm, June 2014
Professor Alan Dilani, PhD
International Academy for Design and Health

Acknowledgements

A book like this is not possible without a spirit of cooperation and collaboration, of sharing and caring, for each other and our planet. In this spirit I give thanks to the support of my wonderful family. Theo, Katia and Adelaide, I would not have done it without you. While researching and writing I have appreciated the wisdom and experience so freely shared by many learned individuals over coffee and via email. Thank you. With thanks also to Louise Fox, my editor at Routledge; to my editorial assistant Katia, thanks for your inspiration but remembering any mistakes are mine alone; to Finn Jackson for the use of your home; to my extended family and friends, the Shere Gang and Mo Coshall for your support and encouragement; particularly to Katy Bott and Bev McAlpine in the UK, Alice Leake in Australia, and the rest of the Greenstone Design team who so ably picked up the slack during the year I have been writing; to Jenny Brown for photos of New York and Boston; Steph Gartrell for software support; staff and management at Sprott House, NZ; staff and management at Norwood, UK; the lovely people at the Autistic Society of South Africa, the National Autistic Society of Cymru (Wales), and the Epilepsy Society; the staff and students at Mary Rose School in Portsmouth; Simon Read at Sowing Success; Sue Dutton and Dr Jan Golembiewski in Sydney; Dr Emma Dunning and Olivier Locoua in Wellington; Dr Pekka Lahdenne in Helsinki; Huiyi Liu in Guangzhou for research, photos and art work; Michael Follett and Tim Gill in London, Brendan Casey in Ireland; Mario Pessegueiro and Teresa Martins in Portugal; Frode Svane in Oslo; Emmanuelle Soubeyran in Grenoble; Marcus Schmidt in Berlin; Dr Kerby Alvy, Professor Tim Beatley, Nancy Evans, Annie Kirk and Naomi Sachs in the USA; Anna Kumacheva and George Doelschin in Russia; and to my fellow author and number one supporter Chris Brown, for believing I would manage to write 100,000 words in twelve months while running two design practices and projects in three different time zones.

Introduction

Landscape and urban design for health and well-being – using healing, sensory and therapeutic gardens

Internationally, populations are ageing, more people are living with disability and there is less money to support them. At the same time environments are being degraded. Fortunately there is a recently rediscovered body of evidence that supports the view that nature generally, and everyday living environments in particular, can have a profound effect on health and well-being. Connecting with nature can restore cognitive attention (Kaplan and Kaplan, 1995, 2002), improve blood pressure and self-esteem (Pretty et al., 2005), support pro-environmental behaviours (Hartig et al., 2001) decrease symptoms of attention deficit disorder (Kuo and Taylor, 2004) and improve community resilience (Moore et al., 2006). Contact with nature is an effective 'upstream health promotion' tool for whole populations. That is, it is useful in prevention of mental health conditions (Maller et al., 2006). Studies have shown that exposure to natural environments enhances our ability to recover from stress, illness and injury, and provides a wide range of social, psychological and physiological benefits (Ulrich, 1984; Kofler, 2010). Across our towns and cities, a connection with nature has been found to be a vital, albeit often unconscious, part of being human. Healing, sensory and therapeutic gardens offer an urban setting to connect.

This text is intentionally accessible. Designed for students and practitioners of design, health and education, it is not a dry academic discourse but rather reflects evidence-based international design experience. It is about using green space to develop livable cities that address the triple bottom line. As an environmental advocate I make no apology for offering solutions that help the planet as they help the people. As a student of economics I understand the need for everything that we provide today within the public realm to be cost-effective and cost-efficient.

Landscape and Urban Design For Health and Well-Being is written to meet the needs of people interested in making a difference socially, economically and environmentally. For the past 100 years or so, architecture has taken the lead role across urban planning and the built environment. The landscape or green component of a development scheme has been seen as an add-on, an additional 'nice-to-have', frequently costed out when there is insufficient money left over at the end of the project. The following chapters show that we need well-designed green space costed in at the project's inception if we are to achieve livable, healthy cities.

E. O. Wilson describes in his seminal book *Biophilia* (1984) our innate love of living things. He coined the term biophilia to describe the connections that human beings subconsciously seek. Trees, small plants, large animals, insects and the weather are all part of that nature connection. I believe it is the fact that we are hardwired to respond that determines the measureable neurological and physiological effects of natural environments. If we lose our connections or do not forge early links with the natural world it is like losing a good friend. We become stressed and depressed and look for ways to replace our loss, often without being aware of our deficit or our actions (Pretty et al., 2005).

The World Health Organization's (WHO) 2010 Global Burden of Disease (GBD) study (Ferrari et al., 2013) reported that depression is now the second largest cause of disability worldwide and a major contributor to suicide and ischemic heart disease. Disease and disability is considered a 'burden' because of the profound social and financial impact on the individual, their community, and the wider economy. The WHO's findings 'reinforce the importance of treating depressive disorders as a public-health priority and of implementing cost-effective interventions to reduce their ubiquitous burden' (Ferrari et al., 2013). The findings, when considered in conjunction with previous research outcomes, are fundamental in establishing the need for green space across our urban centres. The WHO is the international body tasked with monitoring the human health situation globally and assessing health trends. Within the organisation there is growing recognition that the ecological health of our planet is deteriorating. We have cleared forests for farming and built over parks and playgrounds. The United Nations, government leaders, practitioners and academics have spoken of the need to enhance and protect our environment. Now that major international organisations have noted linkages between health and environment, it is time to act.

While almost any green space can provide an association with natural elements, gardens created using evidence-based principles are recognised as being most effective. When guided by a knowledgeable designer and appropriately implemented, gardens can promote stress reduction and enhance health outcomes. This book explores the history of gardens to explain why environmental design is perhaps the most cost-effective tool in the fight against stress and depression. Testimony is provided citing international case studies to highlight user groups most likely to benefit from nature-based interventions. Guidelines are provided for how to design gardens to meet our biophilic need. We conclude with funding options for using landscape and urban design to address the world's second largest cause of disability. As an evidence-based tool for designers from a broad range of disciplines, the book will also be of interest to those interested in self-help, to parents of disabled children, and to stressed execs who need to know why and how to develop green space at home. *Landscape and Urban Design for Health and Well-Being* brings together current knowledge on the topic to provide such a resource.

The text is as much about health promotion as it is about treatment. It is about cost-effective landscape and urban design interventions, broken down to the scale of gardens. When we look at the built environment's relationship with nature, at the complex issues around human health and well-being, we see the need for a new way to look at gardens. Although many schemes we work on are large, master planning exercises, all are made up of gardens. This is an important point to remember. Our postgraduate intern from Guangzhou, China, told me of vast landscape development schemes she had worked on. She wanted to work with us to understand how to take those vast spaces and make them feel personal, somewhere you could feel 'at home' amongst 400 million others. She needed to create gardens, each with an individual feel and character. A garden is hence how we describe a landscape that has been formed to frame our urban existence.

When we think in terms of creating 'gardens' we are less inclined to over-emphasise hard landscapes and we re-emphasise the soft. Hard landscapes are experienced as fast moving, assertive spaces. To vulnerable people they can feel aggressive. How we *feel* in a space is critical to our sense of well-being. Soft landscapes are slower and provide the opportunity to reconnect, to literally stop and smell the roses. Socially and environmentally soft landscape interventions provide a win/win situation. Soft landscapes can restore biodiversity, rebuild wildlife corridors and absorb heat; leaves transpire to locally cool the air, provide natural shade, absorb sound and filter water and airborne pollutants. It is where soft and hard landscapes are out of balance that we most need healing gardens. Each space must work at a human scale. Gardens offer positive distraction from the 'white noise' of modern life, from the information overload that comes from digital media, from physical pain and mental suffering. Gardens can be designed to calm or to stimulate, depending on planting and materials.

At the 9th World Design and Health Congress I met with practitioners, academics and policy makers to discuss how best to deal with the increasing global burden of disease. Due to ageing populations, rising costs and diminishing budgets the current healthcare model is financially unsustainable. The Congress agreed that the best, most cost-effective, cost-efficient treatment is prevention. Without ecological health there can be no human health and well-being. For adults and children, regardless of culture, climate zone or socio-economic status, the most cost-effective health prevention comes through environmental design.[1]

Held in Brisbane, Australia in July 2013, the Congress featured speakers from around the world. I was fortunate to present alongside architects, engineers, finan-ciers, developers and clinicians. We spoke about the need to adapt environments for climate change as the biggest global health challenge today (*Lancet*, 2009), for the growing burden of mental illness, and to counter lifestyle-related health conditions. People spoke passionately of the role that environment plays in health, of taking a preventative approach to healthcare. They spoke of the need for people to be able to access nature as an integral ingredient in the recipe for longevity and quality of life. They also spoke of the financial constraints brought about by increasingly technological healthcare that means governments and private healthcare providers cannot continue to fund the development of hospitals as they have done. While we will always need traditional hospital-based healthcare and treatment models for certain conditions, for non-communicable diseases (NCDs) such as obesity, depression, cardiovascular disease (stroke, heart attacks), cancers, type 2 diabetes and chronic respiratory disease it is much more cost effective to prevent than to treat them.

Dr Sally Fawker told delegates of the need for partnerships in care – novel partnerships. The hard urban form has damaged our health, affected our relationship with nature and had far-reaching impacts throughout society. Education, crime rates, and ultimately economies have been affected. We now need to soften that urban form so that it becomes a supportive environment. Landscape professionals advising and working with healthcare professionals offer the novel partnerships that Dr Fawker seeks. The natural environment in general and the positive role gardens in particular can play, have been undervalued for too long.

Now is the time for landscape to be revalued as the integral part of our urban environment that it is.

> Gardens, as a microcosm of the natural landscape, have an innate ability to bring people together, to encourage healthy, active lifestyles. In the Northern Territories of Australia 5% of the children have gangrene. That is a shocking indictment on their living environment. Through gardens we bring the bio-physical and psycho-social universal health needs of the human species together.
>
> (Golembiewski, 2013)

Mental health has many cultural taboos and superstitions surrounding its causes and effects. A largely invisible disability, mental health disorder often goes unmentioned as it is frequently associated with feelings of shame (Norris, 2013). Without good mental and physical health it is difficult to access education, housing and employment. Everyday tasks become monumental as the disability weighs heavily upon the individual and their family. Society suffers as the individual suffers. It is important to provide cost-effective early intervention and prevention strategies, as stress and depression are strong determinants of physical health. They not only influence ischemic heart disease but also obesity, type 2 diabetes, cancers, and a host of other lifestyle-related conditions such as sexually transmitted disease, rickets, binge drinking, domestic violence and drug abuse.

In 2007 a group convened by the New York Academy of Medicine met to consider what to do about the growing burden of disease. They, like so many others, concluded that urban and landscape design has a significant role to play in public health. They agreed that spaces should be accessible, especially to vulnerable populations. Public green space should respond to needs at the neighbourhood level and create opportunities for social engagement, economic empowerment, nature access and stewardship. Spaces must be community-driven, ecologically sustainable, and answer the very human impulse to seek and create beauty in our everyday surroundings. They are a primary foundation for a resilient community (Campbell and Wiesen, 2011). Subsequent chapters explore these ideas, the broad effects on society, and our need to adapt the public realm for an ageing population from a landscape and urban design viewpoint.

Background

Around the world there is growing concern that human well-being is deteriorating. Advances in medical science have almost eliminated many communicable diseases, that is conditions caused by bacteria and viruses such as polio, tetanus and typhoid. Meanwhile, preventable non-communicable diseases, disabling conditions caused by inactive and self-abusive lifestyles, are increasing. The WHO is concerned that if current trends continue no nation will be able to afford healthcare for its people. Already the NHS, the UK's national health provider, is struggling to keep pace. In the USA the situation is similarly dire.

A recent study found that

> the environment influences our health in many ways – through exposures to physical, chemical and biological risk factors, and through related changes in our behaviour in response to those factors. To answer the question 'how much disease could be prevented through better management of our environment' . . . scientific evidence was summarized and more than 100 experts . . . consulted for their estimates of how much environmental risk factors contribute to the disease burden . . . The evidence shows that environmental risk factors play a role in more than 80% of the diseases regularly reported by the W.H.O. Globally, nearly one quarter of all deaths and of the total disease burden can be attributed to the environment. In children, however, environmental risk factors can account for more than one-third of the disease burden.
>
> (Prüss-Üstün and Corvalán, 2006)

These findings have important policy implications, because the environmental risk factors can be largely modified by established, cost-effective interventions. The interventions promote equity by benefiting everyone in the society, while addressing the needs of those most at risk.

Landscape and Urban Design for Health and Well-Being aims to bridge the divide between public health and landscape. Health professionals, like educators, are trained to base decisions on empirical evidence. This is as it should be. However, intuition and acceptance of the importance of biophilia have their place too. Adding that to traditional knowledge we now have modern science. There is a need for further research but we have sufficient peer reviewed data to act. The data is compelling. It is gathered here to encourage those engaged in urban planning and design related disciplines to regulate for and create spaces that ease the burden of disease, spaces that not only look good and work well but help build sustainable, healthy communities, cost effectively.

To effectively take public health into account in spatial planning requires an acknowledgment of nature's restorative and healing powers. Being outdoors and actively gardening heightens feelings of tranquility, spirituality and peace (Kaplan and Kaplan, 1995; 2002). With this in mind, healing, sensory and therapeutic gardens, urban forests and soft landscape treatments are increasingly being reintroduced across towns and cities as an important support tool.

In the face of ageing, and in some places declining populations, rising incidences of stress and NCDs, we need to look carefully at historic and existing practices, and then change what we can. We need to look at the role landscape can play. The NCDs listed here are known as lifestyle-related diseases. They are preventable illnesses with a strong relationship to the environment in which the person lives, works, plays or goes to school (WHO, *Global Status Report on Noncommunicable Diseases*, 2011). So the question becomes, how do we engage communities to change lifestyles? What are the benefits that may accrue to the community if we do? Can we offer a cost-effective alternative to traditional healthcare treatment models for certain conditions? By using healing, sensory and therapeutic gardens, by re-engaging people with nature, the evidence shows we can effect those changes, save money and ultimately lives.

> As the Global Strategy for the Prevention and Control of Noncommunicable Diseases indicates, NCDs can best be addressed by a combination of primary prevention interventions targeting whole populations, by measures that target high-risk individuals and by improved access to essential health-care interventions for people with NCDs.
>
> (WHO, 2000)

I have been fortunate to work internationally across health, education, housing, disabled children in schools and with their families at home, with disadvantaged youth, migrants, extended and blended families in social housing, with socially isolated older people, with executives wanting to de-stress their lives, with dementia residents in care homes, with indigenous communities, and with people young and old living with disability. Interestingly, we observe a common theme running through each of our client groups. Although each has need of some formal health provision, they also need something quite simple. All of them had disconnected from nature to a greater or lesser degree and all lived, worked, played or went to school in non-supportive environments. Their lifestyles became, or remained, sedentary and their health problems mounted as stress levels rose. From the outset it was obvious that to achieve best value socially, financially and ethically for the client, while respecting and enhancing the the natural environment, a collaborative approach would work best. Using integrated systems thinking, and often working across multi-disciplinary teams including care workers, occupational therapists, social workers, doctors and teachers, we approach design challenges from a joined-up thinking perspective.

Health happens not only at the doctor's office or in the hospital.

Given the accumulated research, we have an opportunity to apply that knowledge. Some would say we have a responsibility. Health as a state of being happens when where we live, work, play and go to school is healthy. The challenge now is to take the emphasis out, to encompass the public realm. Others authors have ably demonstrated the benefits of therapeutic landscapes within health settings (Cooper Marcus and Sachs, 2013), so we can now focus more widely, on the application of gardens for their ability to create livable cities and healthy, sustainable communities.

Divided into four parts, this text looks at the questions of where today's renewed interest in healing gardens has come from, why we need them, how they are relevant today and what we can expect from them. The origins of modern healing, sensory and therapeutic garden design, the issues and challenges of modern society such gardens can address – active ageing, mental and physical ill health, disability due to sensory impairment – why we need to turn to nature and an asset-based healthcare system, are laid out across the following chapters.

Definitions and scope

There is growing recognition that a salutogenic design approach, that is design for health and well-being, offers a cost-effective means to keep indigenous, at-risk and non-indigenous populations healthy and independent throughout life (WHO, 2011). Forward-thinking social scientists and medical practitioners are looking to the past to explore the future potential of landscape. Since the turn of the twenty-first century sensory gardens have been designed to stimulate and soothe the senses of people on the autistic spectrum, as well as those living with post-traumatic stress disorders, dementia, stroke and spinal injuries. Over a similar time span, therapeutic gardens have improved the healing times of surgical patients and reduced their need for pain relief. Refugee children have been eased into their new homes through social and therapeutic horticulture programmes.

The commonly held view is that there are two main types of green space with healing properties: healing and sensory gardens, which offer passive health benefits; and therapeutic gardens, which afford and promote active healing. Traditionally, both types have been located within a private or controlled setting.

Healing gardens heal communities. They not only enhance local aesthetics and biodiversity and improve the mood of the people, but they help build sustainable communities. By boosting tourism and in-bound investment, increasing property values and livability ratings, healing gardens offer benefits to the local economy as well as the local population. They are gardens specifically designed to enhance mental and physical health as places to meditate, to sit quietly and chat with friends or to just relax and get away from it all. Using a careful combination of plantings and materials, they are calming and peaceful garden settings where young and old can escape and emotionally revitalise. Healing, soft landscape treatments provide a necessary balance to the harshness of the modern hard landscape and built environment. By spending time in a healing garden visitors are healed in a passive way, through sensing nature. However, healing gardens are not just for when you have become ill; they are vital in preventing illness through encouraging and enabling an active, healthy lifestyle, and in maintaining and improving a sense of health and well-being.

Many studies have shown the link between health and outdoor nature experiences. Dr William Bird, strategic health advisor to Natural England, emphasises those potential benefits; but perhaps more importantly, the *known harm, particularly to children, that comes from a deficiency of outdoor experience*. Health, design and education professionals around the world agree that children, and adults, need outdoor exercise in stimulating, green environments. What I believe is missing from previous studies is an emphasis on the supportive qualities of the environment.

Whether alone, with random strangers, or close friends, moving in a beautiful natural environment is good for us. People may not recognise the degree their lives are compromised by a lack of quality nature experience until it is provided. Royalty and captains of industry have, for centuries, enjoyed beautiful gardens and woodland as part of their prescription for success. Bird says: 'Prescriptions for nature experiences may sound a far-fetched treatment for mild to moderate depression, but they are [as] efficacious and cost effective [as] anti-depressants' (Bird, 2009). We know the adrenaline rush of fitness junkies, but less strenuous exercise, simply being outside in a beautiful space, can produce powerful endorphins too. Anecdotal reports state that: 'Suddenly it is as if a cloud has lifted and I feel invigorated, re-energised, renewed . . .'

Sensory gardens is a UK-based term widely used in schools, veteran rehab centres and care homes. Sensory gardens awaken the five main senses by providing a

- visually pleasing,
- audible,
- tactile,
- scented,
- tasty experience.

Designed to be attractive to wildlife as well as people, they reconnect us with nature. Sensory gardens work in varied settings as they provide deep memory prompts for people living with dementia, soothe the stressed exec, provide a calm space in a school where experiential learning can be conducted outdoors, assist developmentally delayed children to achieve milestones, and balance the digital information overload.

Therapeutic gardens is a US-based term used principally in corrective and health-care environments. These are the gardens where horticultural therapy, sometimes also known as social and therapeutic horticulture, takes place. They differ from sensory and healing gardens in that they provide active healing through the act of gardening. Examples of therapeutic landscapes include gardens specifically designed for

- dementia,
- mobility,
- rehabilitation,
- community cohesion.

Raised garden beds are commonly associated with therapeutic gardens, as they allow people of all ages and abilities to access the soil and plants.

Inclusive, accessible design is at the heart of healing and therapeutic landscapes. Increasingly the benefits of social and therapeutic horticulture, the gentle art of growing things under a structured programme, is being seen to be more widely applicable as a cost-effective treatment for a range of conditions. As the evidence of using gardens as a successful therapeutic tool builds, increasing numbers of health, social/public housing and education providers are asking for gardens to be included within their setting.

New research challenges us to see that design for health and well-being can occur across controlled and uncontrolled urban space. Citing international reports and case study examples, and showcasing different cultural and climatic conditions, we examine the broad potential of a salutogenic design approach. 'Healing gardens', as the landscape type offering most healing properties, is the umbrella term we will use to describe any garden designed specifically to improve, maintain and enhance the well-being of people and the planet. We will use the term to describe both sensory and therapeutic gardens, as they are specifically designed to restore a community and an individual to health.

Architects, developers, and urban and landscape planners have an opportunity to incorporate healing landscapes into design schemes. Adopting a salutogenic[2] design perspective allows us to consider landscape architecture and design as a valuable tool to boost and maintain human health and well-being, reducing the need for costly social, educational, health and economic interventions.

We talk about resilience and resilient communities today in the way we talked about sustainability yesterday. Here we take resilience to mean 'the capability to anticipate risk, limit impact, and bounce back rapidly through survival, adaptability, evolution, and growth in the face of turbulent change'.[3] We are faced with climate change on a global level, with impacts being felt through extreme weather events locally on every continent. There have been devastating earthquakes, civil unrest and war. In September 2012 the rapid increase in non-communicable diseases was noted for the first time by the WHO as being 'of concern'. Any efforts to promote human well-being must be based on an understanding of the dynamic interplay among diverse environmental and personal factors, rather than on analyses that focus exclusively on environmental, biological or behavioural factors (Stokols, 1992).

Healing gardens and the wider landscape have much to contribute. The USA, followed by Mexico, Australia, New Zealand, the UK, Canada, Ireland, Chile, Iceland and Hungary, are the top ten countries facing an epidemic of obesity and a lack of physical fitness (*IBT*, 2013) . Inactive lifestyles could, according to recent estimates, cause the American adult obesity rate to reach 43 per cent by 2018. This would cost an additional US$344 billion in healthcare expenses related to diabetes and hypertension, among other diseases, in the USA alone. But inactive lifestyles are not just a problem for adults. Obesity threatens to shorten the lifespan of today's children by as much as five years; the first time in two centuries that a generation of children faces a shorter life expectancy than its parents. This issue, along with the significant role it plays in the overall escalating healthcare crisis, could cripple our economies, damage our communities, overstress our businesses and threaten the health security of future generations.

Over a decade of research now clearly links obesity, physical activity and the environment (Allison, 2013). But how, specifically, do we design communities and landscapes to positively and measurably influence physical well-being, health and productivity?

Healing gardens have been recognised as a useful part of the landscape since early walled Islamic gardens and monastic cloister gardens. However, not since medieval times have landscape and urban designers been considered or consulted for the public health potential of using sustainable sensory landscapes and sensitive built environments as early intervention, treatment and prevention strategies. In our quest for cost-engineered, pathogen-free environments we have largely forgotten our ability to use nature for its natural healing properties.

The market for the application of landscape interventions for health and well-being is large, and growing. Our population is ageing and health naturally deteriorates with age. Around the world healthcare and aged care costs are increasing at alarming rates. Costs of education have also gone up as students require more support to achieve learning outcomes. Infrastructure costs to mitigate the effects of climate change are rising with each major flood, storm and drought event. Taken together or even singly, these are burgeoning costs that cannot be met by society.

Through the development of healing, sensory and therapeutic gardens overlaid across the urban plan, incorporated within new social housing and built into public open space, we can ensure developments improve human health and that of the planet, are more efficient, cost effective, functional and ultimately sustainable. We can raise educational aspiration and achievement and reduce crime. If it sounds like we are presenting gardens as a universal panacea, to a certain extent we are. However (there is always a disclaimer), healing garden designers and their promoters need to be mindful of what they are trying to achieve, for without a deep understanding of the complex relationship between people and the land we simply get another ineffectual bed of lavender, three betula and a stamp of 'job done'. Once we understand *why* we need to provide nature connections we can explore where and how to maximise the effect of outputs, while minimising costs to society, within a sustainable ecological framework.

> Local and central governments need to be adaptable and creative in their response to proactive urban design for healthy lifestyles. Appropriate landscape and urban design can be used to prevent and diminish the severity of non-communicable diseases in indigenous, at-risk and non-indigenous populations.

For all the advances in research, the progress has been largely client-led. It is time we, as landscape professionals, put landscape back on the planning and development agenda as the cost-effective tool it is in addressing a variety of social and environmental concerns. Design for health and well-being is nothing new. In our contemporary world, however, it is a new way of looking at the potential of green space, a new way of putting landscape back up the priority list.

In the following chapters we will see that design for health and well-being can be incorporated across any setting. Gardens and playable spaces for children, whether in schools, on street corners, within public parks, healthcare settings or around housing, can be cost-effective developments. The return on investment, or ROI, is marked. Schools, business owners and developers benefit, while the community gains. In shopping strips, footfall numbers increase, properties sell faster, the area becomes known and is marketed for its competitive advantage. For schools it is the same. They gain a healthy environment that boosts the results of their students, so they attract more funding and more students, while building a sustainable community. We can quantify the cost of development and know that if we apply salutogenic design principles we can save the client time, money and heartache. We can improve the public health of the community and at the same time improve the health of the planet.

To achieve cost-effective community health we need to use integrated systems thinking. Rising levels of non-communicable disease and social pathologies erode economies and communities, putting pressure on limited health and welfare resources. We have a solution. Positive links to the environment have been demonstrated in the literature, showing that absenteeism, binge drinking, some cancers, depression, heart disease, inequality, low aspiration, poor parenting and type 2 diabetes can all be influenced by the environment in which people live, work and play. Attracting and retaining a vibrant, healthy population within a changing multicultural community is influenced by the creation and maintenance of a sustainable, diverse ecology and built environment in and around our cities.

Historically, gardens performed a vital role. Garden designers were esteemed, educated people, and even in the early Middle Ages often widely travelled. They brought their knowledge and experience to bear in creative and often spiritually aware ways. Today we have become obsessed with profit margins, client face time, project turn-around times. It has become easy to think of gardens and green space purely in aesthetic terms. We intuitively know they look good and are necessary, but how often do we stop to ask ourselves *why* do we need them and what are they actually *for*?

We have an opportunity to make a fundamental difference to the fabric of society, cost-effectively building healthy, sustainable communities in the process. Social and therapeutic horticulture practitioners, occupational therapists, other healthcare professionals, special education teachers and community volunteers need to be able to reference and justify the development of gardens for health and well-being. *Landscape and Urban Design for Health and Well-Being* will guide you.

Notes

1   Public health promotion programmes are based on the prevention of mental and physical ill health. Because of the complexity of human health and well-being, effective salutogenic design is inherently a multi-disciplinary, multi-method approach.
2   The salutogenic approach aims to prevent illness, to maintain and enhance human health and well-being. Traditional healthcare takes a pathogenic approach, where various means are used to treat someone who is ill. It is generally accepted that it is less expensive to prevent illness than to treat it.
3   Resilience definition from www.resilientus.org/about-us/definition-of-community-resilience.html

References

Allison, M. (2013). America's design and health initiative: an important value proposition for architects. Retrieved from *American Institute of Architects*: www.aia.org/practicing/AIAB088657
Bird, W. M., Dr. (2009, 15 July). Interviewed by the author.
Campbell, L. and Wiesen, A. (2011). *Restorative commons: creating health and well-being through urban landscapes*. Newtown Square, PA: USDA Forest Service.

Cooper Marcus, C. and Sachs, N. A. (2013). *Therapeutic landscapes: an evidence-based approach to designing healing gardens and restorative outdoor spaces*. New York: Wiley.

Ferrari, A. J., Charlson, F. J., Norman, R. E., Patten, S. B., Freedman, G., Murray, C. J., Vos, T. and Whiteford, H. A. (2013). *Burden of depressive disorders by country, sex, age, and year: findings from the Global Burden of Disease Study 2010*. San Francisco: PLOS.

Golembiewski, J. (2013, 12 July). Ph.D. March, BFA. Interviewed by the author.

Hartig, T., Kaiser, F. G. and Bowler, P. A. (2001). Psychological restoration in nature as a positive motivation for ecological behavior. *Environment and Behavior*, 33:590–607.

IBT (*International Business Times*) (2013). Top 10 obese countries. Retrieved December 2013 from www.ibtimes.co.in/articles/517210/20131027/top-10-obese-countries-world-obesity.htm

Kaplan, R. and Kaplan, S. (1995, 2002). *Experience of nature: a psychological perspective*. Ann Arbor, MI: Ulrich's.

Kofler, W. (2010). *Ecology and forests for public health*. Munich: International Council For Scientific Development

Kuo, F. E. and Taylor, A. F. (2004). The potential natural treatment for attention deficit/hyperactivity disorder: evidence for a national study. *American Journal of Public Health*, 94:1580–1586.

Lancet, the (2009, May). Health and climate change. Retrieved 2013, from www.thelancet.com/series/health-and-climate-change

Maller, C., Townsend, M., Pryor, A., Brown, P. and St Leger, L. (2006). Healthy nature healthy people: 'contact with nature' as an upstream health promotion intervention for populations. *Health Promotion International*, 21(1):45–54.

Moore, M., Townsend, M. and Oldroyd, J. (2006). Linking human and ecosystem health: the benefits of community involvement in conservation groups. *EcoHealth Journal*, 3:255–261.

Norris, H. (2013, 31 October). Director of Policy and Development, Mental Health Foundation. Interviewed by the author.

Pretty, J., Peacock, J., Sellens, M. and Griffin, M. (2005). The mental and physical health outcomes of green exercise. *International Journal of Environmental Health Research*, 15:319–337.

Prüss-Üstün., A. and Corvalán, C. (2006). *Preventing disease through healthy environments*. Geneva: WHO.

Stokols, D. (1992). Establishing and maintaining healthy environments: toward a social ecology of health promotion. *American Psychologist*, 47(1):6–22.

Ulrich, R. S. (1984). View through a window may influence recovery from surgery. *Journal of Science*, 224:420–421.

WHO (2000). *Global strategy for the prevention and control of noncommunicable diseases*. Geneva: World Health Organisation.

—— (2011). *Global status report on noncommunicable diseases*. Geneva: World Health Organisation.

Wilson, E. O. (1984). *Biophilia*. Cambridge, MA: Harvard University Press.

PART I

THE ORIGINS AND EVOLUTION
OF HEALING GARDENS

CHAPTER 1

The history

What were gardens for?

Gardens as havens, gardens for health

E. O. Wilson, father of the biophilia hypothesis, says our sense of belonging today comes from time in city parks, from choices we make for habitation, for where we spend our leisure time; time spent in gardens provokes deep memories of our evolutionary time on the African savannah. Wilson believes we are hard-wired to need nature around us, that it is within our genetic make-up that we are part of nature. Since he wrote *Biophilia* in 1984 and co-edited *The Biophilia Hypothesis* in 1993, around the world much research time and effort has gone into proving the case for our need to be surrounded by living things. This deep need is a core part of our being that when denied affects us in multiple ways.

> 'If there is an evolutionary basis for biophilia, then contact with nature is a basic human need: not a cultural amenity, not an individual preference, but a universal primary need. Just as we need healthy food and regular exercise to flourish, we need on-going connections with the natural world.'
>
> Judith Heerwagen, Ph.D.

As places to connect with nature within an urban framework, healing gardens are part of that universal primary need. The relationship between children's ability to learn, our social relations, our productivity at work, our propensity to commit crime and indulge in self-harming lifestyle behaviours, our appreciation and stewardship of the environment and our psychological and physical health, have all been studied in relation to time spent outdoors in nature. Wilson explains:

> All these things are intertwined, and so we have to learn how to look at them as one combined, nonlinear process that's just about going to bear us away unless we handle them now as a whole . . . And if we do it, there's going to be light at the end of that tunnel. We'll be so much better off.
>
> (Tyson, 2008)

Figure 1.1
Healing water garden,
Surrey, UK.

Design for health and well-being requires us to focus first on where we have come from. In order to plan our way forward it is therefore helpful to look to the wisdom of the past. Indigenous peoples of North America, ancient wisdom from China, early philosophers and religious teachings from Europe and elsewhere, all look to the spiritual nature of the land, and its capacity to heal. When surrounded by the beauty, the power and the majesty of nature, our sense of awe and wonder is evoked. It is nature's capacity to inspire, to give peace, to heal, to balance life, that we value when we set out to create new landscapes.

Creating gardens and gardening (the tending of gardens and rearing of plants), along with animal husbandry, was one of our earliest forms of taming nature, bending it to our will. Early gardens were a simplification of Mother Nature herself, formed for the benefit of people but with few modifications of the natural form. Propagation of hybrids and elaborate training and cultivation techniques came later. Natural elements within the garden included flowers, shrubs and all-important trees. Trees were originally planted to provide shade, fruit and to uplift the soul through a view up through a tracery of leaves.

Today we talk about health spas being like 'an oasis in the city'. Early gardens often fitted the description of an oasis. The gardens were leafy, compact, welcoming spaces, developed around a water supply. Resources were scarce and from that scarcity came an understanding of and an appreciation for the need to work with nature, to grow what naturally grew in the local climate, that soil. The gardens were intimate spaces, at a scale easy to tend and comprehend. By being a smaller scale version of the wider landscape, early gardens were presented in a form able to be appreciated and understood by people regardless of age, ability or education.

Medieval gardens were about beauty and respite from the harsh world beyond the garden perimeter. Frequently walled to keep out wild animals or marauding

Figure 1.2 Date palms' tracery of leaves, Dubai.

Figure 1.3 Pergola perspective, Wisley Gardens, UK.

bandits, the gardens had an aesthetic that did more than just green and cool the space. Symmetry and line were balanced with a profusion of plants. The eye was eased down an axis, with resting points along the way.

Initially, using locally available materials, structures were built for the plants to grow over. As communities and economies began to expand, trading allowed for unusual and prized imported materials to be used within the gardens. These small buildings, arbours, pergolas and arches, were used to provide perspective, shade and frame views. In time some gardens evolved as a display of wealth. Most gardens, however, were necessarily low maintenance, as few people could afford the luxury of time to tend a purely decorative garden. They needed to grow plants and tend animals for food. Culinary herbs and vegetables were regularly mixed into herbaceous plantings. The mixed plantings enhanced the low maintenance aspect of the gardens by attracting beneficial insects and pollinators and reducing the risk of major outbreaks of pest infestation or disease. Interestingly that 'fashion' of mixing herbs and flowers, practicality with beauty, is becoming popular again today.

> Gardens, like most art forms, are heavily influenced by their moment in history. The level of cultural and spiritual enlightenment at the time in large part determines the style of garden.

Evidence in paintings and models provides information about our first gardens, such as we know them today, in Egypt. Early Egyptian gardens grew food and flowers,

Figure 1.4 Wellington Botanical Gardens, New Zealand: Edible edging – parsley and tulips.

laid out as temple gardens and domestic gardens. Lilies and roses were also grown by the ancient Egyptians for perfume as an early form of commercial horticulture.

In China, Italy and Greece there is evidence of gardens 5,000 years ago. In China, however, the 'gardens' were more vast royal parks than intimate growing spaces. Smaller temple and domestic gardens came later.

As culture grew so did an appreciation of plants. We learnt how to grow them out of their natural habitat, and developed decorative containers to house them. Over time we placed symbolic sculpture and pots within natural plantings, developed tiled paths and terraces with intricate detailing in colours complementary to the plantings. While practical, the durable surface was also beautiful.

The gardens were relaxing havens, where people could go to 'take the air', walk, sit, pick and eat fruit, admire the colour, scents and sounds of nature.

History is rich with references to gardens and the people's close relationship to and with the affirming, sustaining, and health-giving properties of nature. Today though, how often do we forget the essence of a garden, that basic nature, that ability to heal, when we come to a design project? It has almost become the norm to allow ourselves to be driven by deadlines and budgets to the point where we forget what landscape and nature is about. We have become accustomed to seeing a design or a development scheme that looks good on paper but in reality takes its reference more from 'commercial realities' and the built environment than the natural environment to which we were originally so attracted.

Driven by desires for 'bigger, brighter, better', it is easy to forget *why* we are working on a project before contemplating what we are trying to achieve.

Figure 1.5 Tiled garden, Marrakech, Morocco.

Figure 1.6
Container grown
plants, Marrakech,
Morocco.

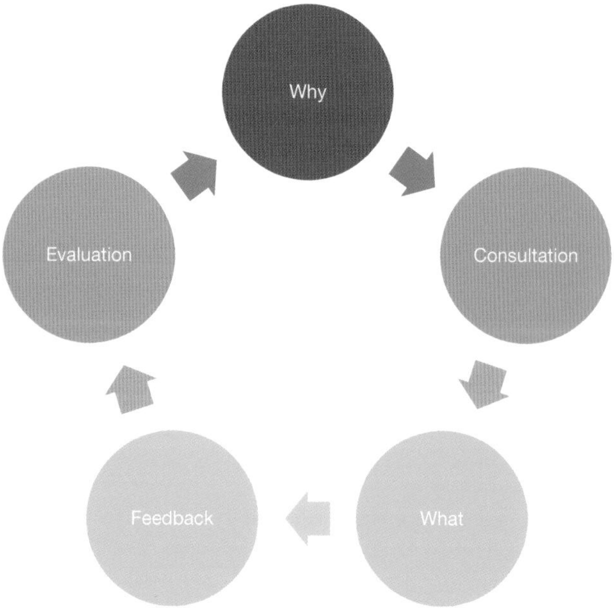

Figure 1.7 The design cycle.

Ancient to modern healing, sensory and therapeutic gardens

When looking to create healing gardens today, it is helpful to consider the healing gardens of yesterday. If we take two of the world's major religions as offering examples of early garden forms, as early as 1,500 years ago we see walled Islamic gardens and monastic cloister gardens being used as healing gardens. Designed and constructed to sustain the local community, the origin of today's model for salutogenic sustainable living can be traced to these gardens. Aiding health and well-being in a time of pestilence and strife, monastic and Islamic gardens shared many characteristics. Based on the belief in paradise on earth, the concept of a paradise garden is an ancient one, pre-dating the three great monotheistic religions, Judaism, Christianity and Islam, by centuries. These were early sensory gardens.

Paradise gardens

Islamic gardens referenced paradise through the Garden of Eden, with the 'river of life' flowing under the garden in irrigating, cooling rills. Fruit trees provided welcome shade as well as food. The fruit blossom provided fragrance, colour and general delight while also attracting beneficial birds, bees and insects. Gardens were laid indoors and out in a pleasing symmetrical fashion, where nothing jarred the eye but rather presented a balanced, calming view. They echoed the fundamental principle that this world is a reflection of a heavenly realm.

From early on in the Jewish and Christian traditions, 'paradise' became associated with the Garden of Eden. Prior even to that, the pre-Islamic Arabs considered the slightest indication of nature's greenness to be sacred. Since people were completely

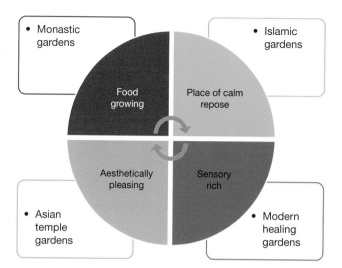

Figure 1.8 Historic religious gardens matrix.

- Monastic gardens
- Islamic gardens

Food growing

Place of calm repose

Aesthetically pleasing

Sensory rich

- Asian temple gardens
- Modern healing gardens

Figure 1.9 Indoor water garden, Marrakech, Morocco.

dependent on the oases for their survival it was natural that they should love and revere nature's vegetation, both for its physical benefits and as a sign of the mysterious power that guided the universe.

This sense of mystery is an important element in garden design that we will come back to throughout the text. Gardens and nature have held and continue to hold a deep spiritual appeal, albeit sometimes on an unconscious level, for many people today. Although by nature humans are suspicious of things they cannot see or understand, we accept simple gardens and wider nature on a deep level, without need or desire to question. When we are in a garden, what bliss not to have to think for a moment! However we define paradise today, a blissful state of being forms a large part of the image. Gardens today, however contemporary in styling, must still reference their origins if they are to be the healing, therapeutic spaces they can be.

The early paradise garden was a private space, hidden away as a place for quiet contemplation. In Persia, as well as in the Arab countries and India, the courtyard garden is like a miniature paradise garden representing our inward, contemplative nature. As a smaller area removed from the dirty, noisy world outside, the paradise garden became an oasis in itself. Within an Islamic context the key elements of flowing water, shade and exuberant foliage powerfully convey ideas of both spiritual and physical refreshment. The gardens nurtured the mind, body and soul of the people, effectively providing for their needs and aiding their health and well-being.

In the Middle Ages, European communities were focussed around the Church, as the predominant local landowner of those times. In the absence of a welfare state, the Church was expected to heal the sick, educate the poor, and employ those without access to their own, usually rented, land. So it followed that the lands of the Church had to perform those functions. Monasteries developed a particular garden style to suit the various needs of their community.

The Islamic and monastic garden styles have much to teach us in terms of healing and therapeutic garden design. As a model for how to design a town centre, a city park, a care home, a school playground or a private courtyard garden in the home of a stressed executive, I can think of no better approach. When I referenced them in a lecture to the Horticulture Society, people commented that they had never expected to see the relevance of monastic garden design to urban gardens today. It was a revelation to the audience that a garden could fulfil so many functions at once.

Monastic gardens

Monastic gardens typically had four main functional areas:

• the kitchen garden,
• the orchard,
• the physic garden,
• the cloister garden.

These areas were sometimes separated but often the functions were mixed and overlapped to good effect.

The monastic kitchen gardens did more than simply provide food for the local inhabitants. They were good examples of early inclusive and accessible gardens. With no welfare provided by the state it was left to the Church to tend to the physical and spiritual needs of the people. This is significant in urban planning and social housing today, as we strive to provide more with less. By providing 'kitchen gardens', or community gardens or urban agriculture, as these projects are sometimes called around our towns and cities, we can provide for those most in need of cheap, fresh, local food.

Social isolation, that silent killer of modern times, was banished through mean-ingful, co-operative activity for all who joined the monastery. Lay priests worked in the gardens to be able to enjoy the welfare and protection of the Church. An early form of 'community garden', a typical kitchen garden would have raised beds to allow easy access for intensive cultivation by even the elderly and infirm monks and lay brothers. To reduce risk from pests the monks grew companion flowers between the vegetables. Modern therapeutic horticulture programmes use this idea to provide vulnerable people with meaningful activity.

The orchards were planted with varieties of fruit and nut. Space-saving espalier techniques, developed in France as a way of training trees along a flat surface such as a wall, were introduced into English monasteries. It meant that an orchard could be planted anywhere where the blossom and fruit could be appreciated. Hop vines for medicinal use (sleep, tension, digestion) as well as beer were also grown using the vertical plane, and provided welcome shade. 'Thus, in the full enjoyment of peace and protection, the monks busied themselves very diligently with the gentle art of gardening, and so reaped calm happiness and the useful fruits of the earth' (Gothein, 1928).

The physic garden was where they grew medicinal herbs. As the plants tended to be invasive, and to aid monks with failing eyesight, the garden contained one bed for each herb. Planting the herbs in neat rows allowed weeds to be easily identified and removed by touch where sight impairment was profound.

The abbey garden of Clairvaux, France, is described by a contemporary of St Bernard in the early twelfth century:

> Behind the abbey, and within the wall of the cloister, there is a wide level ground: here there is an orchard, with a great many different fruit-trees . . . It is close to the infirmary, and is very comforting to the brothers, providing a wide promenade for those who want to walk, and a pleasant resting-place for those who prefer to rest. Where the orchard leaves off, the garden begins, divided into several beds, . . . cut up by little canals, . . . The water fulfills the double purpose of nourishing the fish and watering the vegetables.
>
> (Hobhouse, 2004)

The abbey gardens can be used as a template for modern healing gardens. The gardens were designed to be both practical and beautiful. The little canals, or rills as they are commonly known today, are a sensory-rich way to cool the air (and hands and feet), provide the gentle sound of moving water, and provide drinking water for animals, while also nourishing fish and vegetables. Part of the practicality is position. The wide promenade mentioned allows two people to walk together companionably. Providing space to be together or alone, as one desires, is part of the healing nature of the gardens. Likewise, a resting place or multiple resting places are essential in a healing landscape.

The proposed plan for a monastery at St Gall, drawn by Abbot Haito or Reichenau (763–836) for Abbot Gozbert of St Gall, shows in great detail the various functional gardens. The St Gall plan is the best record of monastic garden details from the early Middle Ages.

Figure 1.10 St Gall monastery plan, France.

Source: www.GardenVisit.com

The gardens include an infirmary garden, a cemetery garden and a gardener's house. Two semi-circular 'paradise' spaces at the east and west ends of the church, confirm the influence of eastern churches on the plan. The word paradise entered Christian Church history as the name for the porticoes adjoining the oldest Byzantine basilicas, planted as gardens (McLean, 1981).

An important part of any monastic garden was the cloister garden, used as a con-templative space. While some cloister gardens had shrubs and flowers, most were a level field of lawn. The following is from 'The Cloister Lawn', in *De Vegetabilibus et Plantis* (1260) by St Albert the Great (1200–1280):

> Care must be taken that the lawn is of such a size that about it in a square may be planted every sweet-smelling herb . . . and likewise all sorts of flowers. At the edge of the lawn set square, let there be a higher bench; and somewhere in the middle provide seats so that men may sit there to take their repose pleasurably when their senses need refreshment.

> Upon the lawn too, against the heat of the sun, trees should be planted or vines trained, so that the lawn may have a delightful and cooling shade, sheltered by their leaves. Let them be sweet trees, with perfumed flowers and agreeable shade.
> (SCU, 2013)

Was this the original model healing garden?

Islamic gardens

Islamic gardens share many similarities with monastic gardens. While feeding mind, body and soul, they also provided a sense of safety and enclosure. Islamic gardens were traditionally divided into four, with four rivers flowing out to the points of the compass dividing the garden spaces. The four-fold form of the 'archetypal Islamic garden is not just a whim of design or a horticultural convenience, but a reflection of a higher reality and symbol of divine unity' (Clark, 2004). It was written in the Quran that the only word spoken in the gardens of paradise was 'peace'. The search for paradise on earth became a search for peace. This was interpreted in Islamic garden design to mean the garden must be beautiful, a sanctuary from the harsh world outside, a place for calm repose. This is a feature of the enduring appeal of the garden. While monastic gardens have largely died out, Islamic gardens as a style have retained their popularity.

Islamic gardens were characterised by four main features

- water and shade,
- symmetry,
- edible, sensory planting,
- peacefulness.

Islamic gardens evolved in a largely arid climate zone. Water was a precious commodity and so plants were chosen for their ability to withstand local conditions. Cooling shade was likewise vital. Roses grew well within the shelter of garden walls.

Palms, lilies and reeds were planted in or beside water.

LEFT: **Figure 1.11** Roses, Sissinghurst, UK.
ABOVE: **Figure 1.12** Water garden.

As a sensory feature water was used sparingly, in decorative fountains in sheltered courtyards where wind would not evaporate excessive amounts of water and in the open gardens in rills to cool the air. It was often contained within sacred, symbolic fountain forms.

Irrigation pipes were largely laid above ground, which meant the water did not get fouled by animals, and the cost of development was reduced as less labour was required.

The symmetry of Islamic gardens was deliberate. Although the series of spaces that made up the garden were enclosed they unfolded one from another logically, with nothing to jar the eye. This allowed the mind to be stilled and the imagination to soar. As places of contemplation and scholarship, the Islamic garden style can be incorporated into schools everywhere.

Within the symmetrical layout, functional areas were defined by planting. The fragrant blossom of almonds was sought close to seating areas. Citrus trees were often planted near dining spaces. Ground cover planting was essential to reduce soil moisture evaporation, so under-planting with lilies, roses, and smaller perennials was common.

Planting included colourful and fragrant flowers, offset by the leafy green of evergreens.

Edible planting within the Islamic garden was an essential, practical feature. To reduce the risk of animals browsing on precious fruit and vegetables, they were enclosed within the garden walls. Proximity to where the food would be used afforded an easy route from garden to table. Placing fruit trees near where people walked and sat promoted a healthy lifestyle and good diet. Edible planting was also part of the sensory-rich experience afforded by the Islamic garden. Eating is the one activity that uses five senses at once. When we use our hands to pick and eat something fresh off a tree or bush we make a connection with nature. This feature of Islamic gardens could

Figure 1.13 Islamic tiled water feature.   **Figure 1.14** Citrus in Islamic courtyard garden.

be used to good effect around modern housing developments, where residents seek somewhere attractive and safe to congregate, rest and rejuvenate.

A sense of peace was found in soothing Islamic gardens. The key design feature was that they were green, secluded spaces, which emphasised the contemplative dimension. Gardens were never created in isolation; they were an extension of the living and working environment. When the architecture balanced the water, planting and symmetry, the gardens allowed a deeply satisfying and harmonious connection with nature. Modern paradise gardens are found in widely diverse countries, from Malaysia to Morocco. They all display the universal concepts of peace and unity. We can learn from history. Contemporary evidence-based design is mindful of what has worked well in the past. Islamic-style planting and the careful use of water is relevant today as we adapt landscape and urban design to climate change, and to positively impact public mental health.

Case study 1: Islamic garden as therapeutic space

In the middle of a busy hospital I met a senior doctor, who requested an Islamic-style garden for his home. I had just designed the spinal unit rehab gardens and he was keen for me to develop his personal garden. He was a classic stressed executive who worked long hours and needed a place to recharge his energies. There was an additional component to the design brief: the garden also had to fit in with the style of his local, very English, village. Bringing history up to date allows an applied science approach. The essential Islamic garden elements of the river running under the garden, fruit trees and symmetry had to be incorporated with planting that evoked a sense of Arabia within rural Buckinghamshire. Before I began the design process I studied the Quran to learn the symbolism inherent within a garden. As a healing style transplanted to Buckinghamshire, this garden had to look, feel and function like a traditional Islamic garden, but with some substitutions.

Symmetry translates into any setting. Originally designed as a foil to the chaotic life beyond the garden walls, the calming Islamic style is the same as we use in gardens for people on the autistic spectrum. Modern landscape architecture is known for its love of outdoor rooms. In the Islamic garden, rooms of hedged and walled enclosures open and connect one space to another, to promote conversation and gentle exploration.

My client wanted the social nature of the traditional Islamic garden to be evident within the design. Outdoor dining spaces, fountains and fruiting shade trees were placed close to the house. A swing was hung from a tree for adult as well as children's delight.

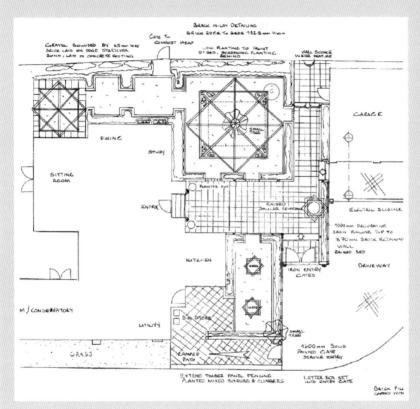

Figure 1.15a
Islamic garden plan.
Designed by
Greenstone Design
UK.

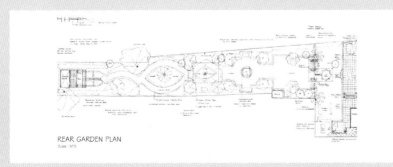

Figure 1.15b
Islamic garden plan.
Designed by
Greenstone Design
UK.

As we reference the history of healing gardens across cultures it is important to distil the essence of each style. To be useful in landscape design today, we must understand why our ancestors developed their gardens. Only then can we interpret that as something useful for individuals and communities today.

Case study 2: a simple, modern physic garden

It was when researching for a project to develop an historic garden, spanning 2,000 years of British gardens from Roman Britain to the present day, that I first came across monastic gardens as a distinct typology. The town the project was in had ruins of a Cistercian Abbey, so it made sense to include reference to the abbey gardens within the historic gardens we were designing. The client, a museum in Surrey, England, had a small space in which to develop a timeline of garden history, showcasing plants and gardening practices introduced by successive conquerors and explorers, immigrants and contemporary fashion. The monastic garden had just a 5m × 5m (15' × 15') space available to demonstrate the style of monastic garden we thought most representative of the time. We chose to develop a physic garden, which is a medieval medicinal herb garden. Laid out in grids, with non-toxic treated timber dividers to avoid root encroachment of the herbs from one space to the next, we placed paths in between for ease of access (visually and physically) and for harvest. It is a simple garden that offers visitors sights, smells, tastes and the buzz of beneficial insects.

Around the edges of the physic garden are walled gardens with espaliered fruit and nut trees, soft fruits, vegetables and flowers. Although the outer gardens showcase the evolution of modern gardens through a series of different time periods, the planting combines to give the effect of being in a kitchen, orchard and cloister garden, adding to the physic garden experience.

Figure 1.16
Monastic physic garden, Museum of Farnham, Surrey. Designed by Greenstone Design UK.

East meets West

The West and the Middle East were not the only places offering their people the benefits of healing gardens. Oriental monasteries concentrated on providing the best education and preparation for life to come. Their Buddhist gardens were the ultimate in quiet, contemplative spaces where the initiates' young minds were free to explore, to ponder their teachings. In moist climates water was and is used extensively. In dry areas, raked sand soundlessly created the impression of water movement.

Figure 1.17
Balinese water garden, Bali, Indonesia.

History brought up to date

A few hundred years after the monks' great gardening feats, the acclaimed English garden designer Gertrude Jekyll wrote in her 1914 book *Colour Schemes for the Flower Garden* that

> Surely my fruit garden would be not only a place of beauty . . . but of leisurely repose . . . There is a pleasure in searching for and eating fruit in this way that is far better than having it picked by the gardener and brought in and set before one on a dish in a tame room. Is this feeling an echo of far-away days of savagery when men hunted for their food and rejoiced to find it, or is it rather the poet's delight of having direct intercourse with the good gift of the growing thing and seeing and feeling through all the senses how good and gracious the thing is?

Whether from medieval times or just last century, when we look at these early examples of healing gardens we recognise places attractive to us today. A well-designed modern healing garden also offers connections to nature. Whether through symbolism or reality there is water, fruiting trees and flowers and the air is alive with birdsong and the hum of beneficial insects.

George Cadbury established one of the first garden suburbs, Bournville, around his chocolate factory in the English Midlands around the turn of the twentieth century. The idea behind Bournville was that people could readily breathe fresh, clean air, enjoy green views and walks, boost their sense of wellness, maintain their social connections, and so improve their productivity in the workplace. The father of modern town planning, Sir Ebenezer Howard, took Bournville as the impetus to carry out his ideas.

It is an idea that has caught on. Business parks are being designed as garden estates, with buildings dotted amongst leafy glades, lakes and walkways. Corporate headquarters of NASDAQ and FTSE 50 companies are choosing to locate on the city fringe, or with roof gardens and balcony spaces that offer an attractive alternative to sitting at a desk. By offering their staff green space to sit and admire the view, meet a friend for lunch, take five minutes' break from a busy day, take a walking meeting in private, or simply enjoy the opportunity for fresh air and exercise, they hope, as George Cadbury did, that their staff will be happier, healthier and more productive and that staff turnover and absence rates will fall.

In Europe, Canada and Australia pocket parks and laneways provide abundant opportunities for workers to get active. The health risks that used to be associated with smoking, the incidence of high cost cardiovascular diseases, dropped significantly as smoking was banned in workplaces and public places, and a massive public education programme was initiated to encourage people to quit their unhealthy habit. Since the 1990s, as previously developing countries have become more globally competitive and their populations more mobile, Western countries' workers, like their counterparts elsewhere, are working harder to

Figure 1.18 Bournville Garden Suburb.

Source: www.bournvilleconservatives.com

maintain their positions. Stress levels have increased and we are more likely to eat lunch at our workstations than take a break and go out for a walk.

> Sitting has become the new smoking. Our inactive lifestyle is killing us, in thousands, slowly and expensively. As we become disabled due to ill health we are robbing families and communities of valued members and our economies of valued taxes. By providing safe, accessible outdoor green space we can counter the effects of a sedentary lifestyle.

In Wellington, New Zealand, walkways ring the city, connecting blue space to green space as city parks fringe the harbour, lace through the urban centre and out to the green belt which serves as backdrop to the suburbs. All parks offer free admission, and although set within a hillside landscape offer a range of inclusive spaces with accessible routes for young and old to enjoy nature.

In New York, USA, the highline walkway connects parts of the city with an attractive walking route, using a disused elevated railway line. Space at ground level is scarce so an elevated park and garden area is ideal. It affords opportunities for local volunteers to get outdoors and actively garden, as well as providing an attraction for tourists and new businesses.

In the UK similar developments have been proposed for London, Manchester and Liverpool to replicate the initiatives of the highline walkway, pocket parks and green

LEFT: **Figure 1.19a** The Highline Park, New York, USA.

Source: Jenny Brown.

BELOW: **Figure 1.19b** New business investment following urban regeneration project, New York, USA.

Source: Jenny Brown.

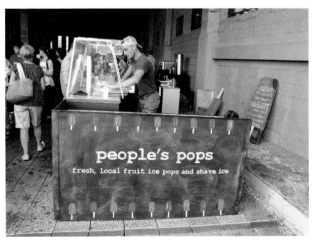

belt walkways. These examples are by no means the full extent of healing green space provision in these countries or cities, but serve to show the breadth and range of where and how recent landscape research is being applied.

The potential

As we will see in later chapters, a salutogenic approach to landscape and urban design has enormous potential. This book was born out of a desire to share that potential, to infect new students and experienced practitioners with enthusiasm for a new way of looking at landscape, as a garden and as a healing, therapeutic, sensory-rich space. In recent times the quest for efficiency and 'lean design' has led many to provide spaces with bland 'contemporary' features. A brief for 'easy care' has been interpreted as low interest rather than as an inspiration for creative high impact, low input, low maintenance schemes. If ancient Islamic and monastic garden designers could provide an oasis in the desert or a calm contemplative respite from daily life, then it is not beyond us with our myriad design tools to step back and think about what we are trying to achieve with a space, within budget and meeting all local constraints and requirements.

Figure 1.20 China: pop-up children's interactive space.

Source: Alice Leake.

Figure 1.21 China: pop-up children's interactive space.

Source: Alice Leake.

Around the world there are multiple examples of grand design schemes built as monuments to people. The might of the machine can be awe-inspiring, but never so much so as an unexpected touch of nature, a swathe of lawn, a grand tree, or a trickling stream. The hard environments that predominate in our towns and cities can add to stress and depression and actually serve to discourage people from strolling along their paths. Although functionally the vast plazas may be designed to move people quickly from point A to point B, we need to balance that with options to take a slow route. Adults and children with sensory impairment can become overloaded when surrounded by the sights and sounds of unrelenting hardscape. They need the sense of enclosure and safety that comes from a more human-scale approach. The softer acoustics provided by living materials are less jarring. In Figures 1.20 and 1.21 a wall of woven straw changes the hardscape into a playful, engaging space. This simple intervention changes the overall dynamic, slows the pace and provides a soft counterpoint to the hard brick.

Historically, gardens were a counter to the harsh life outside the garden. We have the potential to include elements of those gardens into modern cities as the pace is slowed for ageing and disabled populations. Not only do slow routes need to incorporate natural and planted material, they also need seating. Ignoring historic wisdom around the need for balanced active and resting spaces, in many areas seating is being removed from parks and school playgrounds to encourage children and adults to be more active. In other places seating options are removed for the less healthy reason of reducing the potential for 'anti-social behaviour'. This is a short-sighted initiative.

Where streetscape space is tight, window ledges and low walls can afford an ideal low-cost seating option for the elderly, the disabled and parents with young children, or indeed anyone who needs to pause a moment. Over-zealous officials are installing anti-sit spikes across our cities, such as at London's Southwark Council buildings (Figure 1.22). By so doing they add to the stress of moving through the city's streets, making them less liveable, and ultimately less healthy.

As modern society moved away from historic wisdom the landscape profession became marginalised. Horticultural skills were devalued by a public that did not see the benefits that gardens of previous eras provided. In a cost-conscious world landscape became a frippery, a nice-to-have accessory to the main event. However, with health, environmental and financial pressures mounting to unsustainable levels,

Figure 1.22
Non-salutogenic anti-sit
spikes, London.

Figure 1.23 Biophilic urban
green space, Wellington,
New Zealand.

the time is right to reinstate the historic role of landscape. If we think back to the role and four-part design of the early monastic and Islamic gardens, we can model that within our urban schemes. Healing gardens can be developed within city parks, around office blocks, on roof terraces, within and around social housing, or new estates – in fact just about anywhere. Bars and restaurants are using free wi-fi, green walls, rooftop and garden courtyards and comfortable sofas to attract people into their premises. With an engaging space they hope to encourage patrons to linger longer and spend more money in their place of business.

While looking to develop a sustainable community, what better than to offer the livability option, set around a healing garden landscape? Sustainable economies can be developed around local food supplies with local businesses supporting each other. Innovative, entrepreneurial and web-based service industries allow location to be anywhere there is a broadband internet connection. People will congregate wherever it is attractive to do so. Perhaps the idea of green walls, gardens and comfortable seating is not such a bad one?

As an indication of how mainstream the idea of looking after health and well-being has become, increasingly, corporate employers are catering for the well-being of their staff with early intervention programmes as part of their health and safety in the workplace provision. If, for example, the employer tackles a sore muscle by offering a free half-hour massage session during work time, they are less likely to have that staff member take a sick day with incapacitating pain. Employers can see an improvement in their bottom line when they take a preventative approach and look after their staff.

As an advocacy tool for sustainable and environmental education, healing gardens offer a wonderful opportunity for adults and children to engage with nature and connect, perhaps for the first time. The ecological health of our planet is at risk, at the same time as rates of non-communicable diseases are rising. Early sensory gardens were designed to inspire and uplift the senses, with health-giving herbs, clean air and views to heal the mind, body and soul and provide a therapeutic occupation for those in need. The same potential exists today.

'When you sit in a nice garden for two hours, it seems like two minutes; when you sit on a hot stove for two minutes, it seems like two hours. That's relativity.' – with apologies to Albert Einstein.

Early gardens were designed to be sensory-rich. Their designers were mindful of the power of nature to heal, of the need for a local food supply, and to provide gentle outdoor activity for all ages. The five basic senses of sight, smell, hearing, touch and taste were well accounted for. Modern sensory gardens accommodate other senses now being documented, such as awareness of our body in space. When we consider the history of healing gardens we need to look at the details. Local gardens develop as a response to local conditions, and suit the local community. By offering a garden-based response to modern social ills we raise the design profession in the eyes of the community, extend skills back towards those of the early garden designers, and offer the accountants a salve to their itchy red pen. Using similar salutogenic design principles in each setting, a city, school or healthcare agency can tackle problems before they get to the costly stage. Such a preventative approach is at the heart of salutogenic design.

We started the chapter by looking at the work of Edward O. Wilson. He says 'Children who remain out of touch with the natural world are like cattle in a feedlot. They may appear content, but are they children, or cattle, in the fullest sense?' The same is true for adults, whether young or ageing, and especially those with disability involving any form of sensory impairment. When we live without regular contact with the natural world we may appear content, but are we fully engaged and living life to our potential?

> We need nature in our lives more than ever today, and as more of us are living in cities it must be urban nature. Biophilic cities are cities that contain abundant nature; they are cities that care about, seek to protect, restore and grow this nature, and that strive to foster deep connections and daily contact with the natural world. Nature is not something optional, but absolutely essential to living a happy, healthy and meaningful life.
>
> (Beatley, 2010)

When we combine Beatley's view with the thinking of E. O. Wilson, paediatricians, physicians and psychologists, we have a solution to many of society's ills. If we take biophilia and apply the principles of monastic and Islamic garden design, attend to the fine details, the sensory stimuli, we see that what we create is more than the sum of its parts. In that way we can create healing gardens that will keep even the accountants happy. 'The best time to plant a tree was twenty years ago. The second best time is now' – Chinese proverb. Using the wisdom of the past we must take action to protect our future, today.

In subsequent chapters, we will look at applications for healing, sensory and therapeutic gardens in modern times. To account for those readers who wish to dip in and out of the text we will refer back to monastic garden design, and how we can use the design principles of old to feed mind, body and soul today. As we are genetically hard-wired to respond to nature, we must create healing garden environments that support us.

References

Beatley, T. (2010). *Biophilic cities: integrating nature into urban design and planning*. Washington, DC: Island Press.

Clark, E. (2004). *The art of the Islamic garden*. Ramsbury, Wiltshire: Crowood Press.

Gothein, M.-L. (1928). *A history of garden art*. Edited by W. P. Wright. London: Dent. First published Berlin, 1913.

Hobhouse, P. (2004). *Plants in garden history*. London: Pavilion.

Jekyll, G. (1914). *Colour schemes for the flower garden*. London: Country Life.

McLean, T. (1981). *Medieval English gardens*. New York: Viking Press.

SCU (2013). St. Clare Garden. Retrieved from *Santa Clara University*: www.scu.edu/stclaregarden/ethno/layout.cfm

Tyson, P. (2008, 4 January). NOVA: a conversation with E. O. Wilson. Retrieved March 2013, from *PBS*: www.pbs.org/wgbh/nova/nature/conversation-eo-wilson.html

CHAPTER 2

Why do we need gardens for health and well-being today?

Preventative policies and interventions for things like cardiovascular disease take 20 years to show their effect. If we are going to make a difference we need to start now and take a long term view. We will always need hospitals and a robust healthcare system, but for prevention, lifestyle factors make an enormous difference.

(Franklin, 2013)

Healing gardens need to be an integral part of our modern urban framework. Early Persian and later monastic gardens were a fundamental part of their society and communities. Their role was a mix of spiritual, welfare, educational and healing. While modern life has become more complex our basic needs remain unchanged. The contemporary health and well-being benefits of healing gardens spill over into education, crime prevention and social cohesion. Behind the promotion of nature connections as a cost-effective prevention and treatment option for many social and medical ills is an awareness of the big picture, and the economics at play.

We tend to take our health for granted, until compromised in some way. Poor mental or physical health, as a result of illness, injury or congenital condition can make it more difficult to access education, employment and the community in which we live. In discussions with disabled people we find little talk of disability from a physical perspective, but a great concern for and about disabling environments. Healing gardens are, by their nature, enabling environments.

There is a long history of using gardens for their mental and physical support. 'From the earliest times, the culinary and medicinal properties of herbs and aromatic plants have made them a vital part of human existence' (Lawless, 2005). Over the past 200 years or so we have designed towns and cities with parks and gardens to provide access to fresh air and exercise. A healing garden can occur in any setting. It is an area of open or enclosed space. Although traditionally found at ground level, with the demands of urbanisation pushing the price of land ever higher, roof top gardens, balconies and green (living) walls offer alternative healing gardens. Like any good residential garden they need a range of plants to give height, texture, colour, and fragrance, attract wildlife such as native birds and butterflies, and perhaps provide a fresh local food supply. They have comfortable seating from which to absorb and admire nature in all her glory. Varied access ways through the garden allow areas to 'open up', to be discovered, as we move through the space. Vertical gardens require a different design emphasis but can still provide measureable health benefits. Schools, hospitals, children's play grounds, city streets, shopping centres, village streets, homes and factories, offices and warehouses all need gardens to anchor them into the landscape.

Gardens are an important part of public open space. The UK planning document PPG17 specifies that open space should be taken to mean: 'all open space of public value, including not just land, but also areas of water such as rivers, canals, lakes and reservoirs which offer important opportunities for sport and recreation and can also act as a visual amenity' (ODPM, 2002).

Open space plays a vital role in meeting people's recreational needs in both formal and informal roles, from organised sports to walking, bird watching and picnics. Access to open spaces and thus recreational activities is integral to sustaining a decent quality of life. Not only are they places to meet friends, to exercise and to observe nature, they can also perform an important role in conservation and bio-diversity. Through the protection of natural features and the promotion and retention of natural habitats, nature is made obvious to city dwellers. Gardens can be part of active transport systems, movement corridors for pedestrians, cyclists and wildlife. They are a vital part of salutogenic urban design through the improved aesthetic value of the urban environment positively impacting upon people's health. Iconic gardens, such as New York City's High Line Park, are valued for their pro-motion of local, national and even international tourism, and for the subtle yet powerful sustainable and environmental educational message they can give.

Lifestyle related diseases and active, healthy lifestyles

To combat the increasing incidence of lifestyle-related, non-communicable diseases (NCDs) clinical, pharmaceutical and technology-based research is working hard, but at great expense. As the WHO has said, we need to promote active, healthy lifestyles if we are to curb the burden of disease (WHO, 2013a). No country can afford to maintain current levels of care against the epidemics of obesity and depression. To combat the unsustainable rising costs we need prevention strategies to support public health programmes. Fortunately landscape interventions can provide a win/win, achievable solution. Human health and well-being has been found to be inextricably linked to social and environmental factors (Wilkinson, 2003). There is a widespread recognition of the role of active lifestyles and a connection with nature in keeping populations healthy into old age (World Design and Health, 2013).

A healthy, active lifestyle is the basis of most public health promotion pro-grammes around the world. With a shrinking tax base from an ageing and increasingly disabled population, governments need to find new ways to keep people healthy and in the community as long as possible. As the pace of urbanisation and climate change increases, governments are under pressure to supply liveable towns and cities. A salutogenic design approach creates an environment that is nurturing and healing. Encouraging and enabling healthy behaviours using evidence-based urban design makes social, environmental and economic sense. Using land-scape interventions to adopt a preventative approach will create a healthier society and place lower demands on struggling healthcare systems.

Urban landscapes featuring gardens designed for health and well-being can affect both social and environmental determinants of disease. Where nature is valued, protected and enhanced, and ready access to nature is enshrined within local and national planning laws, human health is better than in areas where this is not the case. Obvious examples are in mining towns such as Weipa in Queensland, Australia. The earth is stripped bare and the local population is beset with lifestyle-induced health problems: NCDs such as alcoholism, family violence, obesity, and poor educational outcomes for children at school. In the process of developing the mine, local indigenous Aboriginal people have become dislocated from their traditional spiritual lands and lifestyle, and their health and well-being is, not surprisingly, seriously impacted.

Socially and economically deprived areas historically have had poor access to green space. Public and affordable housing has been characterised by a drab building sat in a patch of grass with perhaps a tree. Little consideration of the health and broader social impacts of the environment is visible, other than the bare acknowledgement that a green view is essential. With increasing migration to towns and cities and limited work opportunities for many, today more people are under stress and in need of affordable housing. Community disability levels are growing as the population ages, and as more adults and children disconnect socially and from nature and succumb to depression. However, the good news is that people not well served by market housing do respond well to integrated, landscape-led community health programmes. The Green Prescription was introduced in recognition of this. The *British Medical Journal* found that 'community walking, exercise and nutrition, and brief advice with exercise on prescription (Green Prescription) were the most cost-effective with respect to cost-utility' (Ministry of Health, 2011). Inequality of access to healing environments is seen as a major threat to public health.

It is difficult to live a healthy lifestyle without an appropriate environment. Healthy choices, whether meeting friends in the park, eating fresh fruit or cycling to school have to be the easy option. When we ignore the effect of environment on productivity, child health and development, we overlook the link between ecological health and that of vulnerable disabled, older or socially disadvantaged people. Our cities and areas within our cities can quickly resemble mining towns. Young and old easily fall prey to malnutrition, asthma, depression, type 2 diabetes and coronary heart disease. These NCDs are preventable illnesses. If governments, housing providers and educators are to be socially and economically accountable, environmental quality and the widespread provision of healing green space must be of major interest and concern.

Hard landscapes and hard politics

Hard landscapes have been, and still are, over-represented in cities and towns around the world. Concrete and asphalt surfaces are laid in abundance. With some notable exceptions, the hard lines of the built environment have become a feature of modern contemporary design. Alongside the rise in popularity of sharp edges, concrete and steel there has been a concomitant rise in rates of cancer, obesity and depression –

the NCDs that soft landscape interventions or healing gardens have been shown to effectively treat or prevent (Stigsdotter et al., 2011). These conditions are not the only problems seen in predominantly hard environments. Aggressive behaviours and a lack of age-appropriate social skills have been noted in school playgrounds such as that shown in Figure 2.1, and particularly in areas where the surrounding urban environment is also hard.

We were brought in to discuss the development of healing gardens and natural play alternatives as an antidote to the effects of the current playground. Staff and student stress levels were high, absenteeism was high and aspirations and general educational outcomes were low. The problem is common in schools around the world. Distracted, fidgeting behaviour exhibited in the classroom leads school administrators and politicians to wrongly believe children need to 'burn off energy', so they allow a plethora of hard surfaces and play structures to dominate. They falsely believe that overweight, stressed and depressed children need to run around to improve their health, so remove outdoor seats from parks and playgrounds. In fact the opposite is true. Local politics needs to be aware of and acknowledge the good that comes from a softer, salutogenic approach, and the damage that is done by a hard environment.

The global burden of disease is such that we need to change the way we look at urban design, education and healthcare. Case study 3 highlights a missed opportunity to develop healthy active lifestyles and improve social cohesion. The inefficient use of public funds is unforgiveable in times of economic recession. Hard political lessons need to be learned. Budget efficiencies are not found by cutting the landscape component from development budgets. Effective community consultation and awareness of the wider issues at stake must inform procurement decisions.

Figure 2.1
Bleak school playground, Enfield, UK.

Case study 3: BSF School, Midlands, England

In 2011 I was invited to address a consortium of school leaders to discuss the benefits from and opportunities for learning outside the classroom. The host venue was a new school, completed as part of the government's school improvement programme. Designed to house 1,400 students between the ages of 11 and 16, it was bright and shiny and had windows with views from the library to the distant hills. While a mainstream school, there was a higher than average number of children with registered special needs on the roll, including students with mobility impairments. The school was part of a strong multicultural community. Outside, the grounds were extensive; spread over 8 hectares (20 acres), they sloped away to the south. Taking account of the sloping site, the main entrance was on the upper level. Internally the building was set around an open central hub. To save children from the possibility of throwing themselves over the balcony railing to the school cafeteria below, clear perspex safety walls, as used in prisons, had been installed. CCTV monitored every corridor. Indoors the environment was experienced as aggressive, distrustful and slightly unnerving. There were two doors the children could use to get outside. One was 'upstairs', requiring an external flight of some sixty steps to access the playground; the other was downstairs, opening onto a windswept, shaded, hard-paved undercroft. The social part of the 'playground' consisted of an open expanse of asphalt with nine backless bench seats set in a long line, and five rubbish bins, for the 1,400 children. At lunchtime the large grass sports field was filled with tough-looking older boys playing football. There was nothing to attract the majority of the young people to leave the building. With no provision for free outdoor play, there was no reason for non-football players to go outside. For the non-sporty types, there were no seats placed to admire the view, no sheltered, inclusive, sunny, soft-landscaped spaces to sit quietly and observe or meet friends. No colour or fragrance enlivened the space. Not surprisingly, most children chose to stay indoors, to 'play' on their own, on their phones.

When we talk about healing gardens we talk about creating a sensory experience. I found the experience of this school disturbing. The school felt like a prison and the children moved around as if they were in one. Even after the investment of many millions on new buildings, aspirations and achievements were low. The learning-outside-the-classroom initiative was a way to break the cycle of poor schooling outcomes indoors. Over the course of the workshop we discussed how best to deal with the problems local schools were experiencing. Below-average achievement and below-average social skills were the principal reasons school leaders wanted to be able to take students outside. From a design perspective, development of accessible paths and connected, protected spaces for individuals, small and medium sized groups, and class sized soft spaces outdoors were seen as essential. The schools also had other problems. Strict local imams would not allow their young people to study music. Rather than having a group of students excluded from the curriculum, we worked with the music department to create new habitats – quiet spaces outdoors where teachers could take small groups to study environmental music. The imams were happy because the consideration brought the students closer to an appreciation of the beauty of paradise on earth. The school was happy because the students could access the curriculum. The students were happy and inspired to explore education 'outside the box'. They found it is possible to create a symphony from natural sounds of birdsong, grass rustling, wind through power wires, insects rasping. The initiative proved popular with non-Islamic students also, as the young people connected with nature for, in some cases, the first time in their lives.

'Article 28. Recognise that effective NCD prevention and control require leadership and multi sectoral approaches for health at the government level, including, as appropriate, health in all policies and whole of government approaches across such sectors as, inter alia, health, education, energy, agriculture, sports, transport, communication, urban planning, environment, labour, employment, industry and trade, finance and social and economic development.'

WHO, NCD Action Plan (WHO, 2013b)

Healing landscape interventions can make a difference to longevity, quality of life, and the general well-being of communities. To be effective, a multi-disciplinary, co-operative approach is essential. If we are to avoid flat, featureless playgrounds such as shown in Figure 2.2, we need to consider what we are aiming to achieve.

Through the development of healing landscapes across schools, towns and cities we can cost-effectively decrease the economic and social threat of NCDs. The United Nations agreed *ad referendum* that the importance of environment and a collaborative approach between inter-disciplinary grounds is such that we must

Acknowledge that the global burden and threat of non-communicable disease constitutes one of the major challenges for development of in the 21st century which undermines social and economic development throughout the word and threatens the achievement of internationally agreed development goals.

(Diess, 2011)

Figure 2.2
Bleak special needs playground, Midlands, UK.

If we ever needed evidence that we can have a positive effect on human health and well-being, the World Health Organisation's Global Strategy on Diet, Physical Activity and Health shows how. It asserts that non-communicable diseases can be prevented and their impacts significantly reduced though regular and intense physical exercise, urban planning, active transport and healthy-lifestyle work sites, and the increased availablity of safe environments in public parks and recreational spaces to encourage physical activity (WHO, 2013a). To apply this guidance requires someone to take the initiatve. Private developers may yet outperform governments as they see the financial benefits of providing for the WHO's strategy.

Government initiatives

Governments are slowly catching on to the need for a different approach to urban design, public health and education. With mounting conflict and pressure on resources around the world, growing numbers of refugees and migrants are expected to become common. This can be to our advantage as we design our towns and cities. The WHO states that we must 'recognize further the potential and contribution of traditional and local knowledge and in this regard, respect, and preserve . . . the knowledge and safe and effective use of traditional medicine, treatments and practices . . .' (WHO, 2013b). Traditional knowledge is often displaced as people move, but with healing gardens it is possible to incorporate that wisdom to the benefit of the relocated community, and hence the supporting economy.

Since the onset of the global financial crisis there has been an increasing awareness across multiple sectors that things cannot go on as before. At roughly the same time as the global banking system went into meltdown, so did the polar ice cap. Extreme weather events have brought drought, snow, flood and hurricane to widespread areas of the UK, Asia, Australasia, Europe and the USA. While some people continue to debate the cause of the changing weather patterns, 97 per cent of climate scientists agree that the effects are anthropogenic, or man-made. But regardless of cause, our climate is changing. While governments fear the cost of doing something, the cost of doing nothing grows. Forced migration, infrastructure upgrades and replacement, and the security of food and drinking water supplies are already affecting communities. We need to think globally but act locally to provide for the health of our communities.

As the changing climate requires us to adapt, so too does the global economic situation. Evidence-based design works on the premise that we change the way we do things when we have seen the evidence to support that change. The evidence is crushingly obvious all around us. Health, education and welfare budgets are decreasing as infrastructure costs rise. The cost of mitigating climate change is currently estimated at 4 per cent of gross domestic product (GDP) (OECD, 2008) if we act now. If we do not act, replacement infrastructure costs are predicted to rise to 20 per cent of GDP. Insurance companies are already paying out on damages caused by uncharacteristic weather events. Claims for weather-related catastrophes have *tripled* since 1980. Within a focus on healing gardens we have an opportunity to put in place environments that will mitigate climate change, consciously use less manufactured resources in the provision of those environments, and cost-effectively

Figure 2.3
Community
gardens raised
beds, London.

support the health and well-being of the people. We can affect the environmental determinants of health. As a result of the convergence of climate, health and financial challenges we must find innovative ways to provide better value from fewer resources. Landscape is uniquely placed to provide a solution.

With major world bodies like the United Nations and the World Health Organisation emphasising the need (a) to act now and (b) to recognise environment as a useful tool in the fight against NCDs, government initiatives must lead the way. Outdated market perceptions that landscape was merely a nice-to-have feature, have meant many environmental components of development schemes have been squeezed out of public and private development budgets. Examples include playgrounds in residential developments, living (green) roofs, green walls, natural shade, rainwater harvesting, green light wells, and general healing soft-landscape treatments. Misconceptions of the value of landscape within the broader design community have meant horticultural knowledge has not been sought as part of the development process.

There has been, however, a growing awareness on the part of politicians, academics and practitioners, of the need to reconnect children in particular, but also their adult community, with nature.

Increasing numbers of children are losing contact with the natural world. Reasons include childcare centers with outdoor spaces that do not support children's developmental needs; the rapid growth of domestic air-conditioning since the 1950s; apprehensive parents who keep their children close to home; state-mandated curricula that do not allow time for study outdoors; and the overly-structured, harried lifestyle of many children today.

(NCSU, 2012)

The UK government's 'Healthy Living Healthy Eating' initiative came about as a response to rising levels of unhealthy lifestyles leading to childhood obesity, depression and low educational aspiration. The programme encourages schools to educate children in the benefits of eating fresh foods and taking exercise. In some places local businesses support the schools with supplies of free fruit for the children. It is placed before them and they are expected to eat it. According to teachers much is thrown away uneaten. For those readers who have children, you will know that it is sometimes difficult to get a child to do what you want. It is so much easier if you can let them think they are deciding for themselves by providing appropriate choices. Think how much simpler and less expensive it would be if the businesses supported schools by providing appropriate trees. In that way children are involved in the growing and have a personal interest in the literal fruits of their labour. When the school is able to grow fruit on site, which the children can then learn about, pick and eat on their way out to play, the uptake is vastly improved. The old saying holds true: If we provide an apple we can feed a child for a day; if we plant an orchard we can feed a village for a year.

Design note: When we design for health and well-being in schools we are mindful that clients will often be working with restricted budgets. In order to make their money go further we need to look, for example, at what other functions an orchard could perform. If designed along monastic principles, an orchard can also become an integral part of an outdoor reading space, rather than relegated to a far corner of the site. Fruit trees can be planted to provide a sensory-rich environment. With that comes the opportunity to provide seating, grass, bug hotels for pollinating insects, birds and bees, fragrance and flowers and the seasonal variation of nature, designed to attract the attention of the most ardent 'plugged in' child.

The US Natural Learning Initiative aims to promote outdoor play and learning. Funded by the Forest Service College of Design, the North Carolina State University-led scheme is developing guidelines for natural play. The Initiative was founded in 2000 with the purpose of promoting the importance of the natural environment as part of the daily experience of all children, through environmental design, action research, education, and dissemination of information. Programmes addressing childhood obesity and depression are making a difference to the quality of life of children and their communities across the United States. There is still much to be done, but the will and impetus is growing. Across the USA and internationally, ideas such as the multi-purpose orchard mentioned before can readily be installed, even in schools with only a fenceline strip of space. Espaliered and other ready-trained fruiting vines and trees are ideal in confined spaces. Government initiatives may be slow in coming, but site managers have abundant opportunities to explore the potential of gardens for health.

Natural play and healing gardens

> For this generation and the last, nature is more an abstraction than reality.
> (Louv, 2005)

The current generation of children is the first for 200 years predicted to have a lower life expectancy than their parents. Many children have been kept indoors by parents and teachers keen to them safe from the perceived threats of the sun, strangers, and in some cases, nature. What no one expected was that a plethora of organised activities and time spent watching TV and other devices would in fact do known harm. Perceptions of risk and fear cripple unnecessarily. We cannot make the world safe. Twenty years of safety surfacing in playgrounds has not reduced the rate of Accident & Emergency admissions. In fact these have gone up, as we think it is safe so take risks (Ball, 2002). Our children, like our forests, have become ill.

Increasing numbers of children have lost contact with the natural world. A recent report by Natural England shows that although 81 per cent of children say they want to play outside, only 10 per cent are actually playing in parks and open space. Play is a fundamental way through which we employ the senses to explore, navigate and come to know the world and its various constituent beings, environs and forces. When playing one adopts openness to the world in the moment, responding to not only the cognitively recognised but also the corporeally sensed (Woodyer, 2011). To turn around the health of a generation we must encourage and enable natural play. We must provide access to suitably unstructured environments, where the children can sense corporeally their environment and respond to it.

In Chapter 5 we shall look at the needs of children specifically, and in Chapter 10 at the design elements required to support the crucial role of play. Play is not just for children. To feel a sense of well-being, adults benefit from a playful sense of humour, and opportunities to 'release their inner child'. Space to simply have fun is vital for us all. Natural play in a healing garden environment is embodied in the collapse of the threshold between 'reality' and 'unreality' that is characteristic of play. Playful gardens are those that entice and excite, allowing imaginations to soar; they are sufficiently rich that we are forced to engage and then suspend reality. When children, and adults, can play hide-and-seek in the long grass, or lie on their backs looking for shapes in the clouds, they are reducing their risk of NCDs. Natural play is not about sending children to an annual 'fat camp' in the woods; it is about providing the healing green spaces where they live, play and go to school and then allowing them to engage with them in their own way.

Traditional and local knowledge

Indigenous populations often have strong links with nature. For some that connection has been lost, as adults and children everywhere become 'plugged in' to electronic media. This breakdown, or disconnection from nature, is reflected in a rising incidence of NCDs, destructive lifestyles and poor educational and social outcomes among indigenous communities in North America, Oceania and South America. The United Nations' political declaration on the Prevention and Control of Non-communicable Disease states that we need to recognise the potential and contribution of traditional and local knowledge, such that we respect and preserve the safe and effective use of traditional medicine. Sometimes that medicine is simply tending the gardens. Other times it involves decoctions of medicinal plants from the garden (United Nations, 2011).

Figure 2.4 Riverside regeneration and public green space, Brisbane, Australia.

In Australia, Brazil, the USA and New Zealand, as indigenous community leaders respond to the problem of NCDs rather than sending their people off to drug and alcohol rehab programmes, it can be more effective to address the issues using landscape interventions. As the UN suggests, traditional medicine can be a powerful tool. A slow, sensitive, consultative approach allows us to quietly draw out traditional and local knowledge to assist in designing gardens along traditional lines, and provide horticultural advice where this knowledge has been lost. Over time the 'medicine' becomes working on the land. This is not the time for rushed corporate or funding provider deadlines. Environmental destruction of and dislocation from traditional lands means the consultation stage can often be a painful process. However, it is essential in developing healing gardens to work collaboratively and to respect local awareness of the environment as told through oral histories.

Using that understanding we can develop expressive gardens that give meaning to the indigenous community. As with monastic gardens, local food and medicinal herb growing is an intrinsic part of how traditional communities worked. Diet and food preparation were linked to locally, seasonally available foods. With 'fast food' outlets spreading across the globe, the incentive for people to grow and prepare nutritious meals has been diminished. Part of the healing process for indigenous communities is to restore local food growing, and, where necessary, teach nutritious food preparation.

The digital age

We now live in a digital age. Post-industrial society has emerged as plugged in and tuned out. Socially it is harder to meet people, although we have more online opportunities than ever before. We use our phones not for talking to people but to send abbreviated messages and access information. Our sensory systems are overloaded with ultra-fast access to data, much of it irrelevant to our daily life.

At the same time as we have plugged ourselves in to the digital world we have tuned out from the natural world and concomitantly witnessed a surge in the incidence of NCDs across our communities. Stress and depression are reported not

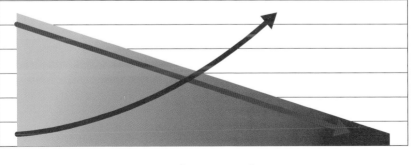

Nature connection as it affects stress and quality of life

■ Sense of well-being   ➡ Stress   ➡ Connection with Nature

Figure 2.5
Nature–stress connection chart.

only by indigenous communities but by adults and children throughout the developed world. As shown in Figure 2.5, as our connection with nature diminishes our levels of stress increase. Over time our quality of life is affected, shown as a direct relationship between a sense of well-being and the proportion of time we spend in nature, or in sight of green space. When connected with nature we report low stress levels and a high sense of well-being, shown as quality of life.

In this digital age it is increasingly common to go through a day without being outside in natural daylight. Many people work long hours, so can leave and arrive home in the dark. Depending on where they work they may or may not have external windows near their workspace. Screen glare means that if we do have external windows we often choose to close the blinds, cutting our connection to life beyond the building. Working environments affect quality and productivity. With increasingly sophisticated technology we create a need for adapted work environments. For example, we expect a surgeon and his/her team to stand at an operating table for 10+ hours. Fatigue could have a serious effect on the outcome of their work. Given our knowledge of the restorative qualities of healing gardens there is an opportunity to bring that into the operating theatre. The research enquiry has often stopped at that point, as in the hospital there is also a need for sterile conditions. The World Design and Health Institute has developed environmental solutions to these problems. Based in Sweden, the Institute draws on global expertise. New hospitals in South Africa, Singapore and Canada show the success of the design innovations. The Institute concentrated on healthcare settings initially, as that is where the research money has been focussed. However, their research-based design innovations are able to be transposed into general architectural design. Anywhere that high cognitive functioning is important can benefit from access to a green view and healing gardens. Regardless of the strength of the testimony, the status quo has been slow to adopt this evidence-based design. We still design buildings that look largely like those of thirty years ago. Clients only know so much, and the brief they provide can only ever reflect their knowledge at the time. It is our responsibility to educate our clients, and our colleagues. New solutions to old challenges are being found; old solutions to old challenges are being rediscovered.

> Aroma scientists are developing chemical scents of nature so they can be piped in to our sealed enclosures, our homes, factories and our hospitals. While academics, developers and practitioners recognise that it is a connection with nature we seek, the first thought has not been to bring the real thing into our (clients') lives but how to manufacture a facsimile of a healing garden experience. The incidence of lower respiratory tract diseases such as asthma is increasing. Airborne chemicals aggravate delicate lungs. Is there a link?

In a discussion of landscapes for health and well-being we find many connections, linkages and associations. It is important to join the dots. As Aristotle said, man is by nature a social animal. Social connections are as important for our health and well-being as connections with nature. Bizarrely, considering the numerous social connections we have through online media, we are more socially isolated than ever before. The newly popular single lifestyle is attributed to increased levels of intolerance for others in their personal space, causing people to choose to live alone. People have few opportunities to get to know people in neutral surroundings. Employers are noticing that people are starting work without the necessary social skills. In hard-edged school environments social skills do not develop through play as they used to, due to parent and teacher communities obsessed with academic results. In 2005 we thought we were fortunate to send our 10-year-old twins to one of the top schools in England. They had been high achievers in previous international schools and enjoyed playing with friends, sport, music, history and geography, as well as the core subjects. We were shocked to discover that here there was no time after school for play as home study pogrammes filled available daylight hours. In school the creative arts and sport curriculum was replaced by extra English, maths and science until the final six weeks of term, after the end-of-year exams. Although the children were supposed to receive a balanced programme throughout the year, the school chose to bend the rules and push hard for academic results. After a year in the school our children knew few of their classmates, and like many others were bored and became disillusioned. Parents clamour for better results, less play time, less time just messing about with friends outside, often without realising the known harm that is done as a result (Louv, 2005).

Like schools, we have allowed our cities and towns to become busy places with few spaces to pause and share a moment with a friend, family member or colleague. While we talk about the importance of place making we have ignored the reasons why we need such places. We have allowed a generation of adults and children to disconnect from nature as we have swept through urban open space developments on a vast scale, spaces that may permit and promote rapid transit but do little to foster social integration.

To counter the ill effects of the fast-paced digital age, we need to slow our personal lives down. Although designed with an emphasis on visual elements, urban environments are experienced by people using their varied sensorium. Different sensory stimuli contribute different layers of meaning and understanding to place, experience and identity, with sensory information sometimes aligned, sometimes contrasting. However, the notion of five separate recognised senses is somewhat misleading, and although scholarly and professional activity has been organised according to these senses, for example by visual artists, acousticians, thermal researchers and perfumiers, there are clear overlaps in sensory phenomena, requiring an inter-disciplinary approach to related urban research and design.

Vulnerable individuals, young and old and their response to healing gardens

While young and old are equally vulnerable, we live in an ageing society. Statistically, as people age they are more likely to develop health concerns. Treatment of such conditions already burdens health budgets. In future the challenge will only get worse.

'The Global Burden of Disease, a study conducted by the World Health Organization and the World Bank, with partial support from the U.S. National Institute on Aging, predicts a very large increase in disability caused by increases in age-related chronic disease in all regions of the world. In a few decades, the loss of health and life worldwide will be greater from non-communicable or chronic diseases (e.g., cardiovascular disease, dementia and Alzheimer's disease, cancer, arthritis, and diabetes) than from infectious diseases, childhood diseases, and accidents.'

(Dobriansky, 2007)

There are three features of the ageing population which soft landscape inter-ventions can actively assist with:

1 Changing family structures. As people choose to live alone and have fewer children, family structures are transformed, leaving older people reduced options for care.
2 The overall ageing population. For the first time in history, people aged 65 and over will soon outnumber children under age 5.
3 The growing burden of non-communicable disease. Chronic non-communicable diseases are now the major cause of death among older people in both more developed and less developed countries.

(Dobriansky, 2007)

While healing gardens will not necessarily facilitate an increase in the birth rate, they do provide places to congregate for social support. In parts of Asia, Africa and Europe older people are cared for by their extended families, in a mutually supportive environment. One of the effects of changing family structures is social isolation. Where children are part of the mix, families are often dislocated by availability of work and so not available for immediate social support. In places where extended family life is not common, we need to provide public space that encourages our ageing population to gather, for friendship and exercise.

With the overall population ageing, it means that our emphasis on the needs of children over the past decade will shift slightly towards more inclusive spaces. We will always need to look after the young, and to ensure they are given time and space to develop social skills and are able to engage and connect with the natural world. However, the weight of numbers will mean that financially more resources will go into active ageing. From a design perspective, the nature and social connection needs of the young are not so different to the needs of senior citizens. Salutogenic urban design needs to acknowledge this. Going forward, 'playgrounds' and sensory-rich adventure gardens may include fitness equipment and features that are equally attractive to young and old, albeit sized and weighted appropriately.

Social isolation is a killer. Chronic NCDs such as depression flourish in areas where people cannot easily connect with each other. Therefore we must be alert to this when designing social housing, public open spaces, and communal areas around schools and parks. Conveniently located gardens with interesting views, planting and wildlife, seating and shelter provide somewhere to go and something to talk about. Gardens that people can actively participate in provide something to do. In order to live meaningful lives our community seniors need to be made welcome. Inclusive design requires more than low maintenance spaces that are accessible for young and old. We need to ensure access from adjacent buildings that allows for easy, independent, transition outdoors. In this way young children can freely explore and master their environment, and older people can carry on living independently for as long as possible, rather than becoming dependents prematurely, disabled by their environment.

We need healing gardens for their salutogenic health benefits through promotion of active healthy lifestyles, nature connections and social connections. The young and the old are not the only vulnerable members of our communities to benefit from healing gardens as enabling spaces. Increasing numbers of immigrants and refugees are seeking the safety, health, education, employment and food security of our countries. One of the ways we can assist with the resettlement process is to provide gardens that allow immigrants access to plants and foods they are familiar with, or where local conditions are unsuitable, familiar planting and cultivation opportunities. Sometimes all it takes to de-stress a young refugee is time out of the classroom and in the garden or greenhouse, surrounded by fresh air, soil, water and plants. The feelgood factor spills out into the community. The young people feel more comfortable in their new home; less violence is seen on the streets, fewer self-harming behaviours are seen and drugs and alcohol become less of a prop. It may sound simple and indeed seem simplistic in its approach, but therapeutic horticulture programmes and healing gardens work.

Figure 2.6 Therapeutic horticulture programme for refugee children, Manchester.

Source: Sowing Success.

The Chicago Botanic Garden, like some other garden bodies around the world, offers a programme in therapeutic horticulture. It is designed to teach students how to run a therapy programme for specific groups of people. Internationally, with increasing numbers of people suffering stress and the debility of inactive lifestyles, demand for the design of areas to facilitate such programmes will increase. Appropriate healing garden spaces will afford more people healthy lifestyles. The more accessible gardens we can provide, close to where people live and work, the better. Landscape interventions are subtle. There is no hard sales pitch required. By supplying the easy option on their doorstep, and in conjunction with health facilitators, healing landscapes offer a cost-effective way to stay healthy and strong. Many older people fear the costs of age and infirmity. Healing gardens and therapeutic green space can reinforce the direct connection that staying active has to keeping their most common medical problems minimised, and ultimately reducing their medical costs.

Older people are often known as time rich but cash poor. It is important to cater to their special needs and requests. Providing accessible open space, whether green or blue, that caters for individual use or within a structured therapy programme is an inexpensive way to keep people active while reducing public costs.

> 96 year old 'Banana George' Blair, an avid bare foot water skier, knows the importance of investing in your health today to prepare for a better tomorrow. Given his achievements smashing world records, he says ' . . . maintaining a fit and healthy lifestyle is important to sustaining your energy levels, enhancing quality of life and ensuring that you can be in good health'.
>
> (Motus, 2009)

Figure 2.7 Banana George – 96-year-old water skier.

Source: MOTUS www.motususfitness equipment.blogspot.com

Other benefits of healing gardens and green space

Urban planners, landscape architects and architects work within the remit of local regulations. In some countries health and education are devolved to the local level but often people wait to be told what to do by those 'at the top'. Organisations such as the UK school grounds charity Learning Through Landscapes acknowledge that the top-down approach needs to be supplemented by community-based action. They have published data (Titman, 1994) showing that when children regularly spend time in quality outdoor environments they value those environments, and develop a deeper understanding of the natural world and a profound respect for it, and for themselves. There are community-led, bottom-up approaches to conservation. When we work with local government to design and develop open space we have an opportunity to create not just a functional space but a beautiful garden space. When we work together with the community and stakeholders to create spaces that showcase seasonal variation, that welcome wildlife, that welcome people of all ages, abilities and cultures, our work has the ability to profoundly affect public mood and support for the environment. In a garden that has been designed for its healing effect, whether that be sensory-rich or deliberately calm and quiet, people will notice nature. They will engage with the space on a fundamental level.

Figure 2.8 Engaging sensory garden, London.

At the moment many people walk in the park or sit on a bench to eat their lunch, without really noticing what is going on around them. For their health and the well-being of the planet we need them to connect, to engage. That means they need something to engage with. A healing garden is more than a collection of plants – it is an ecologically rich space within our urban centres. To be a healing space it will include trees, flowering plants, some sunshine and some shade. It will be somewhere to sit in the cool on a hot summer's day, perhaps listen to flowing water, feed the birds or watch insects at work.

For human health and well-being, it does not matter whether the nature connection is made with colourful introduced plants in herbaceous borders, ducks on the pond or pigeons in the park, or perhaps one day locally rare species attracted back to the city centre by enhanced green space. What is important is that there are opportunities to make those connections.

References

Ball, D. J. (2002). *Playgrounds: risks, benefits and choices*. Contract research report no. 426/2002, Middlesex University, London. Available https://eprints.mdx.ac.uk/4990/1/crr02426.pdf

Diess, J. (2011, 9 September). UN draft political declaration of the high level meeting on the prevention and control of non communicable diseases. Retrieved 12 December 2013, from *United Nations*: www.un.org/en/ga/ncdmeeting2011/pdf/NCD_draft_political_declaration.pdf

Dobriansky, P. J. (2007). *Why population aging matters: a global perspective*. Washington, DC: National Institute on Aging and National Institute of Health, US Department of Health and Human Services, US Department of State.

Franklin, R., Dr. (2013, 6 October). Interviewed by the author.

Lawless, J. (2005). *The fragrant garden*. London: Kyle Cathie Limited.

Louv, R. (2005). *Last child in the woods*. New York: Algonquin Books of Chapel Hill.

Ministry of Health (2011, 25 May). Green prescriptions. Retrieved 12 December 2013, from *Ministry of Health*: www.health.govt.nz/our-work/preventative-health-wellness/physical-activity/green-prescriptions

Motus (2009). Motus USA fitness blog. Retrieved 2013, from *Motus USA Fitness Blog*: http://motususafitnessequipment.blogspot.co.nz/2009_11_01_archive.html

NCSU (2012). Natural play and learning. Retrieved 2013, from NLI: www.natura learning.org/content/natural-play-and-learning-area-guidelines-project

ODPM (Office of the Deputy Prime Minister) (2002, September). Assessing needs and opportunities: a companion guide to PPG17. Retrieved March 2013, from https://www.gov.uk/government/uploads/system/uploads/attachment_data/file/7 660/156780.pdf

OECD (2008). Climate change mitigation: what do we do? Retrieved July 2013, from *OECD*: www.oecd.org/environment/cc/41751042.pdf

Stigsdotter, U. K., Palsdottir, A. M., Burls, A., Chermaz, A., Ferrini, F. and Grahn, P. (2011). Nature-based therapeutic interventions. In: Nilsson, K. and Sangster, M. (eds) *Forests, trees and human health* (pp. 309–342). London: Springer Publications.

Titman, W. (1994). *Special places, special people: the hidden curriculum of school grounds*. Surrey: WWF and LTL.

United Nations (2011, 19 September). Political declaration of the high-level meeting of the General Assembly on the prevention and control of non communicable diseases. New York: United Nations.

WHO (2013a). Global strategy on diet, physical activity and health. Retrieved 2013, from *World Health Organisation*: www.who.int/dietphysicalactivity/en/

—— (2013b). NCD action plan. Geneva: WHO. Retrieved July 2013, from *World Health Organisation*: www.who.int/nmh/publications/ncd_action_plan2013.pdf

Wilkinson, R. G. (2003). *Social determinants of health: the solid facts*. Geneva: WHO.

Woodyer, T. (2011). Allowing for the 'as-if,' 'what-if' and 'something more': the embodiment,vitality, and ethical responsiveness of play. Sawyer Series. University of Edinburgh.

World Design and Health (2013, 9–11 July). 9th World Congress. Brisbane: WDH.

CHAPTER 3

Urban space degradation

> Urban space degradation is impacted by issues of sustainability, environ-
> ment, nature and health. Our perception of and appreciation for urban space
> is in large part determined by the quality of the green space.
>
> (REC Slovakia, 2008)

After development, utilisation and production of waste, areas of urban land are
abandoned and left to decay. Developers know these areas as brownfield sites (EPA,
2011). Degraded sites require a supplementary budget for site investigation and
remediation (Genske, 2003). This chapter connects varied research perspectives to
discuss the issue of urban space degradation as an international issue affecting
quality of life. Landscape design for health and well-being relies on high quality
urban space, developed in close collaboration with local residents, landowners and
policy makers. Community involvement, recognition and support are vital to the
long-term success of any redevelopment project. Where urban areas have become
degraded it is generally because the community and the policy makers have
disconnected from the area.

The linkages between nations, cultures and communities are growing. Urban
degradation does not just affect the American Midwest or the UK's North East. The
health impacts of an economically mobile community are far reaching, and indeed
transnational. In economic boom times development is rapid, often with little
consideration for sustainability and public health. Immigrants flood into an area to
cash in on the opportunity. When economic fortunes change whole communities
are affected. Temporary immigrants become stranded. The environment is often
degraded as the developer/employer withdraws and leaves either a hole in the
ground, decaying buildings or standing machinery.

Urban degradation does not only happen due to economics. With increased
migration predicted as a result of conflict and climate change, further urban areas
are likely to be in danger of becoming degraded. For example, as people move from
flooded, low lying nations such as Tuvalu and Kiribati in search of jobs and liveable
weather, population density will rise in Sydney and Auckland as it falls correspond-
ingly in Funafuti and South Tarawa. Unplanned, rapid population growth could pose
as significant a risk to health and well-being as do declining populations. Where
residual community numbers fall below levels able to support key services, this has
the same effect as oversubscribed schools and hospitals.

Regardless of cause, it is important to recognise and understand that the issues of urban degradation we are facing are universal; that is they will be or have been experienced elsewhere before.

Some 75 per cent of the population of Central Europe currently resides in urban areas – a figure which is likely to continue to grow. The spread of urbanisation removes previously clear boundaries between settlement and surrounding landscape. This puts greater pressure on the natural landscape setting. In many urban areas, such as Paris and Budapest, the historic core is surrounded by new suburbs, which are functionally linked to the urban centre. This requires transport links, which have in turn caused fragmentation of the natural environment and a loss of biodiversity. In this context, open spaces play a vital role. If active transport systems are part of the urban plan, then healing landscapes can be designed into the development. Community-led cycling and walking routes linking the newly expanding suburbs to the historic core create an attractive and liveable city.

Urban degradation and poorly developed green space within towns and cities can influence economic prosperity. For example, in the town of Noosa, Australia, when the adjacent national park was made accessible and a feature, the area began to grow in popularity. As the towns' green infrastructure – the stormwater and sewage treatment, parks, playgrounds and gardens – was enhanced, tourist numbers increased. This attracted additional investment, and permanent residents and businesses were encouraged to establish there.

> Urban development is not only about planning buildings and activities, but also about creating places having a positive impact on their surroundings. The design of high quality urban spaces, involving inputs from community groups, is also an increasingly important aspect of the planning process. Such places help to define the public life of a village or town by strengthening the 'local spirit'.
>
> (REC Slovakia, 2008)

Quality of landscape and quality of life

As the preamble to the European Landscape Convention declares:

> the landscape is an important part of the quality of life for people everywhere . . . it is a key element in individual and social wellbeing . . . in urban areas as in the countryside, in degraded areas as well as areas of high quality, in areas recognised as being of outstanding beauty as well as everyday areas.
>
> (Déjeant-Pons, 2006)

Parks and green spaces naturally form a vital component of the urban landscape, but so do many other elements. These include streets and squares, cemeteries and allotment gardens, housing landscapes and industrial sites, waste ground and urban agriculture.

Although the urban landscape is where the vast majority of people live and work, it appears strangely invisible, in particular to many policy makers. One of the main reasons for the unseen nature of the urban landscape is that we are not used to

Case study 4: London, UK

Former brownfield sites are often redeveloped as housing. Figure 3.1 showcases not so much 'degradation' as missed opportunity. The housing development is surrounded by green space, albeit of low quality in terms of biodiversity, potential for restored habitat, aesthetics and utility. There is little incentive in terms of attraction to use it other than as a cycleway or dog exercise area. Its impact on local human health and well-being is likely to be minimal. Air quality will be improved as some airborne pollutants are filtered and dust levels reduced. However, the biggest opportunities to boost the mental health of the community have largely been missed. Balconies facing the green space are largely absent, or too small to be used to sit out on or to grow and tend containerised plants. There is no communal seating to encourage residents to step outside, meet and enjoy the space. The path is a hard-paved, simple transit route rather than branched and potentially softened through the use of adjacent planting and inexpensive, permeable materials suggesting interesting places to explore.

Figure 3.1 Urban degradation.

Figure 3.2 Urban improvement.

Figure 3.3 Street
fruit trees watered
from house roofs,
New Zealand.

Figure 3.4 Urban
green space
development, France.

Source: Emmanuelle
Soubeyran.

perceiving it in its totality. The downstream effects on health and education have been missed in discussions surrounding landscapes. Often decisions taken for pragmatic reasons mean that we lose sight of the overall strategic importance of the urban landscape as a vital resource.

In fact the urban landscape is central to most, if not all of the issues which are currently seen as being important. It is the strategic resource which can enhance the quality of life, ensure an attractive environment for investors and act as an important basis for the health of the urban population. If our design affords corridors for active transport systems we strengthen social cohesion and even make available the necessary spatial infrastructure for urban water management (EULP, 2008).

One of the impacts of urban degradation is seen in the deteriorating mental health of the community. There is considerable overlap between mental health problems, substance misuse and homelessness. In urban areas without a well-designed and managed community of salutogenic housing and gardens this group of people is in considerable distress for much of the time.

Population growth and economic development are leading to urban space degradation through rapid changes in our global ecosystems. In recognition of this, then United Nations' Secretary-General Kofi Annan, called for the

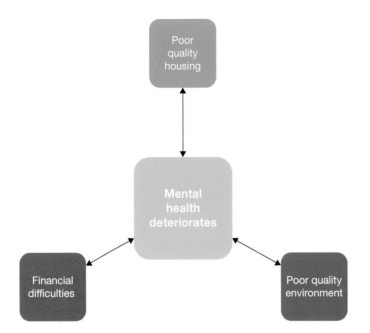

Figure 3.5 Mental health, housing and environment linkages.

Millennium Ecosystem Assessment to be undertaken. The study found that nature's goods and services are the ultimate foundations of life and health, even though in modern societies this fundamental dependency may be indirect, displaced in space and time, and therefore poorly recognized.

(Corvalán et al., 2005)

Using green space across our towns and cities to counter the effects of urban degradation

There are six main beneficial actions that can be taken to improve the quality of green space:

1 Boost biodiversity.
2 Restore habitat.
3 Reduce heat island effect.
4 Reduce storm water runoff.
5 Promote positive interactions between people and nature.
6 Improve interracial and intergenerational interaction.

1 Boost biodiversity

Biodiversity fuels the abundant life cycles on earth. When we look closely at urban areas we see there is an amazing variety of weed species growing up around abandoned sites. When we then compare the species count in the 'wild' space with an average municipal garden plot, that number drops markedly. Nature, left to its own devices, introduces pioneer species to colonise the bare rock and soil. These plants are gradually replaced as over time as the soil layer deepens and can support larger and more complex plants. At the same time a range of animals, small at first and then increasingly large, emerges to fill the gap. In time trees will grow on what was once a bare vacant lot. At some stage during this natural process local people will start to value and visit the space. They will notice its increasing range of plants and animals and come to nurture them and in turn be nurtured. Biodiversity, the number and variety of organisms living in an area, is boosted. This natural process of colonisation and reconnection is interrupted when we fence the area off, put up signs saying 'no loitering', and spray herbicides or put other toxins onto the soil.

2 Restore habitat

Habitat restoration works in tandem with boosting biodiversity. It involves the re-creation of a natural environment that is sufficiently 'healthy' to be able to support a diverse range of plants and animals. While restoration projects are often community-led, some agency intervention may be required to remove pollutants from an area. Urban green space can support a surprisingly large range of plants and animals. As with any programme that will have an impact on the local community, engaging with local people and getting their input, ideas and aspirations for the space is vital for the long term success of the programme.

3 Reduce heat island effect

The urban heat island effect is well known. On the driveway in England the thermometer may read 30°C. On the same day however, on the lawn away from the paved area it may only be 26°C. The heat absorbed and later radiated off the driveway further warms the air. Taken on a large scale over a city, the area of hard paved surfaces reflects an enormous amount of heat. The US Environmental Protection Agency states that 'mean air temperature of a city with 1 million people or more can be 1.8–5.4°F (1–3°C) warmer than its surroundings. In the evening, the difference can be as high as 22°F (12°C)' (EPA, 2013). With global climate change increasing air temperatures in many areas, this exacerbates the heat island effect, creating hot, dry microclimates in our densely packed towns and cities. As we push to increase the density of our urban areas, as part of creating compact urban forms, there is a danger than we could increase the urban heat island effect. Extreme heat, or cold, is bad for our health. Younger and older people are especially at risk, from breathing difficulties and even death. Plants, however, naturally cool the air as they give up moisture to the surrounding air through their leaves, through transpiration. When looking at urban restoration or regeneration projects we must replace or at least shade large expanses of hard paved areas with less heat-absorbent surfaces, and increase the number of shade trees in pedestrian areas.

4 Reduce storm water runoff

Storm water runoff is a threat to human health and well-being, as seen in recent floods in the UK, USA, Australia and Bangladesh. The number of countries and communities affected is in fact wider than our news reports would tell. For example, there are devastating floods in China every year, which have been increasing in severity.

Part of the challenge of climate change is that the computer models cannot tell us what *will* happen, only what is *likely* to happen, based on data received to date. If we accept that alongside drought we are likely to see floods more frequently, we need to take action now to mitigate the effects of these extreme weather events. Storm water runoff becomes a problem when it becomes overland flow. Rather than being absorbed into the ground in natural water courses, large areas of hard surfacing cause the water to flow over the ground, potentially flooding homes, schools and businesses, and damaging urban infrastructure such as the New York City subway system, which flooded during Superstorm Sandy in 2012. Sustainable urban drainage systems can be made beautiful. On flat or sloping streetscapes, planters filter and reduce water flow off roadways. Rain gardens similarly reduce and filter flow off large roofs and other impermeable surfaces.

Figure 3.6 Flooding, Yangtze river, China.

Source:
www.indyposted blog

We know that people are healthier and experience an improved quality of life when regularly exposed to green space. Sustainable urban drainage systems, designed to mitigate storm water runoff, will help. Increasing the use of soft permeable materials and reducing hard impermeable surfacing can only add to the community's sense of well-being.

5 Promote positive interactions between people and nature

Taken together, the above urban interventions help to create a sustainable, healthy community. In this newly softened urban form people are more likely to have positive interactions with nature. With pollutants removed, air and water quality will improve as the natural habitat of the local area is restored. Lung, skin and heart conditions will likewise improve and the social and economic costs associated with these health conditions will be reduced. Abundant, bio-diverse plantings help wildlife corridors to become re-established, and perhaps long-forgotten birds and butterflies will be encouraged back into the community.

6 Improve interracial and intergenerational interaction

When we take a degraded urban space and create softened, planted, bio-diverse landscapes we are in effect creating gardens. Gardens such as the Highline Park in New York City bring local people, and tourists, together. The renewed environment is ideal for people to move freely and indulge in relaxed, playful activities. Inter-generational groups feel included and encouraged to engage socially and with nature.

Overall, the effect is improved health and well-being. It comes from the combination of factors. Taken independently of each other, each of the interventions and design elements mentioned above will improve quality of life. The quality of the built environment, as it relates to the natural environment and as nature responds to it,

in turn affects human health. It is important to acknowledge the interrelatedness of each part of the story. As we know, people are healthier and experience an improved sense of well-being when regularly exposed to green space. So sustainable urban drainage systems, designed to mitigate storm water runoff, can add to the sense of well-being. When combined with habitat restoration and bio-diverse plantings the effect can be profound. As American tribal chief Seattle said, 'the web of life connects us all. Anything we do to the web, we do to ourselves'. If we remember this when we consider design schemes and urban regeneration projects, we will improve the health and well-being of people living in that

Figure 3.7
Environmental influences on health and well-being.

community. As with a wildlife corridor however, the effect flows out across neighbourhood boundaries to adjacent areas, increasing the return on investment (ROI) of the intervention.

Sensory gardens

Beauty and utility are often not considered in the same sentence, let alone the same design brief. Early monastic and Islamic gardens were sensory-rich gardens that were both practical and aesthetically pleasing. A ultilitarian space is necessarily functional, and often developed to a tight budget. However, this is no reason not to give equal weight to the importance of the beauty of the development. If we are to consider the health and well-being of the people using any space, regardless of its function, we must consider how the space will feel, how it will look, and as a result of these factors, how that will affect the functionality of the space.

Educational research conducted through charities such as Learning Through Landscapes (UK) and the Children in Nature Collaborative (USA) has also highlighted the links between time spent outdoors in well-designed spaces and improved aspiration and achievement.

Play, prisons and social isolation

For a variety of reasons some children's playgrounds, schools and social housing developments share much in common with prisons. Mostly this happens as a result

Case study 5: South London Family Centre

As per the design brief, the Centre dealt with problems around anti-social behaviour and mental health. The environment, as provided, was doing nothing to alleviate those challenges. Figure 3.8 shows the environment as it was.

The model shown in Figure 3.10 demonstrates how the barren, paved courtyard area could be greened as part of a joint programme to reduce family violence and provide a calming therapeutic space for vulnerable children and their carers. When family groups arrive they are often in a high emotional state. Abundant planting would cool and soften the overheated environment (which in summer can reach 50°C). The greened courtyard would provide an engaging area to stretch and 'let off steam'. When those receiving counselling are calm they are more receptive to the programme, so it was important that the landscape intervention assist programme delivery.

With an almost non-existent budget, the materials specified had to be inexpensive yet durable and effective. The portable, metal, classroom is shown screened and softened with planted trellis. A living green roof is installed on the classroom and a planted arbour creates a sheltered transition zone at the entrance. To the side a sunflower mural is painted on the wall and hanging play equipment is mounted under the overhanging balcony. Surface interest is provided with flush-mounted, inset, non-toxic, treated log-round detailing, to create a tricycle track. Fragrant and edible planting is placed in rainwater-fed planters atop the prison-like walls of this inner city space.

Figure 3.8 Bleak setting: a family dispute resolution centre, London.

Figure 3.10 Model of proposed environmental improvements.

Figure 3.9 Concept sketch to improve environment at a family dispute resolution centre, London. Designed by Greenstone Design UK.

of a perceived potential for criminal activity. The only way we see to protect the community from potential crime is to barricade people into prisons and out of schools and housing, with physical barriers and signage dictating who may be in the area. Not surprisingly, gates, fences, broken glass or walls topped with razor wire and security cameras do nothing to reduce tension and stress, and in fact can exacerbate an individual's feeling of social isolation and any tendencies towards anti-social behaviour. The area looks degraded even when brand new.

Playgrounds

In Scotland, the 1996 Dunblane massacre shocked the community when sixteen children and their teacher were shot and killed in a school by a 43-year-old unemployed man. In response, in addition to tighter gun control laws, instead of locking the children in and making everything 'secure' the Scottish authorities decided on an open policy. Fences were removed and the environment softened with planting so that the community felt welcomed. The policy has worked. The harsh physical and built environment has been lightened. Social isolation, one of the leading causes of anti-social behaviour, has been reduced as people have somewhere additional to go to meet people, to connect. While it cannot be stated that planting could stop a massacre, inclusive urban green space does aid the mental health of the community. With more people in the area there is a self-policing practice in place. With someone always around, or potentially about to wander through an area, people are less inclined to risk being caught doing something they ought not to be doing.

    This has had a spectacular impact on the development of children's playgrounds. While in many jurisdictions around the world there is a policy of fencing off playgrounds and restricting use to under 12s or adults only when accompanying children, in Scotland, post-Dunblane it was decided to reverse that practice. It is a sensitive issue. With the exclusive, fenced-off policy, anyone who simply wants to sit and watch the joy of children playing is denied access as a potential risk. In Scotland, the authorities have heeded the statistics rather than the perception of risk and decided on an open access policy. Since the massacre, fencing has been largely removed from playgrounds so children can use the whole landscape, rather than being corralled into small areas around the play equipment. Young and old, able bodied and disabled, feel and are in a very practical sense welcomed. Planting and level changes creates spaces within the overall play landscape, which allows for varied users and uses at any one time. Alongside busy roads, fencing is retained to keep young children and those with special needs safe. As restrictions of access have relaxed, site managers have embraced creative, loose play with increased provision of sand and water, set amidst planting for seasonal interest. There is now a reason for the whole community to get out, get together and live a healthier, more active lifestyle.

    Scotland is not the only country that has seen the potential for improving the social fabric of their communities through opening up play spaces. In Scandinavia and other parts of Europe accessible, inclusive public space is common. Some local authorities in England have also embraced the potential, as in the Chapelfield play area in Sussex, shown in Figure 3.12.

Figure 3.11
Children sheltering
in shaded space
within nursery
playground, Takoma
Park.

Source: Lesley
Romanoff.

Figure 3.12
Chapelfield play area –
natural play setting.

When we look at degraded urban environments we notice the comorbid statistics that relate to the environment. 'Comorbidity' is taken out of its usual medical context. Here we use it to describe the symptoms shown by an individual indicating an environmental condition that causes, is caused by, or is otherwise related to another condition in the same individual. Examples include decreased achievement levels in schools, decreased engagement in social activities, increased rates of illness requiring medical intervention including medication and hospital admissions, and increased rates of crime and incarceration. The social cost and subsequent economic cost of the degraded environment is felt across the community.

Prisons

Various prison services have conducted their own research and concluded that therapeutic garden or horticulture programmes calm the inmates, reduce aggressive behaviour and provide useful life skills. Penal garden therapy was the focus of a landscape architecture-based study called 'Designing therapeutic environments for inmates and prison staff in the United States: precedents and contemporary applications' (Lindemuth, 2007). Through the creation of spaces to reflect and grieve, inmates can recover from the circumstances that brought them into the corrections system. From a psychological perspective, the therapeutic qualities found in the gardens may help inmates manage behavioural symptoms exacerbated by the sterility, tension and alienation of the prison environment. For staff, gardens can provide a moment of relief from the harsh social environment of their work place and provide healthy benefits in terms of stress reduction.

In several studies conducted within US correctional facilities, access to external views and the quality of these views have been shown to have a measurable influence on the behaviour and psychological outlook of inmates and staff. Moore (1981) and West (1986) showed that views from prison cells have a significant impact on the physical well-being of inmates. In particular, Moore found that the views from the cell (exterior or interior), the cell's relative privacy, and noise level within the cell are correlated with the number of sick-calls to the infirmary. Cells with exterior views, lower noise levels, and/or more privacy logged fewer sick-calls. Using Moore's methodology, West correlated the number of sick-calls to the type of exterior views from inmates' cells. West's findings show that inmates with a higher percentage of naturalistic elements visible from their cell make fewer sick-calls than those with views dominated by the built environment.

In the 1980s the Los Angeles prison service introduced a therapeutic gardening programme. Hardened gang members with little education and few life skills became proficient in the tender care of seedlings. Although often illiterate, they were able and delighted to learn the Latin names of thousands of plants. Within the gardens was seating and a barbeque. Time was allocated for quiet contemplation within the working day. At regular intervals throughout the growing season they could celebrate their success with a home-grown meal, eaten al fresco. Social skills were improved, alongside literacy and numeracy skills. Self-esteem jumped from low to a healthy high as young men realised they could feed their families through a means other than crime. All it took was access to a garden. For most it was the first time they had any experience of being in or near a garden.

The non-judgemental nature of gardening, of learning to live with nature, cause and effect, sunshine and growth, is of enormous benefit. People who may have missed early nurture and the feeling of security that comes from guided boundaries and consequences especially benefit. For prisoners, many of whom have suffered failure at school, unemployment in the job market and the frustrations of being marginalised in society, horticulture is a process that allows them to control their environment through shared responsibilities – an unspoken contract between person and plant. Accomplishment is its own reward, generating new goals, skills and productive efforts in one's life. As skills develop and projects increase, the individual achieves a greater sense of empowerment along with new-found pride in their role in the workplace. For people disconnected from their actions, for those disconnected from nature, time spent in a well-designed garden space can have a profound effect. If you don't water a plant it may die. It if dies you may not have anything to eat. Simple cause and effect was never so easily demonstrated.

Figure 3.13 Penal therapy garden.

The following quotes from staff and inmates working with US prison gardens further suggest the positive outcomes that these landscapes offer:

> It's just you and the flowers. It gets you away from all the drama of the prison, all the gangs, all the gossip and all the other nonsense.
>
> (Anna Winston, inmate, quoted in Press, 1997)

> Sometimes when I am working on the plants, I'm in my own world, thinking about my life and what I did to get here, and it helps me a lot.
>
>   (Terry Knickerbocker, inmate, quoted in Hiller, 2001)

> When you walked out in the yard [when I first came here], there were 100 eyes looking at you and it was not a good feeling . . . I don't feel that confrontation anymore in the yard and I think it's the plants.
>
>   (Glen Whorton, prison staff, quoted in Hiller, 2001)

Social isolation

Social disconnectedness and perceived isolation combine to be as significant a cause of ill health as smoking and obesity (House, 2001). Social isolation has been linked to ill health across all age groups. While part of the punishment for committing a crime is to be removed from society, it can also be a cause of criminal anti-social behaviour. Where an environment does not afford safe, positive social interaction, mental health and physical health are affected, impacting society in turn through increased expenditures in relation to social, economic and healthcare costs. So what does this have to do with landscape and urban design? The process of urban degradation can erode many of the structures that support social connectedness. Public green space and private gardens combine to provide access to a green view, a green experience. Healing gardens lift the spirit – that is, time spent in nature, with clean air and water and a feeling of safety, meets our basic human needs. In Chapter 4 we will look into those needs in more detail.

The practicalities

Social isolation is caused by many factors. Availability of public services and facilities both adjacent to green space and within the central urban fabric is integral to the accessibility of any city. Within the discussion of healing gardens it is important to consider the needs of the people we are trying to reach. To be valued and of economic use to a community, it is vital that such gardens are set within a broader, salutogenic urban design framework. With an ageing population, vision, hearing and mobility impairments will increase in our communities. As governments and

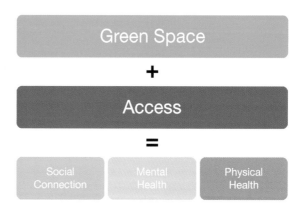

Figure 3.14
Relationship between green space and social isolation.

insurers encourage healthy, active lifestyles and move people away from private car use and on to walking, cycling and public transport we need a concomitant increase in public services such as public toilet provision, as mobility patterns change.

The current renaissance in urban design encompasses attention to user needs as well as aesthetic considerations. Salutogenic urban design requires a more holistic 'joined up thinking' approach to meeting public needs. With social isolation as the consequence of poor urban design it is vital that we consult parents of young children, people who are sight-impaired or have other motion and sensory capabilities, marginalised teenagers, and other representative user groups to ensure that inadequate provision is a thing of the past.

Figure 3.15 Vital infrastructure for accessible design, Seattle, USA.

Source: www.ebay.com

Urban space degradation has allowed many services to be removed from communities. Under the guise of 'cleaning up' a playground, park or neighbourhood green space, communities such as Seattle, USA, sold off almost-new public toilets. When we talk about social isolation we need to remember what causes people to stay at home. Many people require ready access to public conveniences and would rather stay home than risk embarrassment. In 2008 Seattle's standalone self-cleaning facilities, imported from Germany at considerable expense, had only been purchased five years previously but apparently attracted drug users and prostitutes. In an effort to recoup some cost they were listed on eBay for sale for $89,000. Rather than tackling the problems that cause such anti-social behaviour it was deemed politically easier to move the problem elsewhere.

Natural disasters, urban degradation and healing gardens

Urban degradation occurs whenever something happens to a city that affects the economy or social fabric of the community. When an earthquake strikes, a previously healthy community can be reduced to rubble. Indonesia, Japan, Haiti, the USA, Chile, New Zealand, China, Pakistan and Italy have all experienced major quakes. Around the world earthquakes, mudslides, tsunamis and floods affect communities every year. With each event there is an opportunity for the community to come together. In an age of social isolation and a disconnection from the natural world, natural disasters, while causing stress and distress, can perversely offer a chance to get to know your neighbours and to work together for a common goal.

With the effects of climate change becoming more noticeable around the world, insurers and some government agencies, such as the Environment Agency in the UK, have stated that they will not cover future loss to property from natural disasters. While this is bad news for landowners it is good news for communities in need of green space for health and well-being. If it is too expensive to upgrade buildings to ensure they are capable of withstanding natural disasters, planned demolition becomes a positive option, opening up options for healing gardens in the city.

With urban degradation there is an opportunity to retrospectively address some of the issues that have such a profound effect on public health. Urban planners and

Case study 6: Christchurch, Canterbury, New Zealand, after the devastating 2010 and 2011 earthquakes

Christchurch city was built over the past 150 years from stone and brick and believed to be seismically 'safe'. Unfortunately, in November 2010 and again in February 2011, that belief was proved wrong. The centre of what is affectionately known as the 'Garden City' was largely destroyed by two powerful earthquakes. While many people died, many thousands more were left emotionally and physically scarred by the traumatic natural events.

Since the disaster Canterbury District Health Board and other local service providers have noticed an increase in lifestyle-related self-harming behaviours such as recreational drug use, excessive alcohol use and sexual promiscuity, as well as early childhood developmental delays and depression (Kemp et al. 2011). If left unchecked the flow-on effects impacting physical health would create a major burden to public health in the future. Of note, though, is that over time the community is slowly healing itself.

A small, transitional space has evolved as a pocket park (Figure 3.16) while the landowner decides how to develop the land, post the 2011 quake. Prior to the earthquakes the area had no open space within the mixed use office/shopping precinct. The community has taken informal ownership of the healing garden and it is now regularly filled with street performers, artists, gardeners and people who want to stop and chat, play boules or eat lunch al fresco. The demolition of the building has opened up space in the busy mixed-use zone and provided a healing garden area for all to enjoy. In talking with park users there is a feeling that the people do not want a building on the site again. They value the open space more, report feelings of pride in their community, and they especially appreciate having an inclusive space close to where they work and shop. They appreciate somewhere they feel safe outdoors, can meet people and share experiences.

In another part of the city an entire neighbourhood has been 'red zoned', forcing the removal of residents as the land has been deemed uneconomic to rebuild on. Seven thousand detached family homes are to be removed. In early 2012 I was approached by New Zealand's Forest Research Institute (SCION) to develop an urban forest across the residential red zone (RRZ) as an extensive healing garden. As would be expected, the forced removal of residents has created a lot of stress and ill feeling within the community. By incorporating the old gardens of the area, we honour the local residential history and pay tribute to the people who had the foresight to plant long-lived species in their gardens.

The urban forest as a healing garden project has an opportunity to be more than a wilderness in the city. It will also act as a living museum of its former use. We plan to preserve existing mature trees and shrubs, including domestic orchards and, where appropriate, vegetable gardens. The planting plan for the open access forest will include new edible fruiting trees as well as native species, with varied tracks and pathways allowing people of all abilities the freedom to roam, to explore, to garden, and to harvest.[1]

Christchurch's RRZ's new urban forest will be modelled in part on Gyllin's Garden in Malmö, Sweden (Qvistrom, 2012). Gyllin's is the site of an abandoned plant nursery on what was the edge of the city. When the municipal authority announced in 2010 an ambitious programme to transform the wild nature of the garden, complete with adjacent development areas for

Figure 3.16 Urban regeneration project, Christchurch, New Zealand.

Source: Greening the Rubble.

new housing, the people stood up to the authorities and said they wanted logs to sit on, not benches. Benches make a garden a park and no longer a part of nature. Gyllin's history is not as a park, it is something else. I would call it a healing garden, albeit on a wild and forested scale. Christchurch, as the Garden City, has enough old city and new pocket parks but not enough nature. The destruction and general urban degradation brought about by the earthquakes provides the perfect opportunity to bring more healing nature into the city.

In the settlement of Lyttleton, just over the hill from Christchurch city, the port area was devastated by the 2011 quake. The resilient community has rallied and created a strong response to the natural disaster. Where some would see destruction, others see opportunity. When a community embraces the challenge, such as in Lyttleton, mental health benefits help balance the costs of stress. With simple interventions such as the repurposing of vacant land as garden space, there is the chance to strike up conversation with people one has never had cause to speak to before. Social capital grows as healing gardens replace damaged buildings.

The playable ruins sown in Figure 3.17 offer a hint of the devastation alongside a strong message that life goes on. There is no public works development or maintenance budget for healing spaces such as these informal pocket parks.

In Figure 3.18, further along the road, this communal space was built next to the new pocket park by a local entrepreneur using local demolition and recycled materials, offering the community a choice of locations to come together, share experiences, heal and grow. Public funding is going to rebuilding vital infrastructure items, in addition to schools, medical facilities and other public buildings. Community resources are being harnessed to beg, borrow and recycle materials to improve the health and well-being of the community, at a fundamental level.

Figure 3.17 Making playable ruins, Lyttleton, New Zealand.

Figure 3.18 Urban regeneration project, using 'found' materials, Lyttleton, New Zealand.

other built environment professionals, working in collaboration with colleagues in landscape, therapeutic horticulture, psychology, general medicine and public health have a responsibility to use private and public funding wisely. We need to employ 'joined up thinking' as we craft a response to the economic challenge of redeveloping a whole or parts of a city.

In the often degraded, sometimes polluted, sensory overload of the busy, information-rich modern world, we need to provide balance. As we saw with the monastic gardens of old, healing gardens can offer a calming space, where stress levels are reduced and energy levels rejuvenated. Key disabling diseases such as depression can be addressed cost effectively through cohesive healthcare programmes in the fresh air of an appropriately designed healing garden.

Such integrated healthcare facilities are being developed in Christchurch, NZ, since the earthquakes. The new Rangiora Health Hub aims to address indigenous health issues and those of the wider community. It is to be surrounded by community gardens, natural play spaces and healing sensory and therapeutic gardens. Co-located with a school and community centre, the health centre will go to where the people congregate. By creating an environment that naturally encourages an active, socially engaged lifestyle, the 'healthy living' public health message is accessible to those who may otherwise be hard to reach.

In areas of urban degradation, welfare, health and education budgets are often already stretched. Children's play provision and public parks can drop further down the priority list as the tax take is reduced. However, with a collaborative approach the urban area can be redeveloped at minimal cost, and for maximum benefit. In the community-led Christchurch pocket park examples shown above, the people have expressed their previously unknown and unvoiced need for healing gardens. The supporters of Gyllin's Garden in Malmö expressed their need for nature in the city by stipulating that they did not want park benches in their green space – natural logs, whether felled on site after clean-up of storm damage or brought in to add to the natural play and seating provision, allow for the earthy contact Malmö's urban dwellers so value.

Cost-effective public health may not necessarily be on the agenda of the urban renewal team when they first meet. Health economics may traditionally not have been considered as part of the debate around urban degradation. However, if healthcare providers paid landowners of derelict sites the equivalent amount of money saved in treatment programmes to work with the community to transform their land into healing gardens, it would be a win/win situation for all.

Note

1   Freedom to roam is enshrined in law in many countries around the world. In many states of the USA, recreational use statutes encouraging landowners to open their land to hiking, hunting, fishing, swimming and other recreational activities have been enacted. These statutes shield landowners from liability in negligence actions should those using the land recreationally be injured by something on the land; without such statutes, those using the land for these purposes, whether or not they had paid for the privilege, would thus be able to sue the landowner in the event of injury under most circumstances.

References

Corvalán, C., Hales, S. and McMichael, A. (2005). *Ecosystems and human well-being: health synthesis*. Report of the Millennium Ecosystem Assessment for the World Health Organisation. Geneva: WHO.

Déjeant-Pons, M. (2006). Preamble to the European Landscape Convention. Strasbourg: Council of Europe.

EPA (2011). Brownfields and land revitalisation. Retrieved December 2013, from *EPA*: www.epa.gov/brownfields/overview/glossary.htm

—— (2013). Heat island effect. Retrieved 2103, from *EPA*: www.epa.gov/hiri/

EULP (2008). Introduction. Retrieved January 2013, from *European Union Landscape Partnership*: www.urban-landscape.net/content_public/introduction.php

Genske, D. (2003). *Urban land*. Berlin: Springer Verlag.

Hiller, L. (2001, 17 September). Gardening effort: project alters prison. Retrieved 2013, from *Las Vegas Review-Journal*: http://lvrj.com

House, J. S. (2001, 63). Social isolation kills, but how and why? *Psychosomatic Medicine*, 63(2):273–74.

Kemp, S., Helton, W. S., Richardson, J. J., Blampied, N. M. and Grimshaw, M. (2011). Sleeplessness, stress, cognitive disruption and academic performance following the September 4, 2010, Christchurch earthquake. *Australasian Journal of Disaster and Trauma Studies*, 2011–2012:11–18.

Lindemuth, A. L. (2007). Designing therapeutic environments for inmates and prison staff in the United States: precedents and contemporary applications. *Journal of Mediterranean Ecology*, 8:87–97.

Moore, E. O. (1981). A prison environment's effect on health care service demands. *Environmental Systems*, 11:17–34.

Press, A. (1997, 17 August). Hard work in prison yields food for inmates and souls. *Seattle Times*.

Qviström, M. (2012). Taming the wild. In: A. J. Keenan, *Urban wildscapes* (pp. 187–201). Abingdon: Routledge.

REC Slovakia (2008). *Urban Spaces: enhancing the attractiveness and quality of the urban environment*. Bratislava: Regional Environmental Centre for Central and Eastern Europe.

West, M. J. (1986). *Landscape views and stress response*. Seattle, WA: University of Washington Press.

CHAPTER 4

Sustainable communities are healthy communities

Low impact urban design and development (LIUDD) is a sustainable living concept that promotes urban sustainability and health through effective management of stormwater, waste, energy, transport and ecosystem services. An ecosystems approach is a way of looking at the natural environment throughout the decision making process that helps us to think about the way that the natural environment adds value to a community (Defra, 2013). Greening the urban environment through ecological planting is a vital part of the health and well-being of ecosystems and citizens.

The mix of citizens that makes up our communities is changing. Through climate change and conflict it is expected that increasing levels of migration will alter the demographic further. Indigenous peoples, such as the Māori of New Zealand and Native Americans of the USA, have strong and enduring cultural connections with the land. The stronger the connection the more acutely any disconnection from nature is felt. Unsustainable lifestyles and education, employment, social, environmental, economic and health issues result. Extractive activities such as mining, commercial agriculture and forestry degrade the land and strip indigenous people of their spiritual connection. The 2012 US suicide statistics show the highest rates of despair to be among Native American males. Australia is host to the world's highest suicide rate, seen in Aboriginal children (Cunningham, 2009). In Russia and the UK, immigrant and refugee children make up a significant proportion of those accessing social and therapeutic horticulture programmes (Read, 2008). What all these peoples have in common is a displacement from their ancestral lands, and an unsustainable living concept born out of ineffective management of the ecosystem services.

Healing gardens and healthy communities

When we are talking about healing gardens we need a sense of context. Why do we need them (what issues are we hoping to address)? Where do we seek to develop such gardens? What effects can we hope to achieve on the health of the community? How can a garden impact the sustainability of a community? What other flow-on effects can we expect from such developments?

According to the World Health Organisation, health is defined as a complete state of physical, mental, social and spiritual well-being, and not merely the absence of disease or infirmity (WHO, 1948). Healthy communities are defined here as being places where people report feelings of health and well-being and require fewer referrals to healthcare services than their counterparts in unhealthy communities. At the 2013 World Design and Health Congress, many studies were cited detailing the salutogenic benefits of landscape (Baxby, 2013; Hammam, 2013; Wilson, 2013). Experts from fields ranging from finance to psychology spoke of their experience, and success, in taking a preventative healthcare approach. The urban environment has been a source of ill health for too long. With urban immigration patterns showing that by 2020 all major countries will have more people in towns and cities than in the countryside, it is time to make our cities sustainable, and their communities healthy.

Many studies have identified a positive relationship between the natural environment and improved health outcomes. Statements such as 'The greening of cities by planting ecologically with local species is also a vital part of the overall well-being of ecosystems and citizens' (Ignatieva, 2008) are a recurring outcome. That state of well-being, both for people and the environment, is what we aspire to when we set out to create a healing garden. To become a sustainable community, to create that overall balance between the well-being of both citizens and ecosystems, no demands must be made on resources today that would affect the ability of future generations to live. The Brundtland Commission defined sustainable development as: 'development that meets the need of the present generation without compromising the ability of future generations to meet their needs' (IISD, 2013).

Sustainability is at the core of a healthy community. Environmental sustainability cannot be separated from economic sustainability. For economies to function at efficient levels it requires the population to be healthy, so that the workforce is present and the children at school. Hence to be truly sustainable community design must embrace both elements.

> Cost-effective design and development works with nature – creating community environments that respect, conserve, and enhance natural processes and achieve landscape legibility by retaining landforms and remnant vegetation, and using plant signatures to profile biodiversity. Sustainable communities are those that embrace a low impact urban design and development model.
>
> (Ignatieva, 2008)

The low impact design and development model assumes people live to meet their needs and minimise their wants. A 'need' is defined here as a must-have item or element, whereas a 'want' is desirable but not essential for the health and well-being of the individual.

When people can meet their basic needs of housing, food and clothing they are satisfied at that basic level. Abraham Maslow was a psychologist who suggested that all people's different needs could be classified into five distinct groups. What he also suggested was that these groups were arranged in layers or levels – a hierarchy of importance – such that people would only try to satisfy higher-level needs once their needs had been satisfied at the lower (more important) levels (Maslow, 1943). I believe, however, that we value those needs equally. So rather than being a sequence

Figure 4.1 Hierarchy of needs, revised.

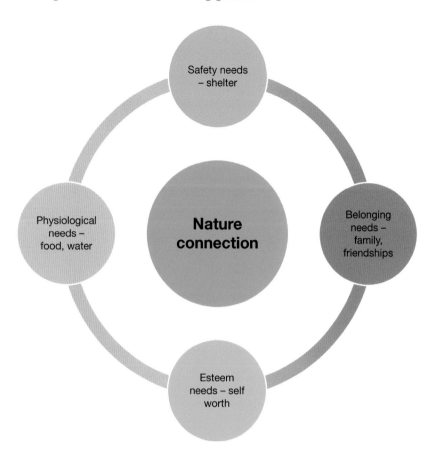

I have shown it as more of a relationship of required dosage, with a nature connection being central to our sense of well-being.

The first level Maslow identified was that of the 'physiological' needs – for air, food and water. These things we need in regular, large doses. Without them we die, quite quickly. Once these primary needs have been taken care of, then the needs for safety and security become important. Shelter is not necessary on a constant basis, we can come and go from our homes, and so we need less of it than air. Maslow's third level covered needs to do with love and belonging, while the fourth level needs were to do with self-esteem and respect for and from others. Both of these layers of needs build on those that have gone before, but equally, without them we will not seek shelter or bother to feed ourselves. The fifth and final level he called 'self-actualisation': the need to realise one's personal potential and find fulfilment. I have placed our nature connection at the centre of our needs for well-being.

The five levels are shared in common by all the people in the world. What is different are the ways in which people try to fulfil those needs. How we meet those needs varies between cultures and at different times in history. In terms of gardens, landscapes, urban design and health, we need to identify what some of those higher order needs look like, so we can determine what it takes to create a healthy community.

How to identify a healing garden

Figure 4.2 shows part of a very simple garden with planting, a stream, a small tree and natural stones. It looks pleasant, but is it a healing garden? From what we can see, it probably is not. While being visually and audibly pleasing the garden is ultimately unsatisfying as it lacks somewhere to sit and ideally, something to eat. There is no wildlife visible; no birds, bees or other insect life. While it is relatively easy to design an attractive garden, a healing garden satisfies our basic needs.

As we saw in Chapter 1, Islamic and monastic gardens historically provided for the health of mind, body and soul. They offered not only fresh air and an attractive

Figure 4.2 Healing garden, water, planting.

place to take some gentle exercise, but also somewhere comfortable to sit, the opportunity for variation between sun and shade, fresh vegetables, fruit or nuts to eat and aromatic herbs and flowers to perfume the air. Healing gardens require a state of health as the outcome from their development. The WHO's definition of health as a 'complete state of physical, mental, social and spiritual wellbeing, and not merely the absence of disease or infirmity' is the one we will use here. Although the WHO's definition has been criticised by some as being too all-encompassing and therefore of little use in scientific applications, it does effectively support the holistic, integrative, critical and community-based perspective. When developing healthy communities it is therefore appropriate to use this definition.

Design, whether landscape, urban or architectural, is a synthesis of art and science. A consequence of adopting the WHO's definition is that health cannot be 'owned' by one specific discipline, be it medical, social, business, planning or environmental sciences; the complete collaboration and interaction between the full range of research and teaching/learning/practising teams is required to move a community towards well-being.

While this text is principally about architecture, landscape and urban design, to understand the full potential we need to understand a little about public health, and in subsequent chapters, health economics. If we accept the biophilic view, that a connection to nature is essential to human health and well-being, we need to accept the science of human bonds with the natural world, including plant and animal interactions (Kahn, 2012).

Exercise and health

The privatisation of health and fitness has contributed to health inequalities. Nature, by virtue of its universal accessibility, allows everyone to benefit. Connecting with nature increases individual health and community well-being. Kahn's study of runners found that exercise in nature results in less fatigue, reduced anxiety, more positive thoughts and an overall feeling of invigoration. The control group exercised in an indoor gym on running machines. While their physical fitness levels, as measured in cardiovascular output, were the same as those of the outdoor runners, they missed out on the additional mental health benefits.

Mental health can have a strong impact on physical health. So-called 'gym junkies' who exercise to excess may have finely-chiselled bodies, but any addiction is debilitating. As Arwa Mahdawi says of Evelyn Waugh's famous quote about his New York gym 'There is neurosis in the air, which the inhabitants mistake for energy', a gym junky's mental health may be fragile, their exercise regime out of equilibrium (Mahdawi, 2013).

Nature constantly seeks a state of equilibrium. High pressure moves to low, warm air to cold. We likewise unconsciously seek balance in life. When we talk about healing gardens having the capacity to heal communities it is about providing spaces where anyone can freely access a healthy, active lifestyle. Positive distractions in the landscape encourage balanced exercise with periods of rest and contemplation. When people are attracted to spend time outdoors daily in nature, multiple benefits spill over into the community.

Case study 7: Paris – softening the built environment

Some years ago I lived in an apartment in Paris, France. We were poor students so had little money for extras like gym membership. In every direction were noisy, busy streets full of pedestrians and traffic, shops, offices and apartment buildings. It would be easy to think of people living in such an urban environment as being disconnected from the natural world. However, like our most of our neighbours we had large windows, access to a balcony and several window boxes. In front of our apartment were tall street trees, creating a leafy outlook.

On each major street intersection was a small park with seats, trees, flowering plants and some play equipment. After school each day we could walk the children two minutes to the nearest park or fifteen minutes to a larger playground. The parks were designed so that children and older people living in apartments could get everything they needed. With either option there was space to stretch, balance, run and play, meet up with friends, sit in the sun, or relax in the shade. With somewhere to go and someone to talk to we made friends with local people. Social bonds in the community were strengthened, local businesses were patronised and our collective mental and physical health was good. Although we were living in the city centre, due to the accessibility of a green, healthy, active lifestyle we felt very much part of the natural world. It was a wonderfully uplifting yet calming, intrinsically healthy place to live.

Figure 4.3 Street trees for green view and to soften built environment.

The lesson from Paris is that with well-provisioned accessible greenspace it is possible to live a healthy active life, very cheaply.

Healthy indigenous and immigrant communities

Indigenous and immigrant peoples are over represented in health and education statistics. As Kahn noted, in many places health is related to an ability to pay. In communities where the only access to a healthy lifestyle is through a paid membership scheme, some people will miss out. Without adequate provision of attractive, accessible green space, stress plays a large part in the poor mental and physical health of immigrant communities in particular. Dislocated from their home culture, language, food, plants, and perhaps climate, it can be more attractive for them to stay home than go out and face a stressful environment. Social isolation impacts mental health. Without socially neutral green space such as the abundant, accessible parks and gardens of Paris, people may feel excluded from their new community.

Case study 8: Wellington – social housing

In Wellington, New Zealand, the city council provides social housing. With restricted budgets, criteria for eligibility have become strict, meaning that those housed by the municipality are genuinely those in greatest need. With only the most vulnerable people being offered support it becomes more important that their health and well-being needs are addressed at a fundamental design and development level. Under Mayor Celia Wade-Brown's patronage a biophilic city programme called Our Living City decided to tackle social housing, as part of a wider campaign to green the city. Old blocks of flats have been retired, some are being renovated and others are being newly developed. Of note is the landscaping around the flats, townhouses and apartment blocks. Amenity trees and flowering plants offer year-round interest. Communal growing space is available; sheltered, private seating areas are balanced with more open communal areas; children's play opportunities allow for hide-and-seek games amongst playable planting; there is space for residents to bring out paddling pools and buckets and spades for sand pits to complement the fixed swings and slides.

Figure 4.4 Social housing playground and gardens, Wellington, New Zealand.

Of course Wellington is not the only city providing social and affordable housing for immigrants and other vulnerable members of the community. In Oslo, Norway, affordable housing is well balanced by green space. With daylight hours being short during the winter months, it is acknowledged as important that people be encouraged by attractive, accessible garden spaces to spend time outside every day.

Like immigrants, indigenous communities are often subject to overcrowded living conditions, inadequate or poor quality housing, and poor access to quality green space. A recent media report on homelessness in Auckland, New Zealand, cited the example of an extended family of thirty-one Māori people living in a three-bedroom house. Non-communicable, lifestyle-related diseases such as asthma, lower respiratory diseases, cardiovascular conditions, obesity and type 2 diabetes are rife within the household, amongst both adults and children. The commentator decided that although the family has a roof over its head the conditions were so inadequate as to constitute 'homeless' status. In Australia, the rate of homelessness for (the indigenous) Aboriginal and Torres Strait Islander people is four times that of non-indigenous Australians (AIHW, 2011).

The health concerns of the Auckland family are mirrored in the immigrant community elsewhere. While people wait for appropriate social housing to become available, much could be done to improve their general health and sense of well-being through the development of local healing landscapes.

Figure 4.5 Social housing playground, Wellington, New Zealand.

Figures 4.6a and 4.6b show an example of barrier-free design in Wellington, NZ. The harbour frontage was redeveloped after the advent of containerised shipping, converting the old bulk goods warehouses into retail, performance and residential space, and the outside areas into engaging spaces, accessible for all. When we design opportunities to engage with the natural environment, we step back from the health and safety mantra that keeps people and nature at a 'safe' distance. We alter the perception and make the natural world visible and readable. City dwellers must be able to see and interact with nature where they live if it is to be culturally relevant and therefore wanted. Only through regular exposure will an awareness and understanding of the significance of natural ecosystems and ecosystem services, especially for human health and well-being, be developed (Ignatieva, 2008). We need to allow adults and children to get up close. Barrier-free design is not just about accessibility. It is also about taking down the physical barriers, the fences and restraints that promote the sense that nature is something to be frightened of.

Playful communities

Playing and having fun is good for our mental health. Play is vital for children but having fun is also important for adults. Just as we talked about balanced exercise regimes so too do we need to balance work and play time. Many cities around the world are starting to embrace forward thinking strategies that encourage people to move towards more sustainable forms of development. While it is important to move away from short-term piecemeal planning and wasteful, highly consumer-oriented behaviour, it is also important to create livable cities. Many infrastructure developments can improve environmental quality while adding a playable resource to the community.

As stated previously, without ecological health there can be no human health and well-being. When we design urban areas around healthy ecologies we can create sustainable communities. When we design for sustainable living, mental health improves, the local economy benefits, and ecologically the situation improves through development of a healing landscape. Sustainable communities evolve as healthy places where people choose to spend time and money.

Guangzhou, China is fortunate to have some large old parks. The trees aid local air quality and offer a green respite from the stress of densely populated living and working conditions. Park policies encourage people to play freely in the parks throughout the day and into the evening. When we spend time exercising and relaxing in nature our adrenal cortex produces less cortisol, the hormone responsible for stress response. Less cortisol means a healthier brain. Prolonged periods of stress can shrink the hippocampus, which is where we form and store memories, as well as being a precursor to various cancer triggers and heart disease (Hildebrandt, 2012).

We live in ageing communities where a significant public health cost is currently related to care due to memory loss. Memory loss in turn triggers myriad broader mental health issues and loss of independence, adding to the cost of care. An early intervention or prevention for dementia is to de-stress in nature, throughout life. This has significance for urban design and provision of public green space to engage people at all life stages. Studies are underway to ascertain how much memory can

LEFT: **Figure 4.6a**
Urban blue space,
accessible design.

BELOW: **Figure 4.6b**
Engaging with
nature: lunchtime
office workers enjoy
the harbour,
Wellington,
New Zealand.

Figure 4.7 Sustainable urban drainage: swale, Taupo, New Zealand.

Figure 4.8 Playable stormwater channel, Christchurch, New Zealand.

Figure 4.9 Public dancing for health and well-being in the park, Guangzhou, China.

Source: Huiyi Liu.

be restored through exposure to healing garden spaces. In Japanese studies, early indications support the theory that time spent in nature can restore memory function.

Playing and simply spending time in natural settings has also been found to alleviate directed-attention fatigue (DAF). DAF occurs when the brain's prefrontal cortex has to constantly manage competing stimuli, as in a busy office or urban centre. As DAF increases, the brain becomes stressed, and as the hippocampus shrinks over time dementia could result. Simple actions, like the sensory-neutral activity of gazing at clouds, can restore both mood and cognitive function (Kaplan, 1995). Hence salutogenic urban centres incorporating gardens designed for health and well-being could become a realistic and highly effective alternative to expensive care options.

Figure 4.10 Rain garden water course.

Sustainable communities are balanced across social, economic and environmental values. When we design engaging environments so people choose to spend time in nature, we reduce the risk not only of common stress, but also dementia, cancers and heart disease. The social cost of these conditions is enormous. For example, a person with heart disease may not be able to work, so may be unable to pay for housing or feed their family. When we consider the economic burden of these conditions in relation to the cost of developing healing gardens we see a real opportunity by improving green space in our urban centres. Adding ecological resources to the urban area aids the development of a sustainable community as it helps the economy and public health.

Designing healthy communities – an ecosystems approach

Ecological resources, or green infrastructure, adds value to our communities. Several recent studies have identified a relationship between the natural environment and public health outcomes. A study entitled 'The relationship between trees and human health' (Donovan et al., 2013) tested whether a major change to the natural environment – the loss of 100 million trees in the USA to the invasive emerald ash borer disease – influenced mortality related to cardiovascular and lower respiratory diseases. The study found an increase in mortality related to cardiovascular and lower respiratory tract illness in counties infested with the emerald ash borer. The magnitude of the effect was greater as infestation progressed and in counties with above-average median household income. The study results have implications for urban design, as they showed just how closely human health is linked to the natural environment. That the effect was more noticeable in areas with above average income is interesting. We will discuss the de-stressing properties of nature and stressed executives further in Chapter 8.

For people living in urban environments trees soften the hard edges and surfaces, shade homes and streets, and enhance neighbourhood aesthetics. However, until recently these benefits were not well quantified. This has made it difficult for urban planners and property owners to weigh their costs and benefits or assess the need for tree cover against competing land uses. Recent studies by Donovan, an economist and research forester, and Butry, an economist, yielded specific dollar values for street and neighborhood trees in Portland, Oregon, and for yard trees that provide summer shade in Sacramento, California. The studies demonstrate that street trees increase home prices and reduce sale time. Combined west- and south-side tree cover reduced summertime electricity bills by an average of $25.16 per household. The study found that citywide, street trees add $1.1 billion to Portland's property value, or $45 million a year. Annual maintenance costs of $4.6 million are a small fraction of the trees' value and are mostly borne by property owners. Thus the case for the cost-effective introduction of more trees to the urban environment is supported (Rodda, 2010).

Trees lend an air of solidity and dependability to an area. By their size, colour or smell they are useful way-finding locator points on personal neighbourhood maps. People of all ages need to feel safe, secure and enjoy a sense of belonging. An ecosystems approach to well-being takes the holistic view that by improving urban ecologies, including planting more trees, we can improve residents' and tourists' connections with nature. How we design neighbourhoods and in particular natural healing elements within communities affects how people feel.

At all life stages we need to be able to engage with living things, whether soil, weather, animals or plants. With increasing urbanisation and reduced contact with the countryside for many people, we need our urban centres to provide access to those ecosystem experiences. 'The more complex the ecosystem, the more success-fully it can resist a stress' (Commoner, 1971). Here we consider an ecosystem to be a defined area of people, buildings, plants and animals.

Ecosystems are at the heart of a salutogenic approach. To be sustainable we must look at urban design as community design; we must embrace both environ-mental and economic elements. Inequality is at the heart of many social problems faced by communities today. Sustainable design then must address the concept of inequality of access, inequality of healthcare, inequality of education. Such con-siderations may seem distant from the day to day work of the landscape architect, but as the early town planners knew, without healthy communities, good sanita-tion, good air quality and access to green space, life expectancy is diminished and populations languish.

Nature deficit disorder is a term first used by Richard Louv to describe the psychological, physical and cognitive costs of human alienation from nature,

Figure 4.11 Natural play: children with fallen leaves.

particularly for children in their vulnerable developing years. Louv has written two ground-breaking books on the subject. The first, *Last Child in the Woods*, tells the story of the 'plugged in' generation, unable and often unwilling to try life outdoors.

> Our society is teaching young people to avoid direct experience in nature. That lesson is delivered in schools, families, even organisations devoted to the outdoors, and codified into the legal and regulatory structures of many of our communities. Our institutions, urban/suburban design, and cultural attitudes unconsciously associate nature with doom – while disassociating the outdoors from joy and solitude. Well-meaning public-school systems, media, and parents are effectively scaring children straight out of the woods and fields.
>
> (Louv, 2005)

A 2003 survey, published in the journal *Psychiatric Services* (Delate et al., 2004) found the rate at which American children are prescribed antidepressants almost doubled in the preceding five years; the steepest increase – 66 per cent – was among preschool children. There is no surprise that these statistics are occurring in tandem with the observed disengagement from nature. North Carolina State University professor Robin Moore has found that:

> Sensory experiences link the child's exterior world with their interior, hidden, affective world. Since the natural environment is the principal source of sensory stimulation, freedom to explore and play with the outdoor environment through the senses in their own space and time is essential for healthy development of the interior life.
>
> (Moore, 1996)

Richard Louv's second book, *The Nature Principle*, tells us that

> the future will belong to the nature-smart – those individuals, families, businesses, and political leaders who develop a deeper understanding of the transformative power of the natural world and who balance the virtual with the real. The more high-tech we become, the more nature we need.
>
> (Louv, 2012)

Bob Sallinger, conservation director at the Audubon Society of Portland, Oregon, USA, agrees. On principle he was averse to the idea of virtual experiences of nature, until the success of Raptor Cam. While believing it is better to engage with nature as a real life experience, he succumbed to a media request and developed a blog to support a reality TV show highlighting the life of urban raptors. A pair of red-tailed hawks had chosen to nest on the fire escape of a city office building in downtown Portland. In conjunction with a local TV station a webcam, 'Raptor Cam', was installed to track the nesting cycle of the birds. The webcam was an instant success and over the next few years each season over a million people kept track of the birds' progress. People who would never have otherwise engaged with nature, would never have looked up and noticed the birds soaring over the city, were suddenly hooked on life in the nest.

Interest in the nest extended beyond the immediate city to gain national coverage. When a chick died many people were outraged that someone hadn't stepped in to save the baby raptor. Others commented that this was nature's way, and harsh as it was, it is good to see and understand how nature nurtures. With people talking about the raptor chicks, interest in local birdlife increased. People out walking their dogs now looked up to see if anything of interest was flying by. In this instance the virtual world has helped the real world, by providing an unadorned 'real' view of life for a pair of native birds in an urban setting.

As seen above, our work as developers of sensory-rich healing spaces and places is of vital importance for the health and well-being of our communities. The 'real' world of nature, with her cycles of life and death, growth and decay, needs to be better presented within our urban areas. We need to provide both the habitat and the quiet viewing areas where people can pause and observe nature. In the case of the red-tailed hawks it required the building owners not to clear the fire escape – it was determined that in the event of a fire people could still use the escape route. The birds found a mix of urban food and nesting material – rats and plastic bags. That was the entire 'habitat' required in that instance. When we seek a more gentle interaction with nature we can provide nectar-rich planting in a local park or garden, in a sunny place to attract butterflies. Nearby seating and informal performance space (Figure 4.12) allows people to take time out of their busy day to pause a moment and enjoy social interactions. Butterfly cams may capture the visitations of particular species on particular plants for a wider audience, but it is important for as many people as possible to have a real experience of nature within their daily life.

Asset-based healthcare

Healing gardens offer biophilic, sensory elements necessary for health and well-being. These environmental assets become social and economic assets when

Figure 4.12 Public space: informal performance space in the park, Guangzhou, China.

Source: Huiyi Liu.

considered in terms of their public health impact. When world health organisations needed a cheaper, more flexible, locally responsive healthcare option they found that a preventive community-based approach worked best. 'An asset based approach makes visible and values the skills, knowledge, connections and potential in a community. It promotes capacity, connectedness and social capital' (GCPH, 2011).

Asset-based healthcare is a new way of looking to the community to provide the resources necessary for good health. Epidemiological tools allow us to link lifestyle factors to an increased risk of disease. Through a salutogenic approach to urban and landscape design we can change lifestyles to decrease the risk of disease, and hence reduce the cost burden to society.

The World Health Organisation states:

> Physical inactivity is the fourth leading risk factor for global mortality. Increasing levels of physical inactivity are seen worldwide, in high-income countries as well as low- and middle-income countries. However, given a supportive environment, increasing levels of physical activity bring health benefits across age groups. All sectors and all levels within governments, international partners, civil society, non-governmental organizations and the private sector have vital roles to play in shaping healthy environments and contributing to the promotion of physical activity.
>
> (WHO, 2013)

In response to the global financial crisis, in 2010 the World Health Organisation noted the need to change the way governments approach healthcare due to unsustainable rising costs, in particular in relation to the treatment of lifestyle-based, non-communicable diseases.

'The shortcomings of taking a "deficits" or "treatment" approach to the delivery of public services, coupled with the cuts to public service provision, have given a renewed impetus to finding better ways of working' (GCPH, 2011).

Asset-based approaches are concerned with identifying the protective factors that support health and well-being. They offer the potential to enhance both the quality and longevity of life through focusing on the resources that promote the self-esteem and coping abilities of individuals and communities. The community benefit of healthcare, when it moves away from the confines of hospitals and formal healthcare settings, comes from improved living conditions for communities and through the prevention of disease by focusing on environmental health, in addition to treatment.

In the rush to develop community health assets, providers have looked to the catalogues of manufactured 'things' they can buy to 'fix' the problem. Designers and health professionals have aided and abetted manufacturers by specifying their wares rather than examining first why we have determined a need, and second, how will the space work for the users, how will it make them feel? The box-ticking, catalogue shopping approach is the downfall of prudent cost-effective public and private spending, however well intentioned. With nature there is no 'instant solution' or quick fix, but rather a slow but measureable change.

Asset-based healthcare is the ideal partner to sustainable communities as it relies on the community, in its broadest ecological sense, to support those at risk. When faced with a need for cost-effective options, through provision of healing garden spaces outdoor therapy becomes available as yet another psychotherapeutic intervention that occupational therapists can recommend. Outdoor work has been used effectively as a therapy to treat those with mood difficulties during the winter season in Denmark (Hahn et al., 2011). As an example, horticulture groups have shown positive impacts on depressive symptoms, which can be associated with psychosocial adaptation leading to healthy occupational performance (Fieldhouse, 2003). Similarly, outdoor walking can provide a therapeutic effect to individuals with seasonal affective disorder (SAD) that is on par with light therapy (Wirz-Justice et al., 1992). With an asset-based approach to healthcare, cost savings can be significant. Walking during daylight hours in the fresh air is a much less expensive option than a practitioner bringing a patient into their facility for artificial light treatment.

In 2002 the health ministries of the United Kingdom and New Zealand devised the 'green prescription'. Originally intended to save money and combat the rising incidence of non-communicable diseases such as diabetes, heart disease and obesity resulting from an inactive lifestyle, it came from research showing that time spent exercising would benefit the patient at a lesser cost and with fewer side effects than traditional pharmaceutical-based interventions. The green prescription programme was backed with a community-based sports agency, such as a local gym, to oversee the exercise and follow up the patient. As an easy option doctors readily prescribed 20–30 minutes exercise five times a week, and saw good results. Ten years and a change of government later, however, funding for the sports agency part of the package has been dropped.

As often happens with good ideas, over time the impetus fades as political mileage diminishes. Green prescriptions as an officially recognised treatment option are now rarely issued in New Zealand. However, informal green prescriptions are still used, mostly for depression but also for other conditions resulting from an inactive lifestyle. The doctor simply tells the patient that they need to walk or swim every day for 30 minutes, and follows up directly with an appointment in 2 weeks to check progress. Neither the patient nor the healthcare provider incur any additional cost of treatment, other, perhaps, than a new pair of walking shoes. The success of the initiative does depend, however, on where the patient lives and what sort of environment they have ready access to. It is important that the area feels safe for the patient, and that it is attractive and designed for the purpose. That is, it needs to offer some variation. Although walking around a bland urban block or sports field ten times may elevate your heart rate and burn some calories, most people would find it boring and be disinclined to continue. To gain the necessary enduring health benefits, the active lifestyle must be attractive.

If there is a destination seating area, walk or cycleway established as part of a planted, interesting loop, perhaps adjacent to a watercourse, close to public trans-port, shops or other amenities, then it encourages people to fit the necessary daily dose of exercise into their routine, free their mind from information overload to explore a little and see if anything is new today – has the water level dropped, are the butterflies feeding, have the bird's eggs in the nest hatched? As the patient connects with nature they develop a relationship with it. For people who have disconnected from society this non-threatening relationship is the first stage in their healing process (Dunning, 2013).

In partnership with local health providers, salutogenic landscape and urban design has the opportunity to provide specific solutions to specific problems. Asset-based healthcare starts with capacity building within the community. Sustainable, healthy communities depend on true partnerships, with high quality, ecologically healthy green space at their heart. A green view's ability to reduce pain and healing time is compromised if the one tree is vandalised and rubbish litters the ground beneath it. Sustainable landscape professionals know how to engage communities

Figure 4.13 Water play and boulder seats: office workers enjoy the nature connection, Auckland, New Zealand.

to design environments that capture the health potential inherit in nature. Existing studies prove the case. Nature health interventions can provide cost-effective management of a range of conditions. What we need now are people prepared to act to achieve the environments people need to live healthy, productive lives.

Evidence-based design

When cost effectiveness and cost efficiencies are important, evidence-based design is the methodology of choice. Design is often ego-driven; the designer thinks that 'this would look nice' so that is what the client gets. Functional, practical design offers much more than simple aesthetics. It still needs to look good if the development is to offer sensory support for the health and well-being of users, but first and foremost it is design based on research tempered with client feedback.

Sustainable communities work on the basis that their ecology is as robust as their social capital and their economy. When looking to design and develop healthy communities it is important to consider not just established practice. Evidence-based design is the process of basing decisions about the built and natural environment on credible research to achieve the best possible outcomes. Included in this process are the following eight steps:

1 Define evidence-based goals and objectives.
2 Find sources for relevant evidence.
3 Critically interpret relevant evidence.
4 Create and innovate evidence-based design concepts.
5 Develop a hypothesis.
6 Collect baseline performance measures.
7 Monitor implementation of design and construction.
8 Perhaps most importantly: measure post-occupancy performance results.

(TCHD, 2013)

A large and growing body of evidence attests to the fact that the physical environment impacts the community. In a healthcare setting patient stress, patient and staff safety, staff effectiveness and quality of care provided in hospitals and other settings are directly and indirectly affected by the design of the space. Like the integrated healthcare facilities of the Rangiora Health Hub discussed in Chapter 3, and Nancy Wilson's study 'Creating healthy communities: rethinking the community centre as a wellness centre' (Wilson, 2013), basing community and healthcare facility planning and design decisions on this evidence achieves the best possible patient, staff and operational outcomes. Landscape-led interventions such as used to prevent dementia provide a cost-effective route to success.

The evidence shows that a quality nature experience leads to both short and long term improvements in health. In subsequent chapters we will see in more detail how all age groups benefit, but particularly the young and the old. The positive outcomes from time spent in well-designed, sensory-rich garden environments are well documented. The cost benefits of green health care are impressive. Experience confirms both nature's ability to provide a cost-effective nationwide health service and the need to work collaboratively. Linking local healthcare providers with built environment and landscape professionals at the initial design phase ensures the development of appropriate green spaces throughout the community.

Conclusion

In conclusion, Part I has shown that since ancient times wild landscapes have been tamed and contained to be used as healing gardens. Historically access to nature was an intrinsic part of daily life. Where modern society has moved away from nature we have seen a decline in public health and an increased need for healing gardens. Today we need nature experiences more than ever to balance the negative effects of the hard-edged built environment coupled with fast-paced, information-overloaded lifestyles.

Soft landscape-led interventions have been found to counter the adverse health effects of urban degradation. Global climate change and unsustainable rising healthcare costs, in conjunction with changing social and economic dynamics, require innovative solutions. Green infrastructure, that is ecologically healthy public green space designed to afford healing nature connections, can meet that need.

When we design urban environments for health and well-being we create sustainable, livable cities. The benefits of using evidence-based design to develop sensory, therapeutic and healing gardens are cost-effective landscapes that promote human health and well-being.

References

AIHW (2011, May). Indigenous housing publications. Retrieved 21 December 2013, from *Australian Institute of Health and Welfare*: www.aihw.gov.au/indigenous-housing-publications

Baxby, L. (2013). Ten major trends in global health systems. 9th Design and Health World Congress, Brisbane, 2013 (p. Day 1). Brisbane: International Academy of Design and Health.

Commoner, B. (1971). *The closing circle: nature, man, and technology* (pp. 34–35). New York: Knopf.

Cunningham, J. C. (2009). *State of the world's indigenous peoples*. New York: United Nations.

Defra (2013, August). Ecosystems services: detailed guidance. Retrieved December 2013, from *Department for Environment, Food and Rural Affairs*: https://www.gov.uk/ecosystems-services

Delate, T., Gelenberg, A. J., Simmons, V. A. and Motheral, B. R. (2004). Trends in the use of antidepressants in a national sample of commercially insured pediatric patients, 1998–2002. *Psychiatric Services*, 55:387–391.

Donovan, G. H., Butry, D. T., Michael, Y. L., Prestemon, J. P., Liebhold, A. M., Gatziolis, D. and Mao, M. Y. (2013). The relationship between trees and human health: evidence from the spread of the emerald ash borer. *American Journal of Preventitive Medicine*, 44(2):139–145.

Dunning, E. B., M.D., MBCHB, (2013, February). Fellow of the Royal New Zealand College of General Practitioners. Interviewed by the author.

Fieldhouse, J. (2003). The impact of an allotment group on mental health clients' health, wellbeing and social networking. *British Journal of Occupational Therapy*, 66(7):286–296.

GCPH (2011, October). Asset based approaches for health imrpovement: redressing the balance. Briefing Paper. Glasgow, Scotland: Glasgow Centre for Population Health.

Hahn, I. H., Grynderup, M. B., Dalsgaard, S. B., Thomsen, J. F., Hansen, A. M., Kaergaard, A., Kaerlev, L., Mors, O., Rugulies, R., Mikkelsen, S., Bonde, J. P. and Kolstad, H. A. (2011). Does outdoor work during the winter season protect against depression and mood difficulties? *Scandinavian Journal of Work, Environment and Health*, 37(5):446–49.

Hammam, C. (2013). The effect on 'mood' of a living (biophilic) work environment. 9th Design and Health World Congress, Brisbane, 2013 (p. Day 3 session 9). Brisbane: International Academy of Design and Health.

Hildebrandt, S. (2012, 6 February). How stress can cause depression. Retrieved 2013, from *Science Nordic*: http://sciencenordic.com/how-stress-can-cause-depression

Ignatieva, M. E. (2008). *How to out nature into our neighbourhoods: application of low impact urban design and development priciples, with a biodiversity focus, for New Zealand developers and homeowners*. Lincoln, New Zealand: Manaaki Whenua Press, Landcare Research, NZ.

IISD (2013). What is sustinale development? Retrieved 12 March 2013, from *International Institute for Sustainable Development*: www.iisd.org/sd

Kahn, M. (2012, December). Free medicine. *Outside Magazine*.

Kaplan, S. (1995). The restorative benefits of nature: toward an integrative framework. *Journal of Environmental Psychology*, 15(3):169–82.

Louv, R. (2005). *Last child in the woods: saving our children from nature deficit disorder*. New York: Algonquin Books of Chapel Hill.

—— (2012). *The nature principle: reconnecting with life in digital age*. Chapel Hill, NC: Algonquin Books.

Mahdawi, A. (2013, 15 March). SoulCycle: an expensive habit for gym junkies to break. *Guardian*.

Maslow, A. H. (1943). A theory of human motivation. *Psychological Review*, 50(4):370–96.

Moore, R. (1996). The need for nature: a childhood right. *Social Justice*, 24(3):203–20.

Read, S. (2008, August). Interviewed by the author.

Rodda, K. (2010, 13 October). Study to calculate dollar value of urban trees. Retrieved September 2013, from *Nursery Management*: www.nurserymag.com/studies-calculate-dollar-value-of-urban-trees.aspx

TCHD (2013). About the Centre for Health Design. Retrieved 2013, from *The Centre for Health Design*: www.healthdesign.org/edac/about

WHO (1948). World Health Organisation: about. Retrieved 2013, from *World Health Organisation*: www.who.int/about/definition/en/print.html

—— (2013). 10 facts on physical activity. Retrieved July 2013, from *World Health Organisation*: www.who.int/features/factfiles/physical_activity/en

Wilson, N. (2013). Creating healthy communities: rethinking the community as a wellness centre. 9th Design and Health World Congress, Brisbane, 2013 (p. Day 4 session 8). Brisbane: International Academy for Design and Health.

Wirz-Justice, A., Van der Velde, P., Bucher, A. and Nil, R. (1992). Comparison of light treatment with citalopram in winter depression: a longitudinal single case study. *International Clinical Psychopharmacology*, 7(2):109–116.

PART II

WHO WILL BENEFIT FROM HEALING GARDENS?

CHAPTER 5

Healing gardens for children

Childhood is a time of discovery, of exploration, learning and growing. It is the time we make neural connections and social connections. Healing gardens for children must offer opportunities that afford development of the whole child.

(Landry, 2005)

While governments are waking up to the requirement for new policies to support an ageing population, it is important we also remember the needs of children. Article 31 of the UN Convention on the Rights of the Child states that every signatory country must uphold the rights of the child to rest and leisure, to engage in play and recreational activities appropriate to the age of the child, and to participate freely in cultural life and the arts (Office of the High Commissioner for Human Rights, 1995).

Children learn through play, imitation and experience. However, in many countries pressures on adults to succeed in a competitive environment have spilled over into the lives of their children. These concerns have seen the removal or reduction of play time seen as 'wasteful', the removal of playground seating considered as 'encouraging sedentary behaviours' and, perhaps not surprisingly, the rise of childhood mental health problems. Childhood stress is evident in increasing rates of depression, anti-social behaviours, and teenage (and younger) suicide. As adults perceive poor results or anti-social behavior to be a problem, authorities react with policies to keep children in structured activites for longer periods.

What we think of as a modern, First World problem is nothing new. Plato complained in the fourth century BC: 'What is happening to our young people? They disrespect their elders, they disobey their parents. They ignore the law. They riot in the streets inflamed with wild notions. Their morals are decaying. What is to become of them?' (Fuller, 1970). What is new is our reaction to normal childhood behaviours. Once we would have sent the children outside to play. Now we restrict them to their room or keep them busy with extra ballet or soccer classes. To improve educational outcomes, lower rates of childhood depression, obesity and youth suicide, we need to redress the balance. Children, like adults, have disconnected from nature, and from each other. To provide play and recreational activities appropriate to the age of the child we need locally accessible safe, inclusive, engaging play spaces. Healing gardens that afford the opportunity for kids to connect socially need to be part of every urban plan. We need more than just the spaces, though; community regulations must allow our children to use and access these spaces.

Natural play areas

'Natural play' and the development of natural playgrounds has become popular as multi-disciplinary research shows the benefits of reconnecting with nature. Natural play describes an affordance to engage freely with nature. At home, at school or in public parks, natural play promotes health and well-being through social connections as it promotes nature connections. To counter public health problems, aid investment and boost economic growth, the South Australian government announced in December 2013 that every school in the state would have a natural playground by 2015.

A sedentary life indoors has meant that many children today have weaker bones, poor muscular coordination (although their thumbs and index fingers may be well developed), rickets and such low life expectancy that today's children are expected to live five years less than their parents (NIH, 2005). Previously life expectancy was related to socio-economic status. Now that is being evened out as poor and affluent alike think they are being good parents by buying their children a virtual life indoors, safe from nature. How wrong they are.

As Richard Louv has described, the fact the current generation of parents has disconnected from nature is a root part of the problem. Parents distrust what they do not know, so a key part to solving the problem of unhealthy children is to work with the parents. It is important to highlight that although most children will actively seek risk in their play, they do not set out to fail or hurt themselves (Little and Wyver, 2008). The vast majority of children seek a level of challenge that they are developmentally capable of achieving.

As Scottish educator and founder of Nature Kindergartens, Claire Warden, says: 'children have a right to feel "the knot in the stomach" – that feeling of anticipation and exhilaration when taking risks during play' (Warden, 2011). She also argues how important it is that children experience the possibilities of now and the promise of 'more to come'.

Natural play provision is important as a means of providing space for children to safely connect with nature in an urban setting. To be effective as a health intervention, however, delivery must be matched with a public education programme that reconnects adults with nature. Even in areas where access to green space is seemingly good, the preference for children to play outdoors is not a given and 'nature deficit', childhood depression and obesity still exist. For example, in New Zealand and Australia, where sport and an outdoor lifestyle prevail, a disturbing increase in the incidence of childhood obesity and related conditions has occurred. While annual camping trips to the beach or the mountains may be part of family life, it is not enough if day-to-day home and school life are spent in organised activities or playing virtual games indoors.

Opportunities to reconnect children with nature can take many forms, from the most basic chair swing in Marrakech to a wildflower meadow in California.

Figure 5.1 Child's swing seat set under shade trees, Middle East.

Figure 5.2 Children happily engaging with nature: playing in mud, California.

Source: The Children in Nature Collaborative. Photo: Roy Gordon.

Natural play opportunities provide children and their families with safe places of reflection, where they can de-stress. Informal swings can be added inexpensively to pergolas, verandah supports and trees – anywhere there is safe space to swing.

Sustainable communities evolve around natural play areas as the mental and physical health benefits spill over into the wider community. In Berlin, Germany, natural playgrounds are common. Developed as a means of mitigating the social disparities and unrest that occurred after reunification, the playgrounds were constructed principally around playable planting, timber, rope, sand and water. Designs include details such as pump-action water spouts on the edge of sand play, allowing 'mud pie' making as well as junior engineering experiments.

These healing elements afford the best nature connection in an urban setting. To achieve maximum health benefit, natural play ideally needs to be located within a green setting. As shown in Figure 5.4, the facades of overlooking apartment buildings have been softened by trees. In the 1950s a local politician decided that many of East Berlin's buildings were ugly, and therefore bad for community morale. Large scale street tree planting ensued, and the result is the greenest city in Europe. Anecdotally, in talking with local schools and preschools, childhood illnesses are found to be uncommon. Asthma, conditions related to lifestyle such as obesity, heart problems and diabetes, allergies, and childhood depression are rare.

What can we learn from this? Natural play promotes healthy whole-child development. The social, environmental and economic benefits of reconnecting children with nature through natural play opportunities are potentially significant.

Figure 5.3
Swing set under
pergola.

Figure 5.4
Neighbourhood
playground, Berlin:
natural play with
timber and ropes set in
large sand pit.

Public health

Multiple studies have shown the link between health and outdoor nature experiences. Dr William Bird, the strategic health advisor to Natural England, emphasises the potential benefits, but perhaps more importantly, the known harm to children that comes from a deficiency of outdoor experience (Bird, 2010). Health, design and education professionals around the world agree that children, and adults, need outdoor exercise in stimulating, green environments.

Including playful spaces for children within the urban realm, by providing access to quality outdoor experiences, we offer a cost-effective health strategy for governments at national and local levels. It is a means to lower the national health bill. It brings social benefits whereby crime rates are reduced. Educational outcomes are improved as children who spend time in green space outdoors become healthy, happy young people who produce the best results. With positive experience of nature, workplace productivity is improved, and relationships are strengthened.

Today's children come from family groups of all shapes and sizes. To build healthy communities we need to ensure children can connect safely and freely with nature outdoors. Children need to be able to play. For a play space to be a true community resource it must offer something for everyone, from teenagers to under-5s, from grandmothers at leisure to office workers enjoying lunch outdoors. Older disabled children often want to be able to play alongside or with younger siblings. Adults want to use the chin press or stretch out in a hammock while the kids are safely in school. All ages benefit from being surrounded by leafy trees and birdsong. As Richard Louv says in *Last Child in the Woods*, 'The woods were my Ritalin.[1] Nature calmed me, focused me, and yet excited my senses.'

Urban planning policy has considered the public health of adults, but not specifically of children. Children, like the elderly, are more susceptible to illness as their immune systems, minds and bodies are vulnerable through their developing years. More than 2,000 years ago, Hippocrates said:

> Whoever wishes to investigate medicine properly, should proceed thus: in the first place consider the seasons of the year, and what effects each of them produces for they are not at all alike, but differ much from themselves in regard to their changes.

Often touted as the father of modern medicine, Hippocrates not only understood the challenges of public health but also nature's potential to heal.

Reconnecting children with nature will go a long way towards building healthy, resilient communities. When we design spaces where children feel welcomed, where they can meet friends and family freely, explore, engage, rest and restore their inner equilibrium, mental health, obesity, diabetes, heart disease, cancers, depression, unemployment and under employment, low aspiration and low life expectancy are managed.

Depression was estimated to cost the UK £8.5 billion in 2009, the USA $57 billion. In Chapter 9 we will look at the cost benefits of landscape interventions in more detail. How best to provide that healing or therapeutic experience requires collaboration with experts from the design and medical professions.

Independent mobility has been shown to be good for children's well-being and general development (Shaw et al., 2013). Restoring parents' faith in their communities is a crucial factor in the success of any development. We need to encourage walking and biking routes, and to reduce the speed limit outside preschools and schools. Dr Mike Knapton, associate medical director of the British Heart Foundation, says we need towns and cities which encourage people to have an active lifestyle (Baker, 2012).

One of the main challenges to children living an active lifestyle lies in adults' attitudes and perceptions. Literature reviews (Bruyere, 2011) show that 'where parents and teachers accept and even encourage children to take risks and challenge themselves mentally, physical risk is more often seen as something negative and dangerous and to be avoided'.

> Very often our playworkers find themselves talking to other adults in the community and helping to address one of the other barriers to play; adult attitudes. We have found that a little bit of misty-eyed reminiscing about childhood 'mischief' is often enough to remind adults that children playing outside in their community is a good thing in a world where, all too often, the young generation are demonized.
>
> (Howard, 2013)

Today's children don't play freely outdoors the way children have always enjoyed in previous generations.

- American children spend an average of less than half an hour per week in unstructured outdoor play.
- On average, children between the ages of 8 and 18 spend 44 hours per week with electronic media.

These facts have significant implications for a wide range of social, environmental, physical and psychological concerns that will affect our society for many years to come.

> There is generally a less than 1% risk of children being run over or molested by a stranger if we let them roam, play freely and experience the local environment. There is a 100% risk of damage if we allow our children to disconnect from nature.
>
> (Louv, 2008)

The above examples and case studies are interesting, but what do they mean for us as designers?

Safe, sterile play

Conceptually, gardens for children and young people have, for the past 20–30 years, largely focused on play. The play areas have looked and felt far from a garden setting, however. Examples of play areas can be seen in towns and cities around the Western world as fenced off areas of manufactured climbing frames, swings, slides and the occasional sand pit set on a rubberised surface. Trees, shade and a feeling of welcome is absent. Some have been described as so 'sterile' as to have no play value at all. Even dog exercise yards compare favourably to what we have provided our children.

The playground in Figure 5.5 shows a client's outdoor play space as provided for thirty-five 2–5 year olds. Surfaced in an impact-attenuating play carpet, the floor is uniformly flat. Plastic play equipment is scattered around the courtyard, lending a generally chaotic feel to the space. When the centre was opened they were sold the playground equipment and play carpet as being easy care and low maintenance. What they were not told is that low maintenance often equates to low interest and low play value. Social play does not develop fully in sterile play spaces, because the children lack a nature connection so are not able to relax. We need an antidote, such as the inclusive sensory-rich play space shown in Figure 5.6.

Forty-seven million Americans now live with covenants prohibiting children playing outside. That means local rules against treehouses, climbing trees, skateboards, basketball nets, even sidewalk chalk, and in some places children hanging out with their friends on the street outside their home. In the USA, UK, Australia and France, compounding the situation, with the rise in fear of litigaton and some unexamined reports from doctors citing injuries from playgrounds, a ban has been

Figure 5.5 Sterile outdoor play space, London: plastic equipment and rubber surfacing heated up in summer to unsafe levels.

Figure 5.6
Axonometric drawing of sensory gardens at Mary Rose special needs school, UK.

Source: Designed by Greenstone Design UK.

placed on some activities and certain types of play equipment have been removed from use. Cartwheels, handstands and even 'high fives' were banned in Australian schools. This has occurred even as child health has deteriorated. The greatest increase in child obesity in our history has occurred during the same decades as the greatest increase in organised after-school activities for children.

As outdoor activity and free play has been restricted, child development has been affected and the adverse health statistics have risen alarmingly. Conditions such as attention deficit disorder (ADD), attention deficit hyperactivity disorder (ADHD), autistic spectrum disorders (ASD) and developmental delays have increased along-side childhood asthma, type 2 diabetes and depression. We are not saying these conditions have been caused by the lack of free play opportunities, but rather that the situation has become exacerbated due to a range of social ills. Restoring parents' faith in their communities is a crucial factor in overcoming these problems.

Adults have a duty to ensure the safety of those in our care, those we are designing for, providing for and working with. However, it is not up to designers to decide whether or not to allow a child to hang from a tree, or which way they must scale play apparatus. The risk benefits of play must be weighed such that we provide access to safe places for children to explore and then stand back and allow children to test themselves and learn as they grow in confidence and competence.

Over the past twenty years child health and development theory has colluded with politics and economics to create a sterile landscape where too often children are confronted with exclusive, inaccessible play spaces that do little to encourage their innate curiosity, develop confidence or increase strength of character.

Provision for children within public parks and urban green space

Historically, public parks and gardens were designed so that people could 'take the air'. Some are managed today like archives, where you can look but it is all too precious to touch. Signs exhort people not to congregate, walk on the grass or remove flowers. While we would never advocate damage, providing accessible green space where children can actively engage with nature requires spaces where they can get up close. Given the immediate appeal of digital media, today's children will be reluctant to engage with nature if kept at arm's length.

The new style of public park needs to be accessible. It has to offer opportunities to test personal limits, ever-changing things to do and see, places to hang out with friends, somewhere to sit and observe the goings-on. That means it needs to (a) offer visiting wildlife and seasonal variation, (b) be close to where children live or hang out, and (c) have safe routes for them to get there without major roads to cross. Much has been written about the risk benefits of play (Gill, 2011). In public spaces, as in schools, the chance of litigation has led many authorities to remove all possible hazards, and in so doing remove opportunities for a very necessary part of child development. Natural play allows children to explore and make their own mistakes in a way that manufactured equipment cannot. While we do not recommend children jump over wide streams, if we do not allow them to test their limits in a relatively safe environment they will experiment with other potentially more harmful risks (Little and Wyver, 2008).

While acknowledging healthy risk, we need to avoid known harm. In keeping children from harm we need to consider air quality. A nature experience should not poison the child! From a safety perspective, even if children do not need to cross a busy road if the park is nearby, if air quality is poor then barrier planting of large trees needs to be included in the park design. Trees absorb carbon dioxide and potentially harmful gases such as sulphur dioxide and carbon monoxide from the air, and release oxygen.

Inclusive, child-friendly environments are an intrinsic part of the development of healthy, sustainable communities. In the heart of Sydney, Australia, the engaging, playable water feature shown in Figure 5.7 allows young and old to socialise and cool off in hot summer weather. Although features of the urban green space may be designed for children, it benefits all sectors of the community. If we create a playful space such as this one in Sydney, it will attract tourists as well as locals. If sufficiently engaging, the space will encourage people to linger and patronise local businesses.

Unique, exciting identities can be created for cities using iconic playgrounds within public parks. Urban centres need to attract people to support investment and ensure livability. Destination playgrounds attract children and adults alike. Using the

Figure 5.7 Playable
public space: water play
in Sydney, Australia.

Figure 5.7 Playable public space: water play in Sydney, Australia.

town's colours, mascot or local historic feature as the basis for themed play areas affords a sense of place. In public parks, as in schools, to achieve maximum health benefits the following should be incorporated:

1 sand and water play;
2 scrambling, climbing and swinging opportunities;
3 playable planting to define exciting areas that entice and stimulate exploring games;
4 discovery zones, such as bog gardens where children can feel mud between their toes;
5 roly-poly slopes, so children are encouraged to feel the earth beneath them;
6 walk and crawl tunnels;
7 open-air theatre;
8 art and outdoor music.

Why we need to take action

With few exceptions, internationally, current provision of public parks and urban green space does not adequately facilitate healing connections with nature. According to Richard Louv (2013):

1 Ninety-one per cent of parents cite TV, computers and video games as the main cause of their children's lack of interest in outdoor play.
2 A study found that young people could identify 1,000 corporate logos but fewer than ten plants or animals native to their backyards.

3 Forty per cent of US schools have cut recess due to funding cuts and/or the need for more instructional time due to pressure created by high-stakes academic testing.
4 There has been a 500 per cent increase in childhood obesity since the 1960s (from 4 per cent to 20 per cent).
5 Children have less time for unstructured, creative play in the outdoors than ever before in human history.

Andrew Curran, research fellow in paediatric neurology at Liverpool's Alder Hay Children's Hospital, says: 'Everything you are, everything you feel and everything you think is because nerve cells in your brain have grown connections to other nerve cells to form a pattern of firing that is hard-wired into you. Every time that pattern fires, you will remember that feeling, relive that moment, recall that fact, re-experience that taste' (Curran, 2010).

Stress in children

Although stress can be a positive influence, as when it stimulates us to reach a deadline, in high doses it can be a negative one and drag us down. It has been linked to poor cognitive performance, heart disease and cancer. As adults we tend to be dismissive of children's concerns and frequently underestimate their effects.

So what does childhood stress have to do with architects, horticulture therapists, landscape designers or urban planners? The 2012 International Forum on Healthcare and Therapeutic Design held at Tunghai University, Taiwan, found an overlap between the interests and research findings of diverse practitioners. The effect of time spent in nature on children's health and educational outcomes was studied, and researchers concluded that a nature connection is necessary for their well-being (Tunghai University, 2012).

Around the world, school-based education programmes have been introduced to try to address various social ills. For example, the UK's 'Healthy Eating, Healthy Living' and 'Learning Through Landscapes' programmes aim to expose children to the natural world. In the USA the Children's Nature Collective encourages free, unstructured outdoor play and use of cross-curricular outdoor learning opportunities. Where schools embrace the programmes the benefits spill out into the wider community with better attention, improved health, and reduced anti-social behaviour.

Why do we need programmes for children and how do we design environments to support them?

As discussed in previous chapters, modern society has become more complex than at any other point in history. This has significantly increased the amount of stress both adults and children are exposed to. Children, who are still growing, developing and building the necessary physical, social, emotional and intellectual toolkits for life,

Figure 5.8 School children pretend, explore and discover nature in their eco school, Hampshire.

are more vulnerable and hence more susceptible to negative experiences. They are experiencing poorer mental health at younger and younger ages.

Tension, anxiety and trauma have been linked to childhood health conditions from depression to eating disorders, allergies to heart disease. When a child is stressed they are more likely to perform below their ability, miss school, turn to crime, develop long-term health conditions and generally have a higher risk of becoming a significant cost to society. For their health and well-being, and to reduce costs to society, it is therefore important we provide environments which reduce stress in the communities in which children grow up.

To counter the stressors that young children today are exposed to – blended families; both parents working outside the home; increased exposure to violence, both real and on the screen; excessive screen time; feeling pressured to perform or behave beyond their ability (Witkin, 1999) – we can design environments to attract young people back to their childhoods and away from excessive screen time, away from dysfunction or disharmony in their home.

Play gardens for babies and children

When we design for the health and well-being of children we need to be mindful of their developmental needs. And we need to start young. Instinctively, a positive association with nature is hardwired into the infant brain. Some parents may have forgotten their biophilia but babies need time outdoors, fresh air and natural daylight every day. For healthy eye development, to build immunity, to build strong bones, to strengthen young lungs and protect against asthma and allergies, regular time outdoors with varied-length focal points, sunlight on their skin and fresh, clean air is vital. If the home situation does not offer the opportunity for their pram to be parked under a tree in the garden for baby's afternoon nap, then the local park or green space around their housing must provide such quiet space. Likewise, as shown in the Danish example in Figure 5.9, for those in daycare that environment must afford the opportunity for infants and young children to be immersed in nature.

Figure 5.9 Babies and children need to spend time outdoors every day; sleeping outdoors is ideal.

Source: Frode Svane.

Inclusive, accessible design starts with plants. Plants soften the built environment and when appropriate species are used, create a play garden for children. Playful gardens allow and support children in their need to explore and express themselves through play. The old-fashioned design precepts of a well-designed garden inviting exploration and unfolding its sensory delights as you traverse the space is as true of gardens for children today as it was for the monks of the Middle Ages.

Table 5.1 gives examples of suitable plants for babies and 1–4 year olds. This list is not exhaustive but covers tropical to temperate climate zones and serves to provide guidance on the sorts of plants that will stimulate young bodies and minds. So long as there is a water supply available there are plants, from trees to shrubby ferns, to suit any environment bar the Arctic. Fruit trees, with their ability to be pruned to shape and low, spreading habit, make them ideal for climbing by older preschool-aged children. Young ones will enjoy gazing up through the leaves. Toddlers and others who don't have the confidence or ability to climb love pushing their way through robust 'jungle' style planting that is just taller than they are.

Politics and economics have played a large part in shaping the landscapes we see today. School yards, playgrounds and public parks provide for organised sport but generally adopt a catalogue shopping approach when it comes to children's play. When finance becomes available, targets must be met and often in ridiculously short time frames, so 'one of those and two of these' are ordered and 'job done' is stamped on the outdoor play provision file for another funding round. This 'box-ticking' may look good on a treasury report but does little for the local environment, the child, or their community. The inherent health-giving, creative impetus that unstructured play provides has been all but designed out of some playgrounds. This is not to say that all manufactured play equipment is bad, but rather that it needs to be set within a playful garden. Designers have a responsibility to educate clients and funders to the potential of a well-designed play space so that the mistakes and missed opportunities are not perpetuated. Healing gardens provide the opportunity to make a difference, to the health and well-being of children and the communities in which they live.

As community awareness of public health concerns is increasing, the politics are shifting. Economics are now being put forward as the reason why we should develop more play gardens for children. Like adults, all children, regardless of whether they are disabled or not, require regular access to nature for their health and well-being.

Table 5.1 Examples of plants suitable for babies and infants in day care situations

Plant	Benefit	Size	Season of interest
Under 1 year			
Acer palmatum	Delicate tracery of leaves	To 3m	Spring–summer leaf, autumn colour
Amelanchier alnifolia (Pacific serviceberry)	Edible fruit, tall shrub, attracts wildlife	To 8m	Spring flowers, summer leaf, autumn colour
Leptospermum scoparium (Manuka/ tea tree)	Edible leaves and honey from blossom, quick-growing evergreen, salt tolerant	To 3m	Year round, fragrant blossom attracts wildlife
Malus (apple tree)	Edible fruit, low spreading branches for dappled shade	2–6m, depending on rootstock	Scented spring blossom, summer leaf, colourful autumn fruit, winter bark
1–4 years			
Blechnum sp. (hard fern)	'Jungle' planting feel	1–3m, depending on variety	Year round
Palms	Spreading for shade, creates exotic 'mood'	To 10m, depending on variety	Year round, wildlife-attracting when in fruit
Phormium sp. (NZ flax)	Cold-hardy 'jungle' planting	To 1m	Red flower spikes in summer, attracts nectar feeders, evergreen
Prunus Lusitanica (Portuguese laurel)	Springy branches for natural bounce, dense evergreen leaves	To 5m but can be pruned	Year round, summer flowers for bees and butterflies, autumn berries for birds

Summary: a wide variety is available and suitable.

There are several aspects to healing gardens for children. We will look at provision for children in schools, in a healthcare setting, in a natural play setting, in public parks, at home and around urban streets.

In schools

As we have seen in earlier chapters, human health and well-being benefits from nature connections. In schools, many grassed play spaces have been sold off or developed. Planting is often minimal or a monoculture.[2] In their 2001 study titled 'Coping with ADD: the surprising connection to green play settings', Taylor, Kuo and Sullivan of the University of Illinois found that children living with the sensory overload that characterises ADD (attention deficit disorder) relaxed and became calm when they spent time playing in green settings (Taylor et al., 2001). In the same study they found that neurotypical[3] girls also do better when connected to nature. Girls with a view of nature from home were studied and found to be better motivated, and perform better in standarised tests than those without access to nature. This point is important to note when designing boarding and day schools, as well as housing developments. Education intervention programmes have found boys are more engaged and attentive when they have spent time outdoors in nature. Green space, gardens and nature have been conclusively shown as key to the educational success of children and young people with attention deficit disorder or attention deficit hyperactivity disorder (ADHD), as well as for neurotypical girls (and anecdotally, boys).

Figure 5.10 Young girl exploring 'jungle planting' in a nursery school.

Source: Matt Dunkinson Photography.

As special interest groups acquire funding, more studies are being conducted into the effects of early interventions on a variety of health conditions affecting children. Early indications are that all children's mental health and physical well-being are improved by time spent playing freely outdoors. Playful healing gardens can be effectively designed to promote the health and development of these children. School playgrounds with the natural shade of tall trees, bio-diverse planting to attract wildlife, edible planting, views of the sky, or distant views create a calming connection for the children. When designers work in conjunction with health and education professionals the outcome for the children is great.

Figure 5.11 shows a school we designed in north London. The neighbourhood had been socially and economically depressed. We have been told that since the introduction of the new natural playground, local housing prices have increased as people have moved into the area, attracted by the community feature.

> Overall it is the variety and quality of experiences offered to children outdoors in the 0–5 years age group that can lead to better outcomes for their learning and development.
>
> (Department for Education, 2012a)

Minimum outdoor play space requirements for children are detailed in some countries. The UK's Building Bulletin 82 (1996) (Department for Education, 2012b) recommended a minimum of 9 square meters (approximately 27 square feet) per 3–5 year old child in a school setting. Interestingly there is no similar guideline for outdoor space requirements in the child's home. As homes become smaller and more crowded it is increasingly important that schools and public space accommodate the activities that thirty years ago would have been enjoyed at home. Splashing about with containers of water, digging in a sand pit and climbing the apple tree were all activities safely accommodated and inexpensively provided for in the home garden. Schools must now fill the gap in provision.

A recent report entitled *Sowing the Seeds: Reconnecting London's Children with Nature* (Gill, 2011) concludes:

Case study 9: Eastwood Nursery School, Centre for Children and Families, Wandsworth, London, UK

The school is located in the second largest (social) housing estate in Europe and falls within the bottom 10 per cent for child and income deprivation in the UK. Wandsworth has one of the worst obesity rates in London and a high prevalence of mental health issues. Many local children do not have a garden or outside space to play in. These facts are related. While the socio-economics of the community cannot be changed overnight, the quality of the school's outdoor environment can. As we did through the new playground in north London, with home–school partnership programmes the school has the opportunity to reach out into the community, to create a hub where healthy eating, healthy living, an active lifestyle and a positive life experience can be delivered inexpensively through the judicious planting of fruit and vegetables, shrubs and trees, and the provision of seating, quiet and active spaces, where families can come together with their children.

> Children want space at all ages. Space, that is ample space, is almost as much wanted as food and air. To move, to run, to find things out by new movement, to feel one's life in every limb, that is the life of early childhood.
>
> (Margaret McMillan, 1930, in Ouvry, 2005)

Even the smallest of outside spaces can be utilised. Asphalt can be greened with small trees, vines and flowering plants in large planter boxes, or ripped up and replaced with permeable surfacing such as grass, gravel, sand or resin-bound aggregates. Small scale spaces are often neglected by schools as unworthy of attention. However, they can seem vast and intriguing through a child's eyes and with some creative thought, provide a space for children to explore and connect with nature.

Figure 5.11 Grass amphitheatre seating as alternative access to earth mound and for audiences of performance area opposite. Designed by Greenstone Design UK.

Figure 5.12 Toddlers and young children watching performance on stage. Designed by Greenstone Design UK.

- Only 10 per cent of London's children regularly play in green space.
- One in seven London families have not been to a green space in the past year.
- Forest schools and similar approaches 'should be promoted and supported London-wide to [sic] the conservation, education and childcare sectors'.

Children spend up to six hours or more in school each day. In this controlled setting we can profoundly influence their health and well-being, through provision of access to quality outdoor environments. We can design fabulous play spaces for the children but they are useless unless the school administration supports children's free play. We have been brought in to schools by board members, science co-ordinators and parent bodies keen to create change. One school had 10 acres of playing fields, ripe for redevelopment, which the children were not allowed to access outside of physical education lessons because it was said to be too far for the playground supervisors to walk! (Figure 5.13).

When we questioned the administration we were told that the situation was 'too hard to change as it was difficult enough to find people to fill the position [of playground supervisor]'. Without full consultation and buy-in from all stakeholders any redevelopment work would be doomed to failure. In that instance we offered a free CPD session for all staff on the benefits of natural play. We were rewarded with a brief to develop the margins of the sports field and a change in mindset of the play supervisors. To make best use of the space we developed a sensory trail of robust planting where the children could play freely, and which whole classes could utilise during science lessons. The school's administration was delighted as their problem was solved and the children were happy as they could access the greenspace they could previously see but not touch. As the schools inspectorate, Ofsted, commented:

Figure 5.13 Extensive grass playing area unused because it is 'too far for supervisors to walk', forcing overcrowding of hard paved area and exacerbating anti-social behaviour.

Without any additional equipment the children have greater freedom born from better communications, consensus of what play . . . should be like, shared expectations about behaviour, greater understanding because parents, children and lunchtime staff have all had a chance to say what it's like for them. This has arisen from changes in attitude and practice e.g. it's OK to get muddy . . .

(Playlink, 2009)

In healthcare settings

Children in hospital are not there by choice. To make life easier for them and their families it is important to provide places to de-stress. Where children cannot get out of bed, an engaging green view is important. Where they are able to move about and go outside it is important to make that space attractive. When life is difficult sometimes children are reluctant to walk and lack confidence in using their hands. In a garden setting we can provide gentle encouragement through interesting spaces to explore, using sensory design elements to create fun and mystery. (In Chapter 12 we shall look at the key elements of these features.)

The usual good design guideline of hiding some parts of the garden so that it unfolds as we move through the space hold true for children's healthcare gardens especially. Children of all ages and developmental stages delight in having some-where to go, a hint of something exciting just around the corner, under a tree or through a gap in a hedge. To encourage children to use their hands, a variety of tactile experiences is useful. Soft, cuddly animals such as trained dogs or rabbits can be introduced to the healthcare garden. A variety of leaf textures alongside a path, especially if attractively coloured, will encourage children to touch or stroke the plants as they move past. Note that trees with interesting bark need to be carefully chosen so that when planted close to the path, within touching distance of a chair, bike or walker, their roots do not break up the path surface.

Whether children are hospitalised as a result of illness or accident, there is often some degree of shock and they may disconnect to a greater or lesser degree from their surroundings. Regardless of cause, for children with sensory impairment shading of colour is important. Development of depth of vision is aided by tunnels of greenery over paths to create areas of light and shade. As a design feature, if archways or pergolas are planted with edibles such as peas, grapes or apples children can pick and eat as they pass through a space. Likewise green structures such as living willow domes offer a seasonally changing playspace.

> Gardens for children provide a vital connection with the natural world. Healing gardens are designed to support children as they learn and grow, whether at home or at school. In health care settings children's physical and mental recovery is improved.
>
> (Said, 2008)

Figure 5.14 Sand play opportunities de-stress children: here the sand is contained within an old rowboat.

Source: 3 Little Pirates blog.

Figure 5.14 shows a very simple play area to one side of the paved entry to the building. The design feature to note is the lack of institutional feel to the play elements. This serves to relax the children and allows them to be supported by nature as they heal, promoting a healthy, active life.

At home

The saying 'home is where the heart is' shows how fundamental our homes are to our sense of self. Whether children live in high rise buildings or detached homes, we need to look closely at the outdoor space and landscapes we provide for them. Developmentally, children need room to grow. They need space to stretch. To stretch their long muscles they need space to run, safely, as fast as they can, in one direction, or along a suddenly changing course.

Today's overscheduled kids are increasingly 'plugged in' to electronic devices and unplugged from nature. Richard Louv, author of *Last Child in the Woods* and more recently *The Nature Principle*, refers to this nature–child disconnect as 'nature deficit disorder'. Louv's books bring together a growing body of research that shows a link between the absence of nature in today's wired generation and some of the most disturbing trends in children, including obesity, attention deficit disorders, depression and shortened life expectancy. The problem of children being disconnected from nature, becoming unhealthy and underperforming, can be summarised in the following five points:

1   Our culture places an increasingly high value on technology, often at the expense of time spent outdoors.
2   With population pressure and mounting land prices there is less green space at home and reduced access to public green space.
3   Parents perceive 'stranger danger' to be a greater issue than in the past and are afraid to allow their children to play outside, exacerbating the problem.

Case study 10: Furzedown, London

Some time ago I met with a client at a small school in London which was tucked into a compact site (Figure 5.15).

They wanted us to plant the edges and develop some contour variations to make the space appear larger and more of an oasis in the city. While taking their brief I observed the children and how they were using the current space. The 4–7 year olds appeared physically 'normal' but had a stilted look to their movements. I questioned the head teacher, as it appeared that their long muscles had not fully developed. I was right. I was told that due to a lifetime growing up in cramped high rise apartment blocks, riding in a buggy or stroller until they were old enough to scoot along on a little bike or scooter, they had not had the chance to run freely or even to walk long distances. Their parents' perception of 'stranger danger' meant they were frightened to let their children move by themselves in anything but the most controlled fashion, even in the local park.

The school's restricted site became a problem because the children had no green space where they could run around safely, stretch and grow at home. When away from home, while their parents thought they were keeping their children safe they were actually doing harm by not letting them explore local green space. The children's development was ultimately compromised as a result of the lack of provision of safe garden space at home.

Figure 5.15 Low socio-economic areas need cost-effective natural play solutions, to avoid playgrounds like this.

4   Children and young people are so over-scheduled that they are not given time to just play. Organised sport or dance classes, for example, replace time spent playing.
5   Schools are eliminating or reducing play/break/recess time due to curriculum demands and indoor behavioural problems. Outdoor/environmental field trips have also been reduced or eliminated when in fact numerous studies show learning outdoors can be the very situation where 'problem children' shine.

To counter these points we need to provide engaging, accessible green space close to where children live. Think back to the principles of monastic and Islamic garden design. Historically, healing gardens were created to fulfil diverse roles. We need to apply those salutogenic principles to green space for children around housing developments today.

Figure 5.16 The original play station was a swing set in a backyard: this clever advertisement by Stihl, Australia, has a clear message.

Source: Stihl.

Case study 11: social and therapeutic horticulture

Natasha is a bright 15-year-old girl with ADD who lives in the city with her mother and younger sister. She has recently moved and has been suffering from stress. Her mother works long hours, so the girls have been in a parade of organised after-school sport, music and dance activities for years.

After six months in her new school she was feeling down most days, avoiding school and finding it hard to relate to peers and her family. She was then (re)introduced to gardens and gardening. The following interview was recorded by the author in January 2013.

Q   *How long have you identified gardens as a fun place to be?*
A   Since I was young and lived in a house with a beautiful big garden being able to lie on the grass and look up through the trees made me feel peaceful, and at one with the world.

Q   *When you moved and felt stressed what did you do to manage that?*
A   Not much until my aunt suggested growing some veggies. We had to write a list of the vegetables I liked to eat, buy the seeds and soil and put them in pots outside the front door at home.

Q   *How did that make you feel?*
A   Proactive, as in instead of lying around wondering what I could do I was doing something, and it was nice to have someone interested, to have some company. It gives you something to be responsible for, and it makes you proud when you see baby tomatoes, and beans and little lettuces growing because you planted and watered them, looked after them. I helped them grow. It's also good to know where your food comes from; it gives you a connection with the earth. It's important for kids to know this. Instead of kids thinking that broccoli and Brussels sprouts are weird alien things they have an extra incentive to eat them because when you've grown it you want to try it.

Q   *If you had had a bad day at school how did you feel when you came home to check on your garden?*
A   Seeing my plants grow and having little vegetables pop up made me happy. I felt great. Very proud.

Q   *Do you enjoy spending time in public gardens and if so why?*

A   Yes, if it's really nice, like a grand big tree or a delicate pretty rose you can appreciate the complexity of everything. Just being able to just accept the complexity of things as they are; if it's a grand tree it's just a tree. It gives you a sense of belonging to the earth, because humans think they rule everything but being in the garden and nature helps you understand we need the trees. Listening to the breeze through the trees makes you feel calm and serene, and think how lucky you are to experience those things. In the gardens, if you are there with other people you can get to know them better by appreciating things because it's cool to share a moment.

Q   *The modern teenager is losing their connection with nature. How do you think this affects school, friends, and your home life?*

A   By losing that connection you are losing the important things in life. The importance of being a teenager is about learning what's right and what's wrong. Losing the connection with Earth by worrying about how many Facebook friends you have means instead teenagers can be worrying about trivial things and forget to stop and smell the roses. I think the value of gardens and the Earth is about appreciation and knowing you, as an individual, are not the most important thing on Earth. Most teenagers think that life revolves around them. I am a normal teenager and of course I like to think I am the most important person in my family, my class, my town, but the more time you get to stop and think about things, how cool some bits of nature are, it reminds that you are just one tiny little part in the great big world.

My friends who sit in front of their computer screens aren't so aware or appreciative of nature, they don't have the same appreciation of life. They get bored easily.

Teenagers are lazy so we want things close – neighbourhood parks within easy walking distance of home where we can safely hang out with friends, where we can mostly just sit and chat, but also be allowed to sit on a swing, or even those spinning things, give you a good laugh. If I was to have the ultimate back yard I would want the coolest treehouse with leaves dangling over the windows, a kids-only retreat where I could study, with wi-fi, of course, if I was studying.

Figure 5.17 Tree houses provide hours of flexible, creative, fun, and afford valuable opportunities for nature and social connections.

Figure 5.18 Water play in a toddler-sized container provides hours of fun on a summer's day: where housing does not provide space for such activities, local parks and public space must step in.

From this we learn that young children need safe places to play and explore, at home or near home. When designing housing we need to rethink landscape design options. Do we place a bald log on a patch of grass and say 'it's natural', lay play carpet and add some play equipment and say 'it's low maintenance' or do we create a planted, playful space, a garden where young and old can come together to rest and play and say 'it's cost-effective, it looks good and it feels great'?

Management of play opportunities

Design for children's health and well-being is not just about formal provision. How we choose to manage local green space affects the opportunities children and young people have. If we fence off areas, or otherwise exclude young people from their environment, we deny an opportunity to connect with the healing effects of nature.

As shown in Figure 5.19, a group of 15 year olds created a productive forest garden in woods near their home. They knew that officially camping was not a permitted activity in the area, so they took steps to mitigate any impact. No live trees were damaged and when they left no trace remained of their occupation. They spent the summer experimenting, testing themselves and nature. The time spent out in the woods was hugely beneficial for the girls. The forestry authorities took a risk in allowing the activity, but with no harm to nature and the development of future supporters of their work, a net gain resulted all round.

In summary, we need to design play space to suit the management needs of landowners, but also to encourage and enable time spent learning and playing outdoors that

- supports the development of a healthy and active lifestyle;
- offers children opportunities for physical activity, freedom and movement;
- provides opportunities for developing harmonious relationships with others through negotiation, turn-taking and co-operation;
- supports those children who learn best through activity and movement;
- provides safe, supervised opportunities for children to experience new challenges, assess risk and develop skills to manage difficult situations;

Figure 5.19 Teenagers need nature connections as much as younger children: this informal den in the woods became a summer 'home from home' for these girls.

- supports children developing creativity and problem-solving skills;
- provides rich opportunities for imagination, inventiveness and resourcefulness;
- gives children contact with the natural world and offers them unique experiences such as direct contact with the weather and the seasons.

(Maller et al., 2008)

See Appendix 2 for a table of accessible and inclusive design features that summarises design elements and associated benefits for children.

Notes

1 Ritalin is a stimulant medication often used in the management of ADHD.
2 Monocultures are large areas with only one type of plant.
3 Neurotypical describes typical or 'normal' brain development.

References

Baker, R. (2012, 13 November). *Reduce speed limits to increase children's fitness.* Retrieved 12 February 2013, from *Day Nurseries.co.uk*: www.daynurseries.co.uk/news/article.cfm/id/1558341/reduce-speed-limits-to-increase-child-fitness-parents-say

Bird, W., Dr. (2010, 16 June). Interviewed by the author.

Bruyere, B. (2011, July). Reexamining the significance of childhood recreation patterns on adult leisure behavior. Retrieved March 2013, from *Larimer County*: larimer.org/plugintonature/lit_review_matrix.xlsx

Curran, A. R. (2010). A paediatric neurologist speaks. Retrieved March 2013, from *Independent Thinking*: www.independentthinking.co.uk

Department for Education (2012a, August). EYFS learning and development requirements. Retrieved March 2013, from *The Early Years Foundation Stage (EYFS)*: https://www.education.gov.uk/publications/standard/EarlyYearseducation andchildcare/Page1/DFE-30007-2012

—— (2012b, 26 April). Area guidelines for schools: Building Bulletin 82. Retrieved 20 December 2013, from *Department for Education – Schools*: www.education. gov.uk/schools/adminandfinance/schoolscapital/buildingsanddesign/a0010896/ area-guidelines-for-schools-building-bulletin-82

Fuller, R. B. (1970). *I seem to be a verb*. New York: Bantam.

Gill, T. (2011). *Sowing the seeds: reconnecting London's children with nature*. London: London City Council.

Howard, R. (2013, 7 February). Lack of outdoor play spaces for children over last 40 years 'highly regrettable'. Retrieved March 2013, from *Day Nurseries.co.uk*: www.daynurseries.co.uk/news/article.cfm/id/1558832/lack-of-outdoor-play-spaces-for-children-over-last-40-years-highly-regrettable

Landry, S. (2005). *Effective early childhood programs: turning knowledge into action*. Houston: University of Texas Press.

Little, H. and Wyver, S. (2008). Outdoor play: does avoiding the risks reduce the benefits? *Australian Journal of Early Childhood*, 33(2):33–40.

Louv, R. (2008). *Last child in the woods: saving our children from nature-deficit disorder*. Chapel Hill, NC: Algonquin Books.

—— (2013). Nature-deficit disorder. Retrieved 2013, from *Getting Kids Outdoors*: www.gettingkidsoutdoors.org/get-involved/about/nature-deficit-disorder

Maller, C., Townsend, M., St Leger, L., Henderson-Wilson, C., Pryor, A., Prosser, L. and Moore, M. (2008). *The health benefits of contact with nature in a park context: a review of relevant literature*. Melbourne: Deakin University and Parks Victoria.

NIH (2005, 16 March). *NIHS News*. Retrieved December 20, 2013, from *National Institute of Health*: www.nih.gov/news/pr/mar2005/nia-16.htm

Office of the High Commissioner for Human Rights (1995). Convention on the rights of the child. Retrieved 2013, from *United Nations Human Rights*: www.ohchr.org/ en/professionalinterest/pages/crc.aspx

Ouvry, M. (2005). *Exercising muscles and minds*. London: NCB.

Playlink (2009). *Play at schools*. London: Playlink.

Said, I. (2008). *Garden as a restorative environment for hospitalised children*. Jahor Darul Ta'Zim: Universiti Teknologi Malaysia.

Shaw, B., Watson, B., Frauendienst, B., Redecker, A., Jones, T. and Hillman, M. (2013). *Children's independent mobility: a comparative study in England and Germany (1971–2010)*. London: Policy Studies Institute, University of Westminster.

Taylor, A. F., Kuo, F. E. and Sullivan, W. C. (2001). Coping with ADD: the surprising connection to green play settings. *Environment and Behavior*, 33(1):54–77.

Tunghai University (2012). 2012 International Forum on Healthcare and Therapeutic Design, Taichung City, Taiwan. http://sng.thu.edu.tw/thunews/detail.php?news ID=1782&prevID=38

Warden, C. (2011, Autumn). Rattler. Retrieved 20 December 2013, from *Mind Stretchers*: www.mindstretchers.co.uk/File/publications/rattler97.pdf

Witkin, G. (1999). *Kid stress*. New York: Viking.

CHAPTER 6

Healing gardens for adults

We need an active lifestyle to stay healthy into old age. To facilitate health and well-being we need healing green space across our towns and cities. Great emphasis is placed on children connecting with nature, learning the joys and benefits of an active lifestyle, so they take their healthy habits into adulthood. Seniors and the elderly are also being targeted by government programmes. Organisations promoting an active lifestyle into old age are keen to capture the growing market. While those agendas are good and necessary we also need to focus on the middle years. The burden of supporting the young and old falls to the working population. Those people perhaps more than any other need environments which enable and encourage a healthy lifestyle.

While there is a natural tendency to concentrate resources on the very young and very old, we need to provide healing gardens to redress the balance. From a government funding perspective, the most vulnerable members of the community tend to take the most from welfare, education and health budgets. However, as working-aged adults are the main people sustaining the economy it is vital that we also provide supportive environments that help keep them happy, healthy and fully productive. To do this we need to acknowledge our innate biophilia and provide opportunities for people to connect with nature.

This chapter is dedicated to the middle age group. Working-aged adults are the ones who increasingly have to juggle maintaining a relationship with a life partner, while building and maintaining their career. They potentially have to manage concern for ageing parents alongside care of a family. In addition to the current taxpayer we will also focus on retired people: those often discarded by society as no longer able to play a useful part.

In previous chapters we have seen that a salutogenic design approach is useful. Preventing lifestyle-related health problems through environmental design can be a powerful tool. So-called healing gardens offer opportunities to heal communities as well as individuals. The up and coming 'Generation Y' is known for its high expectations and concurrent low tolerance for the less-than-perfect. Nature, while striving for perfection, seeks harmony and a state of balance above all. As we have disconnected from nature we have allowed a generation or two to forget the importance of the simple natural balance of living things. Biophilic sensory stimulation connects us with the natural rhythms of life. In countries like Brazil, France, Spain and Portugal where culturally, the individual is not defined by their job, mental health is stronger, and the demands of family and the transition from work to being retired, redundant or unemployed is not felt so negatively. In countries like the USA, Australia and the UK, without a job to build their lives around, people can become socially isolated, and without a reason to get up in the morning they can quickly become depressed, fall prey to physical illness and find their quality of life deteriorates rapidly.

Historically, families supported their children and adult children supported their parents. Household stress levels were, by today's standards, low. Political unrest, natural disasters and growing financial pressures around the world mean that increasing numbers of young and middle aged people move to where the work is rather than staying close to their families. Expatriates, immigrants, refugees and local-born are thrown together in unfamiliar towns and cities, with a need to stay healthy enough to work. Perhaps not surprisingly, many young people are saying 'it's too hard' and are opting out of intimate relationships. They are disconnecting from (potential) partners and choosing to live alone. In many countries the extended family unit has largely broken down. In other areas, financial pressures in the family require elderly grandparents to take over child rearing to allow the parents to earn sufficient money to support their family. This is not necessarily a bad thing, as it strengthens communities, and provides a way for older people to contribute in meaningful ways.

Around the world as countries are becoming more urbanised, city land values have increased and the proportion of people living in apartments and townhouses is rising. At the same time as more people are living in high rise and multi-dwelling units, more people are living alone. According to the US Census data released in May 2012, 31 million households in 2010 consisted of just one person, 4 million more than in 2000. Singles now make up 27 per cent of US households overall; in several large cities, including New York, San Francisco, Atlanta and Washington, DC, they account for more than 40 per cent of the population. The singles are primarily women. New York University sociology professor Eric Klinenberg's (2012) recent book, *Going solo: the extraordinary rise and surprising appeal of living alone* has studied the trend and concluded that it is unlikely to reverse in the near future. The impact of this on green space design means that we need to provide safe, attractive spaces for single women to (a) enjoy a healthy, active lifestyle, and (b) to meet people.

Leisure time has changed as working hours have increased. Unhealthy sedentary lifestyles and poor diets become the easy option. The changing ways people choose to live are adding to the burden of disease. Stress levels are rising as adults have disconnected from their traditional social networks and from nature. In conjunction with the altered household makeup, these international trends combine to form a demographic typology that has implications for salutogenic landscape and urban design. Put bluntly, we need more healing gardens and green space to balance and counter the effects of modern lifestyles. Adults, whether living alone and away from family support, or close by and in need of family assistance, all require social and nature connections to enable a healthy lifestyle.

As we saw in Part I, to ensure the long-term health and well-being of our communities we need to soften the edges of our urban environments. When appropriately designed, gardens and urban green space can become engaging healing environments, inclusive spaces that support adult mental and physical health. The key point to remember is the need for appropriate design. As the architect Giancarlo de Carlo famously said, 'Architecture is too important to leave to architects.' He went on to say

> Post-modern architecture has largely forgotten why we are working on design and development schemes and instead is focused on how to create symbolic spaces. Everybody should be able to find a meaning in architecture that is able to correspond with his or her cultural level, history or background.
>
> (de Carlo, 2010)

To reduce stress in the adult population we need to ensure, as a minimum, that working environments have green views. Pockets parks and attractive human-scaled plazas are important close to workplaces so that people can take a break during their working day. When we are designing to cost-effectively prevent non-communicable disease, and improve ecological, social and economic outcomes, it is a very different paradigm to developing an amenity planting strip. For the past fifty years landscape has largely been considered little more than a way to improve the aesthetics of a city. Planning regulations have required buildings to be set within landscaped settings, but in ignorance of the potential health benefits of green space little guidance is given as to either how those areas should function and for what purpose they need to be developed. While developers and architects remain unguided as to why the landscape is important, it will continue to be easy to cost out anything more elaborate than an expensive pavement and possibly a few token shrubs.

It's a hard life

So much of the contemporary 'green space' that has been developed in the past thirty years is hard paved and further hard edged with concrete and brick walls, often with metal spikes preventing people sitting or playing on them. We may never stop to investigate, to wonder why we feel slightly stressed when moving through such an environment, but the effect on our bodies is noticeable in increased cortisol, heart rate and blood pressure levels. Financially and socially stressed adults require a supportive environment to thrive. Modern competitive lifestyles require a softer edged city to balance the harsh reality of redundancies, mortgage repayments, school fees and healthcare. But we need more than just a generic, softer, landscape-led space: we need to look at who makes up the local community and create a local design response based on their needs.

If, as Wellington has done, we accept that adults, as with children, benefit from the biophilic sensory stimulation of nature, that we need to be connected with nature to enjoy a good state of mental and physical health, and that landscaped urban settings can provide such a connection, it is important to look at how and where we can create such connections. Acceptance is not universal, however. A. C. Lee and R. Maheswaran of the University of Sheffield, UK, in their 2011 study 'The health benefits of urban green spaces: a review of the evidence', concluded that

Case study 12: Wellington, New Zealand. From a conversation with a senior urban planner

In Wellington, New Zealand, a vibrant film animation industry requires the city centre to provide places and policies to support the creative adult community. Streetscapes and cycle/pedestrian routes through the city centre enable professionals who don't take the bus to walk, run, skate or scoot to work. Varied seating affordances – walls, rocks and formal benches – allow people to stop and sit with friends on the pavement edge. Soft grass provides a comfortable space to lie out on a bean bag, sit under a tree or stretch out in the sun for a quick nap. Lawn areas also offer somewhere to play frisbee during breaks, supplemented by good coffee vendors every 50 metres.

To remain healthy, alert and at the top of their competitive game people need to balance their long work hours with time spent in nature. They also need somewhere close to their workplace, and close to public transport, where they can spend time with their families; precious time in the middle of the working day where partner, nanny or carer can bring the kids in after school to spend half an hour having fun, before the kids head home to homework and dinner and their parent heads back, refreshed, into their creative work zone.

The central city gardens, green space and harbourside bluespace that make up the local landscape has to multi-task, such that in the early morning it provides calm, inspirational space for city dwellers to enjoy tai chi; a little later a through route for people on their way to work; by mid-morning a safe, pleasant walking environment for retired people to maintain a healthy active lifestyle and meet their friends; at lunchtime room for joggers and city workers who enjoy dining al fresco while refreshing their lungs from potentially polluted indoor air; mid-afternoon a playful environment where workers can take a break to have fun with their children; by late afternoon a chill-out young adult zone; and all the while offering inclusive features such as being accessible to disabled people and a mix of open and smaller, more enclosed spaces for people to meet and socialise.

Figure 6.1 Natural play boulders and planting – the Meets All Age skate park – meets inclusive urban public space as part of the Biophilic City project, Wellington, New Zealand.

Fortunately the biophilic sympathies of the mayor have allowed and indeed promoted the development of supportive soft landscape spaces. By linking broad corridors of green belt to the city centre with a mix of native planting and appropriate exotics, rare and endangered birds and supporting insect life are being encouraged back into the city. Urban parks and playgrounds offer all ages a range of manufactured and natural play opportunities. The photos below feature Waitangi Park, on the east side of central Wellington. The park is a maximum ten-minute walk from most creative art-house offices and offers something for everyone. The images were taken on a winter's afternoon in 2012. Young and old can skate or rollerblade with routes of varied skill levels and freestyle opportunities throughout the space. Planting is as yet immature but in a few years will provide summer shade and winter interest. Shrub species chosen for their robust nature and compact habit make them safe, playable features of the landscape. There is a rain garden to the edge of the space, both as a practical means to deal with stormwater but also as a public education tool. There is no signage, no rules stating what is acceptable behaviour, what you can and cannot do. In this creative community, that is important. By the nature of the multi-generational use throughout the day, the area is self-policing, with a high level of respect shown for other users. Adults like to walk along the tops of walls, just as children do, and here there are no signs, park attendants or security guards telling people not to explore their limits and have fun.

Like many cities, Wellington's population is ageing. While the city attracts bright, younger, creative people from around the world, it also has an increasing number of elderly people with a range of mental and physical disabilities. Part of the salutogenic test for any city is: how easy is it to get around? How comfortable do older people feel in the middle of the bustling environment that characterises the modern city? How easy is it to navigate your way through public transport from home to shopping, to office to green space areas? How clean is the air? How inspiring is the environment? Does it encourage you to want to explore, to linger? Are there opportunities to sit comfortably and observe? Is there public art and sculpture? Is there public performance space?

Figure 6.2 Safe, engaging public space: family-friendly hide-and-seek games are afforded by this rain garden in central Wellington, New Zealand.

Wellington has started to work on its main streets to create 'slow zones' where the previously fast paced pedestrian area is slowed with street trees and seating along the road edge. In some places roadways have been narrowed to allow for more street furniture. Cars and buses still travel the routes, but the people who have chosen to be out walking are able and indeed have been encouraged to slow down a little, to be able to pause in their busy lives and smell the roses. By making the pedestrian experience more attractive it is hoped that more people, of all ages, will leave their cars at home and embrace a healthy, active lifestyle. Early signs are that the plan is working. Since work began on making Wellington a healthier place to live, work and play, in the past ten years there has been a huge drop in car usage, and in 2013, 11 per cent of people walked to work, compared with 3 per cent in 2003.

Along with the success stories come some challenges. For a time a Parks Department manager was a little autocratic and things happened because he said so, rather than because there was a particular need for a certain feature or area to be developed. He forgot why he was developing and maintaining parks. The system is not flawless, but by acknowledging the community's inherent love of living things the Council has been successful overall in creating a healthy, liveable city. Over time the city will no doubt adapt as climate changes, its local economy changes and so too does its community. How planning and parks managers respond to those changing needs, whether and how widely they collaborate during the design and (re)development phase to consult with healthcare, education, finance and play practitioners, will determine to a large degree the future health, vitality and liveability of the city.

Figure 6.3 Intergenerational natural play space promotes healthy active lifestyles and brings young and old together to watch the spectacle of scooters and skaters.

most studies reported findings that generally supported the view that green spaces have a beneficial health effect. Establishing a causal relationship is difficult, as the relationship is complex. Simplistic urban interventions may therefore fail to address the underlying determinants of urban health that are not remediable by landscape redesign.

(Lee and Maheswaran, 2011)

So-called 'simplistic urban interventions' may not address the issues in their totality. I agree that a lack of understanding of what is encompassed by the biophilic sensory stimulation that we seek when connecting with nature has created some inadequate attempts at healing gardens.

Space to sprawl

The modern preference for a single-person lifestyle may be a sign of stress. As land prices go up residential plots become smaller. A feeling of overcrowding is common in many parts of the world. To counter this some cities are providing public green space close to residential areas where people can stretch out, relax and enjoy activities such as entertaining around a barbeque they may have once shared at home. New Farm Park, in Brisbane, Australia, is described by the local newspaper, the *Courier Mail*: 'Kids love it for the great playground near the fig trees, couples love it for the swathes of grass beside the rose gardens, groups love it for the barbecues, tables and inner-urban space to sprawl' (TCM, 2011)

Brisbane city provides coin operated public barbeques, with adjacent covered seating and table areas. Couples and small groups regularly bring food and drink, a tablecloth, candles, friends and family, to a beautiful outdoor setting. The barbeques provide the city authorities with sufficient income to maintain the facilities, while remaining affordable and accessible for all.

It is that 'space to sprawl' that we so often miss when we live in multi-dwelling units – terraced housing, apartments, flats. Regardless of whether we live alone or in groups, when all we have by way of outdoor space at home is a window ledge, our biophilic inner self cries out, albeit often unconsciously, for that space to stretch out that can make a real difference to our sense of health and well-being. Healing gardens for adults, when designed as expansive, protected communal spaces, where people can come together in small groups or large, are invaluable in developing social relationships, and creating connections with nature.

Public healing gardens can create a feeling of oasis in the city. A sensory-rich space, the garden is designed to stimulate the biophilic senses, our love of living things. For those people without adequate outdoor space at home, public space must meet their need, with spaces to relax, spaces to entertain, space to play, space to stop and admire a bird, a nest or distant view or a colourful flower, a scent, a memory prompt, or to sit quietly and listen to the birdsong or the buzz of insects.

Public parks are not just for city apartment dwellers, however. As we noted in the Wellington case study earlier, it is important to provide tourists, day visitors and city workers space to socialise, to relax and play, during the working day, even if they have a detached house and garden to go home to. When people travel or work long hours they may see little of their home garden during daylight hours. Public space must therefore do double duty; it must provide room for personal space such that we can feel as if we have a private oasis of calm in the city, as well as provide room to meet with a group of friends.

Non-communicable diseases, the lifestyle-related diseases such as obesity, binge drinking, some cancers, heart and lung disease, and mental health disorders such as stress and depression, become costly to society when basic public health preventions are not in place. A salutogenic design approach to landscape and urban design accounts for nature connections, as well as social connections.

Social benefits of healing gardens

> London boroughs face a £900m adult social care funding shortfall within the next five years, according to a report published today.
>
> (Hailstone, 2013)

The study referred to here, by London borough councils and consultants Ernst and Young, warns that municipalities within the UK's capital are already spending one-third of their total budgets on adult social care – and the figure will increase as the number of Londoners aged 65 and over rises.

To mitigate the costs of social care it is important to provide freely accessible spaces where people can de-stress and relax. Sheltered areas and open sunny spaces outdoors enable year-round places to walk, meet friends and relax. Seating must reflect this. Indoors the standard seat depth is 400mm; outdoors we need to allow 500mm so people can perhaps fit a cushion at their back, sprawl a little, tuck up their feet and get comfortable. Some local bodies are concerned about homeless people taking up space and their outdoor seating attracting the 'wrong type' of person. I would argue that healthy communities are those that look after the needs of all their citizens and residents.

Opportunities for public health promotion and environmental education come wherever people congregate. Thus we can show everyone who comes in contact with sensitively designed environments how easy it is to grow plants. They do not need to be told of the health benefits; if people can see, touch and taste the plants, feel good in their presence, they will more readily adopt a healthy lifestyle naturally. We can place edible plants in surgeries, in schools, by bus stops, anywhere there is a little space and light.

Part of the benefit of experiencing nature outdoors comes from being under natural light. It is bizarre that UK planning regulations for medical rooms should require more natural light than residential settings. We know people are healthier when they have more natural light but we legislate only to improve their state once they are ill and at the medical centre. If we are alert to this, we can ensure social housing – traditionally built with small windows and few opportunities for opening them, or for fresh air and personal outdoor space – provides the most vulnerable in our communities with the health-giving environment they need. We can design safe, attractive green space so when counselled to spend an additional half hour per day outdoors, children and their carers can do so, easily. The investment today costs little and the benefits last long. When co-designed, developed in conjunction with the local community, a salutogenic design approach brings huge potential gains.

In a well-designed environment chronic stress is reduced. When we exercise outdoors we tend to smile more. Multi-generational gatherings in appropriately designed public space will bring social, health, economic and environmental benefits to our communities. By investing in cost-effective natural health interventions, although there are (design) costs initially, better process = better outcomes = cost savings now and in the future.

We value what we know and experience on a daily basis. Thus we value our new car perhaps more than our ability to walk strongly for thirty minutes. Once we have started walking along a beautiful, convenient, safe route regularly we may well revalue our fitness over the car. When we learn to appreciate and enjoy our local environment we will be motivated to protect and conserve it. Climate change offers challenges and opportunities for us all. Without the health of the planet the health of people seems trivial.

Active ageing

Healing gardens work for all ages. In Guangzhou, China, the old parks have areas laid out within them as gardens for people to rest, relax with friends, and recreate. In the morning the men come to read the paper. There are comfortable seats to sit with a cup of tea in the early sunshine. The young mothers bring their babies out for a walk late morning. At lunchtime office workers sit outdoors in the gardens to eat their lunch with friends under the leafy shade of trees. After lunch the older women come to meet their friends. After school the children play in the gardens on their way home. Later, in the early evening the young adults meet in the park. There are kiosks and concession stands selling snack foods and drink. After dinner the middle aged congregate to dance in the gardens. They bring a portable music player, and enjoy the space and freedom to express themselves, through dance, outdoors.

Central city parks and playgrounds

Public playgrounds set within central city parks, as the places where people go to relax, restore their equilibrium, rest and rejuvenate, are an important part of the social fabric of the city. While some people are fortunate to have appropriate outdoor space at home, many do not. It is these people, those who do not have adequate space as part of their home environment, who are most reliant on public space provision. The benefits are universal, however. We all win when we have a healthy ecology supporting a healthy human population. For everyone who lives in, works or passes through the city, having an oasis, a small, human-scaled piece of paradise, is an essential part of a healthy city.

Relationships between humans and nature are complex. To provide central city parks that afford contact with nature we need to de-emphasise built structures and re-emphasise natural materials: trees, plants, soil, sand and timber. The fact that most studies support the fact that green space has a beneficial effect on human health is our starting point. There is no end point, no limit to our creativity when it comes to designing biophilic environments that support adult health and well-being.

Case study 13: central city parks

In city centres, playgrounds, as part of the city green infrastructure, need to work for children and for adults too. The photos below show a newly opened park space in the centre of South Australia's capital, Adelaide. The 'play equipment' is made of concrete and is set in rubber wet pour. Play value from the site, equipment and surfacing is minimal. The park is ringed by mature trees, but the play area is devoid of shade. No one came into the park during the thirty minutes we were on site. The photos (Figures 6.4 and 6.5) were taken at lunchtime on a sunny day during the school spring holiday. Designed for under 12s, local office workers and their families have chosen to spend their time elsewhere.

Figure 6.4 An expensive mistake: this concrete play space in Adelaide, Australia, offers little to engage and encourage nature or social connections, and as a result remains largely unused.

Source: Alice Leake.

Figure 6.5 The rubber safety surfacing around the concrete 'play' elements absorbs and radiates heat, making the space unsafe and uninviting.

Source: Alice Leake.

An alternative, sculptural, inner city adult-friendly play space could be this example from Berlin (Figures 6.6 and 6.7).

Figure 6.6 Berlin, Germany: earth mounding with inset trampoline.

Figure 6.7 Berlin, Germany: mini soccer pitch with natural shade, surrounded by sand surfacing.

Or this from London (Figure 6.8).

Figure 6.8 Tower Hill urban park, London: a multigenerational playspace with informal seating opportunities for office workers, children and their families.

Both the German and the English examples show spaces where adults are welcomed to perch on a boulder, play with their children, or sit quietly under a tree. The Berlin park uses a mix of rubber safety surfacing, grass and sand. Artificial surfacings can be used within a salutogenic framework, but must be balanced by abundant planting. The Adelaide example is a bald space, whereas both the Berlin and London examples are set within a virtual forest of trees and perennial plantings.

When employed as part of a health-in-all-policies approach, thoughtfully designed parks can and do make a difference.

Residential green space

In an urban setting, gardens or green space are often located around detached and multi-unit housing and within neighbourhood or city parks. These are supplemented by marginal amenity strips surrounding service outlets and shopping malls. Some office, hotel and retail spaces have internal atrium gardens, roof gardens and vertical gardens creating living walls. Singapore is making rapid progress towards becoming the greenest country in the world, largely through the use of green walls. Some cities, such as Berlin and Moscow, have deliberately planted street trees to soften the facades of buildings (Figures 6.12 and 6.13).

All these 'gardens' combine with the weather and resident or visiting wildlife to create the natural environment adults encounter in their daily lives. While the gardens may vary greatly in quality of design and planting, each helps soften the hard edges of the urban form.

One feature of a healthy lifestyle is a healthy diet. Fresh fruit and vegetables can be expensive to buy. We have an opportunity to connect adults with nature through inexpensive food growing initiatives. Residential green space is the ideal location for tending, picking and eating fresh fruit and vegetables. Keeping ducks or chickens likewise requires few skills or resources other than a dedicated space for the birds to forage, roost and lay their eggs safely, away from traffic and potential predators. To enable more people to engage with food growing we need to provide appropriate spaces to facilitate that. Raised beds allow able bodied young and old to tend gardens alongside those with strength, mobility, hip or back problems.

Figure 6.9
Composting information in a community gardens for an immigrant community, Wapping, London.

Figure 6.10 Therapeutic community gardens for an immigrant community: vertical gardens and horizontal beds, Wapping, London.

Figure 6.11 Attractive, accessible green space around social housing, Wapping, London.

Figure 6.12 Berlin, Germany: community gardens as accessible green space for mental health, with seating, growing areas and shade trees.

Figure 6.13 Moscow, Russia: urban green space with children's play area and shade trees in a residential area.

Figure 6.14 Inexpensive, corrugated iron raised beds for accessible gardening in a public space.

Public green space: healing gardens

To enjoy good mental and physical health adults need to be connected with nature. In an urban setting public green space must afford that connection. If we take the park as the overall space, a 'garden' is an area or areas within the park designed not as a simplistic planted bed but as a complex affordance to feed mind, body and soul. A garden is necessarily a soft space, planted and furnished to balance the hard-edged urban existence of the built environment. Just as with gardens for children, healing gardens for adults need to be inclusive and accessible. Healing gardens can only do their job when they are designed to welcome people to stop and sit, to meet friends, provide a safe space for exercise, inspire through spontaneous and planned performance, art and music, and invite exploration.

The size of the space is not as important as the location. Studies have found that people are more likely to exercise outdoors when there is easy access close to their workplace or home (Mowen et al., 2007). Attractive circuits of 3–5km (1–3 miles) from the central business area, allow people interested in building and maintaining their fitness to engage with nature and walk, dance, stretch, run or cycle in their lunch hour, or after work.

Healing gardens provide the equilibrium we seek. In Moscow, parks are plentiful but many neighbourhood spaces lack engaging design elements such as comfortable seating (Figure 6.16). They are, however, attractive in their simplicity. Like Islamic gardens; their style works with the local architecture. Planting is designed so that their slightly overgrown, informal feel balances the heaviness of the adjacent built environment. Further south, in Milan, Italy, spiky architectural planting in public parks is softened by the rounded forms of terracotta pots and urns dotted throughout the gardens (Figure 6.17).

Figure 6.15
Guangzhou Park, China, provides space for informal sport activities under the trees.

Source: Huiyi Liu.

Figure 6.16 Healing gardens: urban green space for mental health, Moscow, Russia.

Figure 6.17 A terracotta pot set amidst grasses contrasts shapes and texture to provide a rich sensory space in Milan, Italy.

Public green space has been described as the lungs of the city. It is also the heart and soul of the city. For adults, the character of a town is described in terms of parks and gardens in relation to the buildings. Work opportunities and good shopping may be of interest, but if the environment is unattractive few people will be enticed to spend time there. Healing gardens provide the aesthetic that creates an attractive urban centre.

Eco resorts and health spas

For adult mental health, when home and local urban space does not adequately support the population's biophilic need, health spas and eco resorts are desirable. An eco resort provides accommodation in a natural setting. Designed to the highest green buildings standards, eco resorts are a way of sharing the health properties of nature with people who do not wish to hike or camp. Views of the surrounding landscape are incorporated into indoor and outdoor spaces such that the visitor feels a part of the land. To be effective the development needs to be mindful of the early healing garden forms. Temple gardens, monastic and Islamic gardens fulfilled particular functions, including meditation, medicinal, food and cooperative activity. In a commercial setting such as a resort, where different users will place potentially competing demands on the environment, it is important to provide spaces to accommodate those needs. A mix of enclosed green space, water, light and shade, edible, flowering and fragrant planting, with comfortable seating, comfortable (soft) paths (and no wi-fi!) will help reconnect adults with nature.

Health spas offer a day visitor the benefits of nature. While traditional healing treatments are offered, without an appropriate setting the effect is reduced. Imagine a massage in an artificially lit barn compared to the same massage in a small palm or fern-filled space filled with natural daylight. Healing gardens require a salutogenic design approach equally indoors and out.

Design for adult health and well-being requires opportunities to engage socially and with nature. To encourage people to connect, cities need to be designed for comfort as well as utility. Regardless of the location, to prevent the NCDs mentioned in previous chapters, obesity, depression, cancer, heart and lung disease, the same biophilic needs must be met.

Figure 6.18 Phuket, Thailand: eco resort combines water with fragrant planting.

References

de Carlo, G. (2010). Architecture is too important to leave to the architects. Interview with Roemer van Toorn. Available at www.roemervantoorn.nl/Resources/De%20Carlo%20Interview.pdf

Hailstone, J. (2013, 9 January). London facing £900m adult social care shortfall. *Local Gov*: www.localgov.co.uk/London-facing-900m-adult-social-care-shortfall/27041

Klinenberg, E. (2012). *Going solo: the extraordinary rise and surprising appeal of living alone*. New York: Penguin Press.

Lee, A. C. and Maheswaran, R. (2011). The health benefits of urban green space. *Journal of Public Health*, 33(2):212–222.

Mowen, A., Orsega-Smith, E., Payne, L., Ainsworth, B. and Godbey, G. (2007). The role of park proximity and social support in shaping park visitation, physical activity, and perceived health among older adults. *Journal of Physical and Active Health*, 4(2):167–179.

TCM (2011, 28 September). Lifestyle. *The Courier Mail*, p. 1.

Figure 6.19
Massachusetts, USA: street trees provide wildlife habitat and welcome shade in this Boston street.

Source: Jenny Brown.

CHAPTER 7

Healing gardens and cityscapes for disabled children and adults

A nature connection decreases stress and reduces risk of many NCDs in the non-disabled population. It also offers significant health and well-being benefits to people living with disability. As we have seen, healing gardens afford a nature connection which offers measureable results for both mental and physical health. With any form of disability some sensory impairment is usually involved. For example, when we are in pain we notice and are more sensitive to bright light. If we lose our sight our hearing becomes more acute. With senses easily becoming overloaded it is important to provide opportunities to calm senses that need calming and excite those that require additional stimulation.

In a residential care setting it is relatively easy to evaluate the effect of various environmental interventions. At home and in urban public space, where most people living with disability spend their time, it is more difficult. In this chapter we will use evidence gained in residential care settings to inform the design of public space.

Disability, accessibility and universal design are often thought of in terms of wheelchair users, ramps and handrails. With depression the second largest cause of disability globally (Medscape, 2013), ageing populations and myriad other congenital and acquired health conditions, we need to broaden our understanding of disability and of the individuals we are designing for. We need to understand *why* we are making provision for a growing segment of our population in order to best discover *how* to make that provision.

In determining why we need healing gardens for disabled adults and children throughout our urban environment, we need to understand first that we are providing for people living with either or both physical and mental disabilities. Mental health conditions are often largely invisible. People living with, for example, Asperger's syndrome (ASD), depression (MDD) or attention deficit disorder (ADD), look like anyone else but often live very differently. Some physical disabilities are likewise invisible to the casual observer but have no less a profound effect on everyday life. Significantly, most individuals are capable of leading meaningful, productive lives; however, if the living, working, playing or schooling environment is disabling rather than enabling they may retreat to a world of dependency.

As we saw in Chapter 2, gardens and green space are vital to our health and well-being, regardless of ability. Valued for their beauty and public health promotion, public and private parks and gardens are good for all. A 2013 UK report commissioned by Natural England, Defra and the Forestry Commission, the *Monitor of*

Engagement with the Natural Environment (MENE) showed that one visit to green space per week for between 10 and 60 minutes is enough to raise self-esteem – which is a facet of mental health; while 10–15 minutes' outdoor exercise at least three times per week will allow the human body to synthesise enough vitamin D to supplement physiological health (Natural England, 2013).

How we create healing gardens and green space around housing, in schools, around workplaces, shops and bus stops, is in some ways universal and in some ways specific to the user group. Although titled 'for disabled children and adults' rather than focussing exclusively on a small population group, in this chapter we are mindful of the needs of all users, from parents with strollers to the health tourist. In the past we have labelled population groups around funding streams. With diminished budgets and increased competition for public funding, it is useful to remember that while for ease of classification we may identify the needs of a particular group, it is likely that there will be some overlap.

However much we advocate a broad understanding and application of salutogenic design solutions, healing, sensory and therapeutic gardens are often associated with disability. Here we are interested in how we address issues of inclusion and universal access. Enabling environments are where people of all ages, abilities and cultures can enjoy a sense of independence.

As the population ages and numbers of people living with disability increase, future landscape and urban design projects will need to include better provision for disability. Spaces within a school, hospital, public park, housing, care home, shopping mall or playground need to feel welcoming to all people. To meet the need it is important that planners and designers understand how disability can affect people's daily lives, and the impact this may have on their family and carers, and hence their community. The typical design professional is well educated and statistically likely to be fit and healthy. It can be hard to imagine life in poor health or with a disability without personal experience. Fortunately there is a wealth of useful material published by charities and support groups associated with each condition, detailing both how the condition presents and suggestions for ways to make life easier. As the parent of a child on the autistic spectrum and as someone living with a spinal cord injury, I understand the impact environmental design can have on quality of life. Uneven paving, a lack of public toilets, long stretches of hard paving, a lack of seats, pot holes, camber and step height are simple things one becomes acutely aware of while moving through a space. For those living with other conditions, a range of design elements become problematic. As we explore healing gardens design for disability you will note the similarities and cross-overs between many conditions.

Universal or barrier free design

'Barrier free design' is the term used in Japan, Korea and Europe to describe accessible ramps and paths. Also known as 'universal design', the idea was first described in 1960 by Ronald L. Mace to explain the concept of designing 'all products and the built environment to be aesthetic and usable to the greatest extent possible by everyone, regardless of their age, ability, or status in life' (NCSU, 2013). While barrier free design generally refers to the retrofitting of modifications to existing spaces, universal design has largely superseded the idea, as it seeks to design spaces from the outset to support easy access. In a sector with as many innovative thinkers as there are disabilities, 'design for all' is another programme that considers the needs of disabled users, focusing on design for human diversity, social inclusion and equality (Neumann et al., 2011).

Disability, whether temporary or permanent, evokes a passionate response from those affected and those close to them. From personal experience I know how environments and attitudes can enable or disable. Whichever term we use, however, it is a mistake to think that one design will suit all user groups. Universal design is not in fact a universal panacea but rather a design approach that aims to break down the barriers to access.

While universal design guidelines were originally intended for products and the built environment, it is important we provide for health and well-being for all ages and abilities through access to the natural environment. We need to ensure environments are accessible and inclusive so that we can *design out* social isolation. Social isolation is a silent killer. Members of the disabled community who do not feel welcomed by society, who are alienated by difficult or disjointed access, who do not feel safe, will not venture outside of their comfort zone.

As the cause or background to many physical health conditions, we will look at provision for mental illness first.

Case study 14: Norwood's Ravenswood Village, Berkshire, England

In early 2013 we were asked to develop sensory gardens for a mental health residential care home at Ravenswood. The facility caters for the long term care of individuals over the age of 18 years. The brief was to provide two separate but adjoining gardens to de-stress the residents, keep them physically active and provide meaningful activity. The Pamela Barnett and Tager gardens are designed using universal design principles as inclusive spaces, but they each offer very specific therapeutic elements. Each garden had to keep tightly to its individual brief as the users had particular and very different, mutually exclusive, needs. The two gardens border each other, with a hedge planted on either side to hide a 2m (6ft) high timber fence. On one side is a sensory-rich space, with scents, tastes, colour, movement, wildlife and texture in abundance. On the other side is a very logical, predictable, calming environment.

The first garden, called Pamela Barnett after the house the residents live in, caters for adults with intellectual disabilities. This group requires additional sensory stimulus as they are harder to reach, requiring more of an input to prompt a response. We spent a long time working with staff and residents to get to know their needs, likes and dislikes. Some design elements became obvious; others needed careful guidance from the client. The residents delight in nature and will happily squelch through mud barefoot; they love to sit and giggle at the antics of insects, and enjoy gardening and growing things. They need a variety of surfaces underfoot, but laid so as not to create any trip hazards. One woman in the house enjoys self-induced epileptic fits when exposed to any reflective surface, so staff were keen to ensure all features within the garden had a matte finish. This meant that the desired water feature had to be shaded so that water droplets did not offer a reflection. Carefully chosen, varied planting with abundant flowers and edible fruit would allow residents to pick and taste anything they want to know more about. When it is difficult to make sense of things, humans intuitively seek to understand, using as many sensors as possible. Our mouths offer the greatest concentration of neural receptors, so as with a baby, many items are 'tasted' by the residents to find out more about them.

It is important that residents are able to access the garden area on their own, safely, so that they can enjoy a sense of independence and self-mastery. As the philosopher Lao-tzu (sixth century BC) said, 'He who controls others may be powerful, but he who has mastered himself is mightier still.' Indoors, the residents can become agitated as they get frustrated easily. They find it hard to self-motivate and self-regulate, so tend to sit or pace for long periods. Their stress can result in vocal and physical outbursts which are difficult to manage for staff and other residents. Outdoors the view is always changing and residents find there is always something to do, to watch or listen to. Stress levels are lowered and staff can concentrate on providing interesting occupational programmes rather than spending time on behaviour management.

Developing self-control is a major part of the therapy programme for residents of Pamela Barnett. The garden is designed to provide opportunities to explore jungle planting, to try out new routes and discover fishponds, trickling water features, a walkable bog garden, dragonflies, birds, butterflies, squirrels, flowers and fruits. It gives them the opportunity to sit outside and listen to the rain on the roof of a small shelter, the chance to feel the sun on their face and the wind in their hair, to work in the greenhouse or create patterns in the gravels of the zen garden. The garden offers quiet spaces where people can be alone, as well as communal spaces, so residents and visiting family can gather privately or with a larger group, as desired.

Figure 7.1 shows the garden designed by my colleague Katy Bott. The Pamela Barnett garden is a sensory-rich space designed to include multiple opportunities for self-discovery and self-mastery. Of

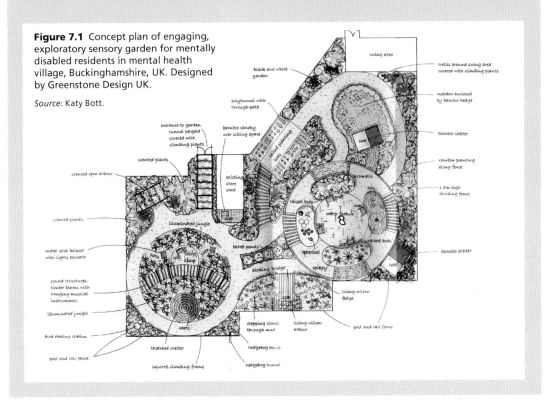

Figure 7.1 Concept plan of engaging, exploratory sensory garden for mentally disabled residents in mental health village, Buckinghamshire, UK. Designed by Greenstone Design UK.

Source: Katy Bott.

note, the client was delighted to receive a hand-drawn image. Interestingly, we have found that when designing sensory gardens the clients almost always prefer a hand-drawn sketch to a computer-aided design image. We use AutoCAD or Vectorworks for technical drawings but the hands-on approach of a hand-coloured image evokes a stronger response as clients relate to a picture and get a 'feeling' for a space in a way they report as difficult to achieve from a computer-generated image.

The garden is crossed with interconnecting paths, with a mix of covered walkways under densely planted pergolas, open beam structures and open areas where the sun can shine through. The surfacing changes from self-binding aggregate to a sleeper-and-gravel path to stone pavers. The following figures show individual design elements within the garden. In Figure 7.2 wind chimes, bird feeders and sensory balls hang from the overhead beams. The beams create interesting shadow patterns on the path below and frame the walkway. Some paths are fully enclosed by planting and some open along the route to a seating area.

Figure 7.2 Sketch of path under pergola in high needs sensory garden for residential mental health village, Buckinghamshire, UK.

Source: Katy Bott.

Multiple seating areas allow for individual choice, depending on mood, weather conditions, and the number of people who wish to socialise on a given day. Each area allows for a minimum of two people, so a carer can sit with a resident if required. Free standing seats are located throughout the garden so if another chair is required in one area an extra seat can easily be moved into position.

Figure 7.3 shows an enclosed roof and seats angled to observe life in the depths of the garden. Seating areas such as the one shown in Figure 7.4 offer the delights of thornless overhead roses, and ground level ferns and fragrant herbs.

Due to the extreme sensitivity of the residents in the adjoining Tager House garden it was important to ensure that the fragrant part of the Pamela Barnett garden be as far away as possible. At each stage of the design process we referred back to the reason why we were creating the particular garden. Overlaid on the basic brief were the constraints of the site whereby we needed to ensure not just a physical barrier between the two gardens but also that to as great a degree as possible sound, scent and visual stimuli did not intrude on the neighbouring garden.

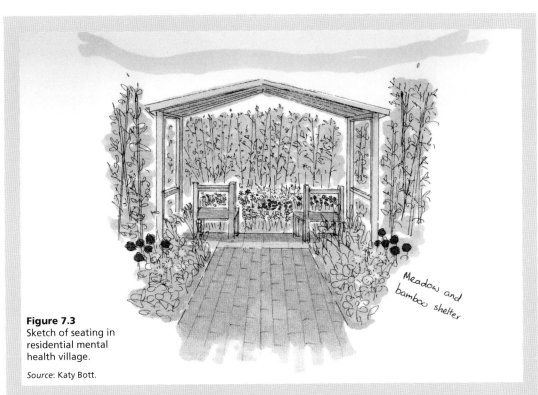

Figure 7.3
Sketch of seating in residential mental health village.

Source: Katy Bott.

Figure 7.4
Sketch of seating under a pergola for residential mental health village.

Source: Katy Bott.

One element the staff favoured was water. The brief was for a stand-alone water feature, some mud for the residents to squelch though in their bare feet and some fish that the residents could see but not sample. We had to ensure the main water feature trickled and made the right noises, was touchable but not sit-in-able. The difficult part was to guarantee it would not reflect light. In Figure 7.5 we see the central dull CorTen steel feature raised on a plinth so residents in wheelchairs can reach the reservoir to touch the water. The chosen location for the feature was the central area, which is shaded by mature trees on the south side of the boundary fence, thereby reducing any potential reflection off the dull-finish oxidised steel.

Figure 7.5 Sketch of non-reflective central water feature for residential mental health village.

Source: Katy Bott.

Figure 7.6 Sketch of safe, interactive oak barrel ponds for residential mental health village.

Source: Katy Bott.

For the fish ponds we used a selection of oak half-barrels, planted with water lilies, reeds, and fitted with a fog machine and a small fountain. Not shown is an additional fish pond water feature which is a clear sided, acrylic outdoor aquarium-style feature. Fish provide the residents of Pamela Barnett with a source of interest with their bright colours and almost constant movement.

In contrast, the Tager garden is formal and almost stark in its planting and layout. Designed for people with severe autism, this garden has to be predictable and offer very low sensory stimulus. No flowering plants were allowed and seasonal variation was kept to a minimum. In order for the garden to provide the required calming, de-stressing natural elements, we had to frame the space with evergreen hedging, topiary and a monastic-styled flat lawn.

If you compare Figure 7.7 to Figure 7.1 you will note the difference. Both can be described as sensory gardens but each design reflects the very different needs of the specific user group.

In the Tager garden the residents need to know what they will see and encounter on a daily basis, and be able to rely on their intimate knowledge of the space to feel safe and secure. As with the Pamela Barnett residents, in the confined space indoors residents can feel anxious and stressed. Out in the garden nature has a calming influence. The gentle diurnal rhythms and distant views reduce stress cortisol levels, allowing staff to spend more time on interesting programmes.

People on the autistic spectrum are often physically strong and as with all people, need regular exercise to keep fit and healthy. Autistic children and adults love the vestibular balance derived from spinning. They also like to swing.

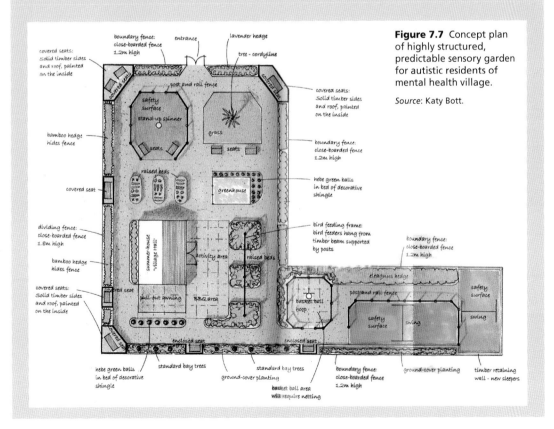

Figure 7.7 Concept plan of highly structured, predictable sensory garden for autistic residents of mental health village.

Source: Katy Bott.

In addition to the design elements shown in the concept drawings, the Centre had some existing outdoor fitness equipment which needed to be included in the design. The autistic residents require relatively strenuous physical exercise to stay fit and healthy. The equipment was placed along the fenceline, opposite the swing area, in the 'active zone' of the garden.

Summer-house with awning

ABOVE: Figure 7.8 Sketch of garden house pavilion for autistic residents of mental health village.

Source: Katy Bott.

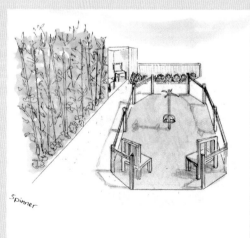

Spinner

Figure 7.9 Sketch of spinner adult play equipment within sensory garden for autistic residents of mental health village.

Source: Katy Bott.

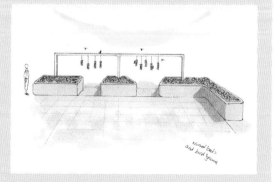

sensory beds and bird frame

Figure 7.10 Sketch of bird feeding station within sensory garden for autistic residents of mental health village.

Source: Katy Bott.

From these examples we see a need for varied spaces around our urban centres. To keep people in the community for as long as possible we need to ensure needs for calm, quiet space are met. For others we need to ensure some spaces are bright and filled with colour, texture and movement. While at times the needs may be conflicting, with thought accommodations can be made across the public realm.

Children in a special school environment

There are many conditions that need to be provided for within a special school environment. For example, children with cerebral palsy (CP) usually need physical, occupational, or speech therapy to help them develop skills like walking, sitting, swallowing, and using their hands. Like all children, disabled children need to be able to play, to discover, to explore, have fun. As a positive distraction from their health condition, playful environments are essential. Recent investment in special education environments has had mixed results. While there are no doubt some good examples, a lot of public money has been wasted on ill-conceived and poorly executed spaces.

Children living with disabilities need the same access to outdoor play spaces as their non-disabled peers. Natural play and a nature connection are important for all children. Opportunities to safely test personal boundaries, experiment and enjoy risk taking are also important. Schools have an opportunity to provide those experiences that the child may not get at home.

Depression

Depression is disabling. Physical health, relationships, work productivity and education are all negatively impacted by symptoms of depression (Moussavi et al., 2007). It is not something we can turn off or on at will; however, lifestyle choices make a big difference to our mental health. Poor choices can aggravate the symptoms of depression and anxiety. On the other hand, making positive changes can have a big impact on recovery. Of the six lifestyle factors that can affect our mental health, a lack of physical exercise is number one (Ministry of Health, 2009). Providing appropriate public green space is where funders, decision makers, landscape architects and urban designers can collaborate to make a real difference.

According to the New Zealand Ministry of Health, getting physically active has been proven to be one of the most effective ways to help adults and children deal with depression. Their mental health guidelines show regular physical activity – such as walking, swimming, dancing, playing sport, or gardening – is likely to be helpful, even for quite severe depression (Ministry of Health, 2009). Unlike many medications, nature experiences have no adverse side effects and, when supplied liberally throughout the public realm, can be taken at any time of day.

Adding exercise to the daily routine is helpful for maintaining both mental and physical health for everyone, depressed or not. People who are socially isolated have an increased risk of developing depression and take longer to recover from illness, so having accessible, engaging, safe places to exercise regularly outdoors, where there is a greater chance of meeting people, makes good economic and social policy sense.

Case study 15: Mary Elliot School, Midlands, England

This school was designed and built in 2008 for children with severe, profound and complex learning difficulties. In 2010 we were brought in to (re)design the sensory gardens. When it was opened the school had been supplied with a space designated by the architects as 'sensory gardens' but the bleak area did little to soothe or stimulate any senses.

As at Ravenswood, some children had mutually exclusive needs. We designed safe spaces for each user group, according to their developmental level, as an educational and therapeutic space for the children to access with a carer.

Within large developments landscape details can be overlooked under the guise of budget constraints. For the cost of the pavers, contoured paths and mulch supplying a richly planted space could have been developed. Where budget is an issue, a sensory design can be as simple as a well-placed open-canopy tree under which to safely park a push chair or stroller.

RIGHT: Figure 7.11 'Sensory garden' as provided within contract for new build special needs school, Midlands, UK.

BELOW: Figure 7.12 Concept plan to develop sensory garden at new build special needs school, Midlands, UK. Designed by Greenstone Design UK.

Source: Katy Bott.

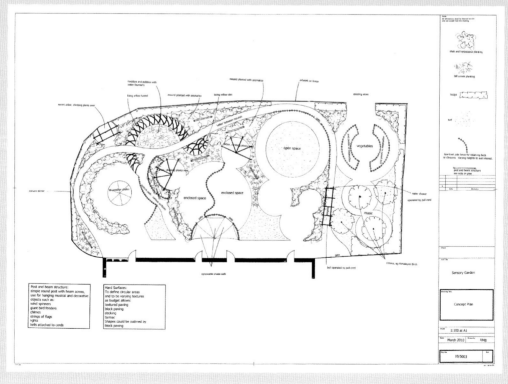

Case study 16: Pyrford Grange School, Surrey

This mainstream school has an integrated special needs unit. The client was unusual; usually we deal with adults. In this case we were contacted by the School Council. The Council includes representatives from every class in the school, and one teacher. Fifteen 5–11 year olds with a range of abilities and disabilities greeted me for the briefing meeting. Cerebral palsy, impaired vision, spina bifida and Tourette's syndrome were just some of the conditions brought to the design table. Although taught separately, the children played together and were keen to have more things to be able to do together. We designed a sensory playground with multiple dual access routes so children could race alongside each other, equally handicapped by obstacles, aids and surfaces. The wheelchairs users could negotiate a route using low overhead bars to pull their chairs through, while their ambulatory peers had to hop and balance between stepping logs. The children helped design the space and told us how they wanted to be able to engage with their friends in the play garden. Views and hidey holes, quiet corners and open space, sun and shade were all incorporated. We transformed a blank asphalt courtyard at minimal expense using recycled and found materials, with abundant edible planting. Fruit trees and currant bushes, strawberries and herbs provide seasonal interest and tasty treats. Outdoor art panels allow non-verbal children to express themselves. Percussive poles give non-auditory children the feeling of sound deep within their bellies. Mesh-topped recycled oak barrels meant each class could safely have a fish pond and freshwater habitat outside their classroom. The children were delighted, the staff also. Equality of provision is about providing a universal solution, a design scheme that suits one user and benefits all.

A number of studies have shown that physical activity can prevent or reduce mental health problems (NHS, 2011). Generally speaking, the evidence suggests that the more physical activity you do, the more you enhance your mental health. This is because:

- Mood enhancing chemicals are released into your bloodstream when you exercise.
- Physical activity improves your health – it works on your heart function and increases blood flow, reducing the risk of obesity, cancer, heart disease, stroke and depression. It can even help you sleep better.
- Regular activity outdoors helps you feel better about yourself – you feel more in control of things. It also provides opportunities for increased social interactions.

Given the importance of outdoor exercise for positive mental health, we need to provide open space in public parks where people can meet and congregate. In Guangzhou, China, ancient wisdom and understanding of the need for people to connect with nature led to the development of grand public parks. With modern population and economic pressures the old public parks now perform many functions. By morning the parks welcome elderly men to read the paper, play chess and chat. Around lunchtime, young mothers come with their children for some time with their friends. In late afternoon children stop to play on their way home from school. In the early evening young adults converge to meet friends and play table

Figure 7.13 Healthy, active lifestyles, with social and nature connections facilitated by public green space in Guangzhou, China.

Source: Huiyi Liu.

tennis. By late evening the mix changes again as middle-aged couples come out for a spontaneous dance and music event. All of this is set under mature trees, with sports arenas, fields and children's play areas to one side, and enclosed squares opening off pathways, giving shelter to the dancers.

In Paris, France, the public parks perform similar functions. As in China, with people around at all times of the day and night there is little vandalism or anti-social behaviour. Community mental health is boosted so that even the homeless feel socially connected. The city's parks and gardens become a draw-card for tourists and local businesses, and depression, stress and anxiety are eased.

Exercise on prescription or 'green prescriptions' have been introduced to New Zealand, Canada, the UK and USA as an inexpensive intervention (Figure 7.14). Australia has recently noted the success of the scheme in New Zealand and is introducing the nature therapy. A green prescription is an inexpensive counselling programme that aims to combat depression, obesity, heart disease and diabetes. Rather than prescribing expensive medication, general practitioners provide a written prescription with community contacts and exercise suggestions to encourage patients to get off the couch and to exercise outdoors for a certain period each week. The success of the scheme is dependent on provision of appropriate local green space so that exercise becomes an attractive, easy option.

Autistic spectrum disorders

Like depression, autistic spectrum disorders (ASD) are increasing throughout the community. Characterised by delayed or poor development of social interaction skills and extreme sensory sensitivity to one's surroundings, Asperger's syndrome, high

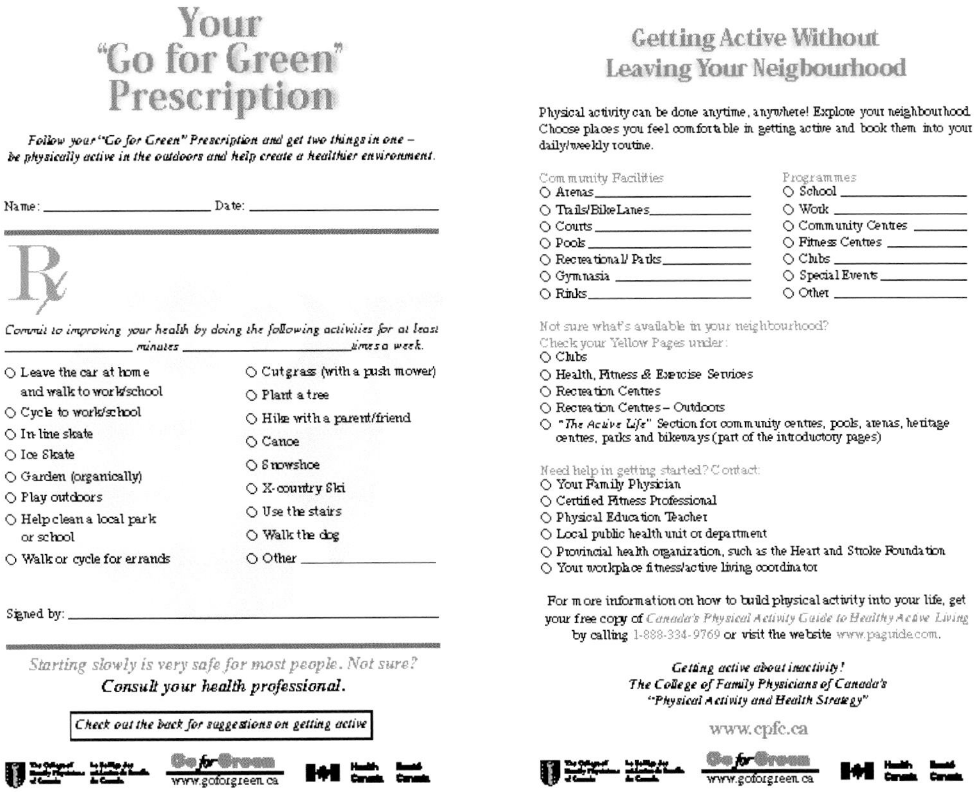

Your "Go for Green" Prescription

Follow your "Go for Green" Prescription and get two things in one – be physically active in the outdoors and help create a healthier environment.

Name: _____ Date: _____

℞

Commit to improving your health by doing the following activities for at least _____ minutes _____ times a week.

- ○ Leave the car at home and walk to work/school
- ○ Cycle to work/school
- ○ In-line skate
- ○ Ice Skate
- ○ Garden (organically)
- ○ Play outdoors
- ○ Help clean a local park or school
- ○ Walk or cycle for errands
- ○ Cut grass (with a push mower)
- ○ Plant a tree
- ○ Hike with a parent/friend
- ○ Canoe
- ○ Snowshoe
- ○ X-country Ski
- ○ Use the stairs
- ○ Walk the dog
- ○ Other _____

Signed by: _____

Starting slowly is very safe for most people. Not sure?
Consult your health professional.

Check out the back for suggestions on getting active

www.goforgreen.ca

Getting Active Without Leaving Your Neigbourhood

Physical activity can be done anytime, anywhere! Explore your neighbourhood. Choose places you feel comfortable in getting active and book them into your daily/weekly routine.

Community Facilities
- ○ Arenas _____
- ○ Trails/BikeLanes _____
- ○ Courts _____
- ○ Pools _____
- ○ Recreational/Parks _____
- ○ Gymnasia _____
- ○ Rinks _____

Programmes
- ○ School _____
- ○ Work _____
- ○ Community Centres _____
- ○ Fitness Centres _____
- ○ Clubs _____
- ○ Special Events _____
- ○ Other _____

Not sure what's available in your neighbourhood? Check your Yellow Pages under:
- ○ Clubs
- ○ Health, Fitness & Exercise Services
- ○ Recreation Centres
- ○ Recreation Centres – Outdoors
- ○ "The Active Life" Section for community centres, pools, arenas, heritage centres, parks and bikeways (part of the introductory pages)

Need help in getting started? Contact:
- ○ Your Family Physician
- ○ Certified Fitness Professional
- ○ Physical Education Teacher
- ○ Local public health unit or department
- ○ Provincial health organization, such as the Heart and Stroke Foundation
- ○ Your workplace fitness/active living coordinator

For more information on how to build physical activity into your life, get your free copy of *Canada's Physical Activity Guide to Healthy Active Living* by calling 1-888-334-9769 or visit the website www.paguide.com.

Getting active about inactivity!
The College of Family Physicians of Canada's
"Physical Activity and Health Strategy"

www.cpfc.ca

www.goforgreen.ca

Figure 7.14 Green prescription, from Pace Canada.

Source: Pace Canada.

functioning autism, Rett's syndrome and classic autism are all conditions on the spectrum. Although a full range of emotions is felt, children and adults living with ASD find it difficult to express those emotions. In fear and frustration they may lash out. In joy they may whoop and yell. Dustin Hoffman's performance as Ray Babbitt in the film *Rain Man*[1] shows the classic shy individual who avoids eye contact, shows little emotion and lives in a very literal world. Upset by any change or break in routine, adults and children living with ASD may become severely upset. There is evidence to suggest that a predictable life is best for the families and individuals living with the condition. However, there is also contrary anecdotal evidence that ASD children exposed to change can be supported to adapt and learn previously unavailable emotional responses. Environments that change through visiting wildlife or seasonal leaf drop offer gentle, slow-paced natural variation.

Design guidelines:

Our occupational therapist Bev McAlpine kindly supplied the following guidelines:

Sensation
- Consistent, low-arousal gardens in which levels of stimulation can be easily calibrated provide a sense of control and empowerment instead of sensory overload; an example is the Tager garden in case study 14.

- Someone with autism may experience hyper- and hypo-sensitivities across a range of senses, and so both extremes need to be catered for within the garden.
- A person with autism may respond to textures in contrasting ways. A person who experiences hypo-sensitivity may want to touch and feel everything around them, while someone who experiences hyper-sensitivity may want to avoid touching things altogether, becoming distressed by unexpected contact with a plant or even the anticipation of it.
- Many therapists try to de-sensitise hyper-sensitive children, for example by lining pathways with plants to brush against.

Perception
- Many adults and children with autism find it difficult to distinguish between foreground and background information. It is a good idea to compartmentalise a garden into easy-to-understand units clearly dedicated to different activities, for example exercise, occupation and leisure.
- Some may have poor depth of perception which will affect the way they judge distances, orientate, navigate and manoeuvre around objects. Garden layout should be logical, orderly and structured with spaces that flow easily from one to another.
- Navigation, organisation and consistent flow are best achieved through repetition of colour, form or texture to create a recognisable pattern.
- Gestalt perception difficulty can occur if a single thing is changed, as it can make an entire space unfamiliar, which may prompt anxiety.

Refuge
- Offer private and withdrawal spaces alongside communal areas for enjoyment and to allow retreat when group situations become too overwhelming.

Predictability and control
- Balance planting between examples that do not change dramatically and perennials that reflect seasonal changes.
- Make vistas and paths clear in order that people can see what they are about to encounter.
- Design for routine and order so that people can predict their progress.
- Features should be stable and non-portable to avoid unintended and unexpected movement.

Flexibility
- Since people with autism have differing needs, garden spaces should have potential to be modified as required to meet changing interests and aspirations, although arbitrary change is to be avoided.

Communication and social interaction
- Use focal points and shared spaces to hold activities and events – such as barbecues – for group gatherings.
- Provide spaces that can be easily accessed and that encourage sharing.

Unobtrusive monitoring
- Create vistas to enable staff to monitor the people they support from a distance without making individuals feel they are constantly under observation.
- Design planting and fencing with a level of permeability so that spaces beyond can be casually checked as needed.

Accommodating hyper-sensitivity
- Create an enclosed quiet space that is calm, restful and undisturbed. Position it away from the social areas of the garden.
- Consider the positioning of sensory spaces, particularly ones involving sound or smell, which are likely to 'leak' into other spaces. Be sure to place such spaces away from more neutral ones designated for escape or solitude.
- The floral scents of a garden are one of its great pleasures; however, this aspect has to be carefully considered and managed for the benefit of those who might find it overwhelming.
- Remember that temperature and location can exaggerate the effects of scent.
- Avoid creating too many sounds at the same time, i.e. mowing a lawn with music playing in the background.
- Be mindful of the materials you use for ground cover in communal spaces, avoiding noisy substances such as gravel, and consider using sound-absorbent alternatives (for example cork, bark or sand).
- Mask unwanted noise with soothing sounds such as water or swishing grasses.
- As some may find it challenging to walk along uneven or unstable surfaces, ensure that ground surfaces are sturdy, bound and continuous. Gravel and pebbles may feel too unstable.
- Those anxious about heights will respond better to slopes than steps, appreciate sturdy seating and feel more comfortable when a garden swing is of a height that allows the feet to touch the ground.
- For those who need to avoid excessive head movement, provide raised flower beds that involve little bending, and supply a clutch stick to pull the apples from a tree or pick up the leaves. A watering hose requires less tilting of the head to use than a watering can.

Accommodating hypo-sensitivity
- A person who seeks sensory input may not be able to tolerate silence and will create their own sounds by tapping and banging. Consider the materials used for garden features and furniture from this point of view.
- Tapping on wood, metal and plastic will all produce different sounds.
- Introduce sculptures and focal points made of materials that amplify the sound of the rain.
- Include nectar-producing plants and feeders to attract birds.
- Provide a garden space for running. A perimeter garden path may be a convenient solution.
- Consider providing a trampoline and exercise ball. The movement of bouncing up and down can produce a very calming effect for those who enjoy it.

- Provide a space with safe, soft flooring for spinning activities. The rotational movement of spinning can be very activating.
- Provide space for craft pursuits – such as making hanging baskets or birdfeeders – in sheltered spaces in the garden. Herbs grown in the garden can be brought indoors and used in cooking

Principles
- A veranda or porch can be used to provide transitional space between being indoors and outdoors, and shelter from poor weather conditions.
- Lighting can make a garden accessible for more hours. The transition from dark to light should not be abrupt, so the use of timed lighting rather than motion-sensitive lighting should be used.
- Winding paths are known to bring a sense of calm and create a flow that promotes calm progress through a space. Curves and slopes are gentle ways of transitioning spaces and can be used as an alternative to steps or angular paths.
- Vertical features interspersed through the garden can help draw the eye upwards and take advantage of the three-dimensional space.
- Obelisks and other structures can be used to mark points of interest and should be visible from vantage points to orientate people.
- Position social spaces in ways that allow several entrances and exits, as this enables people to come and go independently.
- Some people with autism prefer to avoid bright sunlight. If possible provide shading, particularly in areas where people will be spending a lot of time. This can be achieved through natural surroundings such as trees, or by adding structures or canopies.
- Those who might not immediately want to participate in social activities should not be excluded completely. They may appreciate options that allow them to sit a little apart from the main social space.
- Consider all-year garden use and provide a shelter. This can be as modest as a shed or as lavish as a summer house to host indoor activities that can be temporarily relocated to the garden for variety.
- Choose materials for furniture, flooring and partitions that are consistent in texture and non-heat absorbent, as unfamiliar textures and temperatures may trigger anxiety.
- 'Designing in' activities that incorporate resistance – for example climbing, lifting, pulling or pushing – promotes deep pressure for relaxation which is well-documented as a positive stimulant
- Provide a garden space where people can circulate and run. A perimeter path is a good idea if there is sufficient space
- Provide space with safe, soft flooring for a person to spin. The rotational movement of spinning can be very captivating for adults with autism.
- Gardens have great potential to offer opportunities to practise motor skills, balance and coordination. This can be achieved by using objects such as spinning plates or balance beams.
- Interactive equipment can be dotted along pathways throughout the garden to intrigue and encourage exercise and engagement (for example large exercise balls, exercycles, climbing walls or balance beams).

- In a shared garden it is a good idea to contain exercise areas, as the sights and sounds generated may be distracting for others. A well-shielded and designated location is therefore desirable.

Ageing population

Age is not a disability, but with ageing comes a natural degeneration of nerves, muscle and bone. 'Repairs and maintenance' costs, as my mother likes to call her increasingly frequent trips to the hospital, increase with age, just as they do with an old piece of machinery. To counter this, governments need to keep people active for as long as possible, both mentally and physically. Healthy, active ageing is a priority.

> Investing in healthy ageing has become key for the sustainability of health and social policies in Europe. A closing window of opportunity of relative growth of the labour force along with unfavourable economic prospects in many countries in Europe have made the need to step up the implementation of policies for active ageing particularly urgent.
>
> (World Health Organisation Europe, 2012)

Europe is not alone in having a rapidly ageing population. As the demographic changes in the USA, Japan, China, Canada, Australasia and elsewhere, the incidence of disability within communities globally is increasing at unsustainable levels. It is essential we find innovative, cost-effective ways now of ensuring that the state's burden of care is reduced. Government policies and investment will necessarily follow, but we have an opportunity to improve urban environments while addressing a pressing public health concern. Healthy communities offer inclusive spaces regardless of age or ability. Environments that support active ageing include parks and gardens, community gardens and, importantly, spaces and facilities that afford social connections.

Active ageing policies support the development of environments to promote and maintain mobility – the lack of which is a key cause of disability in older age groups, in the USA in particular. Adapted free-to-use adult fitness equipment in public parks; safe, attractive places to go and to congregate; accessible nature experiences that stimulate cognitive function and improve memory – all are needed (Churchill et al., 2002). Healing gardens are by nature inclusive and beneficial spaces. All people benefit from health-affirming healing gardens and cityscapes to remain active mentally and physically, including senior citizens.

Ageing, in the absence of an active lifestyle, can be tremendously socially isolating. Stress and depression can arise from a disconnection from the natural world. Such mental health conditions can also prevent people from feeling safe and welcomed within the community, causing people to disconnect and thus further exacerbating the problem. Figure 7.15 illustrates this cycle.

An active life outdoors helps retain social connections and facilitates independence into old age. Outings improve social health. With that comes an improvement in physical health. Providing accessible natural experiences means more than wheelchair access. Sensory stimulation is important for people with cognitive, hearing, sight

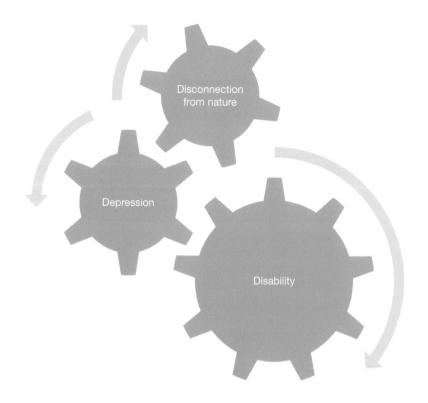

Gearing increases the effect of one condition on another

and mobility impairments. They benefit from the memory prompt of freshly picked mint, the touch of wind in their hair, rain on their skin.

To create a sense of belonging within a community we need to manage spaces that allow and engender a sense of connection and ownership. Sensitive urban design is crucial to keeping older people socially connected. After the death of a partner, older people often live alone. Craving company and the enjoyment and positive distraction of young people, they often seek a sunny spot to sit and watch children play. Too often playgrounds have signs stating 'no unaccompanied adults'. Even where there is no restrictive signage there is often nowhere to sit or the area is open and wind-swept. When housing providers choose to develop accommodation for older people adjacent to existing green space, planners have an opportunity to grant permission on the basis that appropriate seating, natural shade and edible planting is incorporated into the neighbouring park or playground, so that the health and well-being of the residents is promoted rather than frustrated.

In the photo of a senior residence in Berlin, Germany (Figure 7.16) the man is sitting alone in his wheelchair in a fairly bleak, square-edged space. The stone gabion wall and depth of garden shuts him off from passers-by so he is isolated from the community. With impaired sight and hearing he needs to be able to get close to pedestrians to be able to interact. Safety is paramount, and the residence requested the architects provide a barrier or physical reminder to stop people wandering out

Figure 7.16 Berlin, Germany: a lonely disabled man sits outside his seniors' residential housing in a relatively stark, hard paved environment. Although the sign says the centre promotes health, the environmental design does not. The area would be improved by varied surfacing, accessible raised beds, wildlife-attracting shrub planting, and some small flowering or fruiting trees.

into the street. A low kerb would have sufficed. Although the planting is there to soften the space and provide a therapeutic horticultural growing area, it does not fulfil its functional role. If the planting had been developed around a circuit of paths, with variously sized spaces away from and up close to the building, bringing nature indoors on days when residents were unable to go out, with a mix of raised and ground level bed heights, the therapeutic effect would have been far greater.

Dementia

With an ageing population, dementia is a growing concern. As with other disabled user groups, dementia has a profound effect on quality of life. A study of healing garden designs for Alzheimer's patients by researchers from Rutgers University (Flahive-DiNardo et al., 2013) found that the nature connection was a significant memory prompt. Small groups were given access to an indoor Japanese-style garden for fifteen minutes over several weeks. At one point during the testing, there was a cricket singing in a chrysanthemum plant. Ten days passed before the next garden visit. When the study participants returned to the garden, two of the four patients who had heard the chirping asked: 'Where is the cricket?'

That these people could associate the cricket with the garden after one brief exposure – and retain this association for ten days – is significant. One of the researchers subsequently created a small Japanese garden at one end of an Alzheimer's unit:

in these brief exposures interesting things happened. Many of these patients don't know who they are. Many get confused at a certain time of day. Yet immediately upon being in the garden they calmed down, even if they were in the midst of screaming. They smiled and stayed calm for the rest of the day. The doctor said this was more effective than medications that can take time to work and leave patients listless.

(Flahive-DiNardo et al., 2013)

Japanese gardens can be very small and installed indoors. 'They can be put in anywhere at low cost. If they reduce stress, this could mean lower healthcare costs, less medicine, and fewer calls to the nurse. This could have huge implications' (Flahive-DiNardo et al., 2013).

We need to include many more opportunities for nature connections across our towns and cities to keep people engaged and prevent memory loss (Kaplan and Kaplan, 2005). Provision for those with dementia relies on early intervention or primary care options. The World Health Organisation states that community mental health initiatives are more accessible and effective, lessen social exclusion, and are likely to have fewer possibilities for the neglect and violations of human rights than were often encountered in mental hospitals (Brundtland, 2001). However, the WHO also notes that in many countries, the closing of mental hospitals has not been accompanied by the development of community services, leaving a service vacuum with far too many receiving no care. In these communities in particular, healing gardens and general environmental improvements can make a major difference. While it may seem unusual to include landscape and urban design within primary healthcare, when taken as part of a holistic treatment programme it can be key to cost-effective early management of mental illness leading to disability.

Post-traumatic stress disorder

People living with post-traumatic stress disorder (and others requiring a supportive environment) benefit from time spent in a purpose-designed, healing, sensory or therapeutic garden. Such gardens work to support the individual through a gradual reconnection with nature. Not only do healing gardens work for the veteran, they also provide respite for their families and caregivers, and a de-stressing environment for other staff.

Healing gardens for PTSD patients require:

1   natural leafy shade;
2   clear sight lines to give a sense of safety and security;
3   a homelike environment, so no institutional furniture or surfacing;
4   flat walking surfaces without camber, but also some walkways that provide more of a challenge;
5   surfacings chosen to reduce glare;
6   lush planting to absorb sound and create a feeling of oasis in the city;

7   positive sound interference, such as water, to mask local traffic noise and attract wildlife;

8   plants that specifically attract butterflies, in addition to diverse wildlife-attracting flora;

9   abundant seating – spaced at intervals no further than 50m (150ft) apart, with a mix of tables or wide-armed seats to promote casual picnicking;

10   covered areas – when supplied with cooling fans and/or heaters these allow vulnerable people to be outside in inclement weather;

11   playful areas, for adults and children, that include outdoor music, a performance space, a dance space, climbable sculpture, swings and balance beams;

12   a choice of sunny and shaded spaces that allow for quiet contemplation, private conversation, or larger communal interaction;

13   opportunities for light and more strenuous exercise.

Figure 7.17
A healing garden provides somewhere to sit, somewhere to chat with a friend, wildlife-attractive planting, and an attractive outlook.

The important point to note from a salutogenic urban design perspective is that anyone can suffer from post-traumatic stress. Therefore the above design elements need not be limited to specialist gardens within veteran and defence ministry health-care facilities. If we plan our city parks, our schools, our pocket parks and neighbourhood spaces to include the above, then anyone suffering stress or requiring gentle rehabilitation into the community will benefit. It costs no more to choose plants for their function rather than their aesthetic. We will look at the cost benefits further in Chapter 9.

Inclusive urban design for disability

The evidence is clear. Nature and social connections aid health and well-being. Research tells us that if you are able to get about independently, on foot, bike or public transport, it improves community cohesion, and creates a healthier population in terms of their physical and mental well-being, and offers a range of economic benefits. Active public transport, slow pedestrian zones for older or frail individuals, walkways and cycleways are known to benefit economies and individuals (Health Impact Project, 2011). However, although much touted, evidence-based design is rarely applied to urban design. With economies struggling to keep up with infrastructure, health and education costs, it is timely to take action, to include a broader definition of disability in universal and inclusive design.

To create truly liveable cities, therapeutic landscapes as a concept need to be applied across the public realm. Disability, regardless of cause, has been kept away from society, separated by invisible barriers to access. We need to look at other countries, in Europe especially, that have excellent evidence-based urban design. Our depression, obesity and diabetes epidemics cannot be solved by the health system alone. We need high level policy leadership and innovative landscape interventions that include improvements in our urban design, transport and food policies. We need to recognise that depression causes significant disability and disengagement from employment and education. Disability robs individuals, families, communities and economies. The design ideas presented above and within the case studies can be adapted and applied for use in public space. The key to success is ensuring that the healthy choice is the easiest choice. Regardless of their type of disability, adults and children need to be able to easily get outdoors, so as to engage with nature and with their community.

Note

1   *Rain Man* is a 1988 American film directed by Barry Levinson and written by Barry Morrow and Ronald Bass, showcasing an autistic savant and often taken to depict a 'classic' autistic individual.

References

Brundtland, G. H. (2001). *Mental health: a call to action by world health ministers.* Geneva: World Health Organisation.

Churchill, J. D., Galvez, R., Colcombe, S., Swain, R. F., Kramer, A. F. and Greenough, W. T. (2002). Exercise, experience and the aging brain. *Neurobiology of Aging*, 23:941–955.

Flahive-DiNardo, M., DePrado, L., Flagler, J. and Polanin, N. (2013). *Enabling gardens: the practical side of horticultural therapy.* New Brunswick, NJ: Rutgers University Agricultural Experiment Station.

Health Impact Project (2011). *Case study: East-Bay Greenway.* Oakland, CA: A Collaboration of the Robert Wood Johnson Foundation and the PEW Charitable Trusts.

Kaplan, R. and Kaplan, S. (2005). Preference, restoration, and meaningful action in the context of nearby nature. In P. F. Barlett (ed.), *Urban Place: Reconnecting with the natural world*, pp. 271–298. Cambridge, MA: The MIT Press.

Lao-tzu (sixth century BC). Lao-tzu quotes. Retrieved August 2013, from *En Theos*: www.entheos.com/quotes/by_teacher/Lao-tzu

Medscape (2013, 6 November). Depression now world's second leading cause of disability. Retrieved 6 November 2013, from *Med Scape Multi Speciality*: www.medscape.com/viewarticle/813896

Ministry of Health (2009). Depression: lifestyle. Retrieved April 2013, from *Depression*: www.depression.org.nz/cause/lifestyle

Moussavi, S., Chatterji, S.,Verdes, E., Tandon, A., Patel, V. and Ustun, B. (2007). Depression, chronic diseases, and decrements in health: results from the World Health Surveys. *Lancet*, 370(9590):851–858.

Natural England (2013, 13 July). Interest grows in the benefits of being outside for health. Retrieved 12 October 2013, from *Natural England*: www.naturalengland. org.uk/about_us/news/2013/300713.aspx

NCSU (2013, 27 July). Universal design. Retrieved 1 August 2013, from *Wikipedia*: https://en.wikipedia.org/wiki/Universal_design

Neumann, P., Carpinell, S., Heilemann, M. and Unger, C. (2011). Design for all. Intelligent Furniture Project. *Akademie Gestaltung*: www.adam-europe.eu/prj/ 7610/prd/5/3/TP1_DetailedCurriculum_version4_2011-01-24.pdf

NHS (2011, 21 August). Stress-anxiety-depression. Retrieved 10 December 2013, from *NHS Choices*: www.nhs.uk/Conditions/stress-anxiety-depression/Pages/ exercise-for-depression.aspx

World Health Organisation Europe (2012, 11–13 September). EUR/RC62/10 Rev.1 strategy and action plan for healthy ageing in Europe, 2012–2020. Retrieved 6 December 2013, from *World Health Organisation Europe*: www.euro.who. int/__data/assets/pdf_file/0008/175544/RC62wd10Rev1-Eng.pdf

CHAPTER 8

Healing gardens for stressed executives

Landscape and urban design for health and well-being is not just an expression of concern for the unhealthy, the disabled, or for the socially and economically deprived. It is fundamental to creating and sustaining resilient communities. People in executive positions, like any other group, need nature points in their lives to ensure good mental and physical health.

Healing gardens are needed for executives as much as they are for children and the infirm, and for the same reasons. Since the global financial crisis became readily apparent in 2008, very few organisations and few individuals have remained unaffected. The urgency to both grow the business and make it leaner and more competitive in the process has placed the men and women at the top under increased stress. Green space is also under pressure to deliver. In 2011 the UK's Department for Environment Food and Rural Affairs (Defra) calculated the financial value of green space in terms of its contribution to the overall economy. They found that 'with a greater focus on efficiency, productivity and effectiveness, expenditure on (green infrastructure) services will increasingly be judged in terms of the contribution they make to improving the outcomes that matter to people; health and wellbeing, the local economy' (Defra, 2011). The study also calculated the value of green space as an aid to well-being. It concluded that provision of green space is a cost-effective means to counter rising healthcare costs.

This book aims to show that overall, healing gardens are both time- and cost-effective investments. Executives value time and money. By reducing health costs, staff absence and personal stress, healing gardens save governments', employers' and individuals' money. They offer a win/win scenario for all. When we improve the environment for one group, due to the inclusive nature of salutogenic design everyone benefits. The difference with the group that this chapter focusses on is that they, more than any other, have individual and collective money to spend. Executives are willing to pay for services and solutions they see as offering good value, a positive return on investment or that will help make them stand out from the competition. Life is stressful at the top. Provision of healing gardens at home and near the workplace can help make life less stressful.

Stressed executives are found in management positions around the world. That means urban designers everywhere need to be mindful of the environments they create. To create destinations where people want to invest, live and work we need to create healthy environments. Business leaders, by nature of their skills and experience, are frequently community leaders as well. These people often describe themselves as cash rich but time poor. It is important to keep them healthy. The men and women who guide and shape our communities serve us best when they are mentally and physically well. When well, executives make better decisions and value and care for themselves, their families and their communities, and the environment on which we all depend.

Effects of stress

Healing gardens are designed to de-stress, regardless of whom they are targeting. They are about making a difference socially, economically and environmentally. Culturally healing gardens can and do nurture everyone. When we meet the health needs of people in each sector within society, we build strong, resilient communities.

Development of healing green space supports individuals at risk from burn-out, relationship breakdown, depression and feelings of despair. When people are disconnected from nature they are more likely to be negatively affected by stress (Abbott, 2012). Alarming statistics for suicide in the USA were released in May 2013. The suicide rate among middle-aged white Americans climbed by a startling 28 per cent in the decade from 1999. This group includes, but is not exclusive to, executives. Possible contributing factors include the economic downturn (historically, suicide rates tend to correlate with business cycles, with higher rates observed during times of economic hardship). In terms of additional risk factors I would posit that many middle-aged people are likely to suffer from a disconnection from nature. Modern commuter lifestyles often leave little time for a nature connection. As we see in Figure 8.1, cars move people from home to work and back again, leaving little

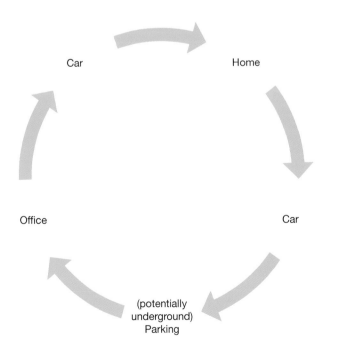

Car

Home

Office

Car

(potentially underground) Parking

Figure 8.1
The commuter stress cycle occurs when there is no opportunity to engage with nature on the route to or from the workplace.

opportunity to experience the sights, scents and sounds of nature. A nature deficit appears most pronounced in groups where it is not replaced by social or religious connections (Sullivan et al., 2013).

As various public bodies have now stated (the UN, the WHO), we need to find innovative solutions to the problems of our time. Stress is a strong influence on depression, which is already the second largest cause of disability globally. Work pressures are ongoing. The financial burden of traditional health treatment options is increasing. A cost-effective way to counter the effect of stress is through environmental interventions. Internally, workplaces can be softened with external windows and green views. Outdoors, adjacent open space can be developed as welcoming spaces, so that people are encouraged to de-stress, to balance work with time spent walking and sitting with friends, outdoors. Using the principles of monastic and Islamic garden design, the green space can be rich with attractive mixed plantings, seats and a mix of sun and shade. In this way workers from the immediate area will be more likely to use the space. Stress levels are reduced and the mental and hence physical health of the people improves.

Biophilic cities – how do they help?

Biophilic cities are developed around the premise that humans inherently love living things. To de-stress executives we need to provide abundant opportunities within urban centres to facilitate nature connections.

Case study 17: the tree seat

In 2013, British designer Andrew Fisher Tomlin, designed a novel conceptual garden as his entry for the Ellerslie International Flower Show, shown in Figure 8.2. He said 'the visitor will be asked to celebrate the beauty of the individual tree itself. By taking the traditional outward focused tree seat and turning it inwards, the visitor is encouraged to examine what is usually behind them' (Source Wire, 2012). Providing the novel opportunity to wrap people around a tree is a powerful way to bring them together in a shared experience of nature. The soft bark chip underfoot, the comfortable seating and the ferns planted behind create a very calming, sensory-rich space that is at the same time a very social space. It is the sort of garden that equally inspires one to quiet contemplation or to strike up conversation.

Figure 8.2 Christchurch, New Zealand: an inward-facing tree seat allows people to focus inwards on the tree as a healing intervention in urban green space.

Cities that are full of pocket parks and open space planted with bio-diverse, wildlife-attracting trees, shrubs and flowers provide sensory interest and a positive distraction from the pressures of work. Roof gardens and living walls help soften the city environment, and provide a green view from high rise buildings.

While distant contact with nature has been found to lower blood pressure and stress hormones, the effect is greatest when people can engage additional senses such as hearing, touch and smell (Maller et al., 2006). Parks and urban green space owners and managers need to allow for senior executives to get up close with nature. To encourage people unused to exercising in nature into parks and gardens they need clean access points in amongst the grass and trees. The natural bark chip shown in Figure 8.2 is ideal in a biophilic garden space. For the gardens to be fully inclusive, grades of bark are available to facilitate wheeled access.

In the city much of nature is kept off-limits or out of sight. Water is piped underground. Plants are kept behind barriers. To create biophilic touch points we need to uncover waterways and add bio-diverse planting, whether self-seeded amongst the ruins of a previous building, or carefully planted in a controlled environment. The early British landscape architect Patrick Geddes lived by the motto *vivendo discimus* (by living, we learn). He understood the enormous multi-sensory benefit of time spent creating and destroying, building a log den, of damming a water channel, of bouncing on a branch until it breaks. All this childhood limit testing

Figure 8.3
Lightweight, high-impact healing roof gardens can be developed above offices, apartments, shopping malls and hospitals, and as sky decks on skyscrapers as sensory-rich, bio-diverse social spaces.

is of practical application when it comes to making business decisions. Knowing when to trust instinct, when to pause to observe, when to take action, which risks are worth taking, whom you can depend on, are all vital skills in the world of the senior executive.

When we examine the architecture of many of our cities and the lifestyles of the busy people who live there, it is easy to see the disconnect between nature and commerce. Commerce has evolved in steel and glass cubicles, set apart from the world outside. Where once commercial buildings were made of wood and stone and featured ornamentation that referenced nature, since the mid-twentieth century they have lost their nature connection. Through a combination of urban design, planning, commercial and architectural factors, cities can make us healthy or unhealthy, and keep us from being as healthy as we could be. City layouts that rely on personal cars to commute from housing in the outer suburbs to the city centre make it possible to stay inside an air-conditioned, manufactured environment all day and forgo the sensory pleasure and health-giving properties of fresh air in our lungs and sun on our skin. Researchers at Texas A&M University found that Houston is a good example of a city that has developed without attention to its population's biophilic need. Set on the edge of a desert, its climate is harsh and the distances between home and office great. Attractive, shaded walking and cycling routes have been included in some residential areas, but they do not link to create an active transport option into the city centre (Zhu et al., 2013). If at any point we break the cycle by inserting an active lifestyle alternative such as walking, cycling or public transport, we have an opportunity to provide a healing nature experience along the route to de-stress the commuter.

However much executives know they *should* seek nature experiences, the design of cities and buildings can make it difficult to get outside of the hard manufactured environment. We can change that.

Figure 8.4 The commuter stress cycle becomes the nature connection commuter cycle when active transport and public transport are utilised.

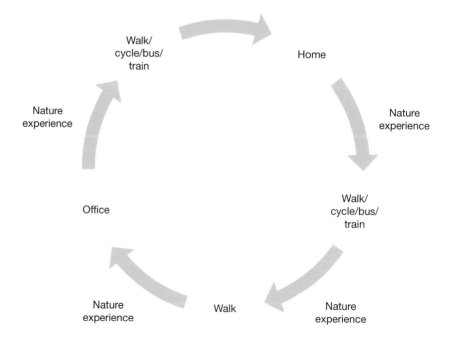

1 Permeable paving options, such as shown in Figure 8.5 and used on the Highline Park in New York, channel and filter rainwater runoff, and provide texture visually and underfoot.
2 Living walls (also known as green walls) soften the harsh built environment, counter the urban heat island effect, provide habitat for insects, birds and invertebrates and absorb air pollutants. As with horizontal gardens, they increase demand for commercial space in the area, attracting higher inbound investment in the district, and increased tourism.
3 Green roofs on office buildings, as on schools, factories and elsewhere, provide de-stressing, healing green views and can also allow access to engaging green space during the working day. Food growing and urban bee-keeping have become popular on the roofs of buildings from Seoul to Sydney, London to Vancouver. Paris, known for its chic yet relaxed executive lifestyle, is the urban bee-keeping capital of the world, with over 400 hives registered in 2010. Some chefs use honey harvested on the roof to provide fresh organic produce in the restaurants. Overall, the city's rates of NCDs are low. Diet and exercise levels are good.

In towns and cities where busy people can pause to experience nature in the city, stress levels tend to be lower and productivity higher. Andreas Meyer-Lindenberg, director of the Central Institute for Mental Health in Mannheim, Germany, says in a study of executive stress:

> city-stress is a big, messy concept, but . . . brains of city-dwellers looked somehow different . . . the stress receptors responded more strongly to negative stress in those brought up in large cities than in those brought up in the countryside, irrespective of where they lived now.
>
> (Abbott, 2012)

Is the urban nature connection the key addition necessary to support feelings of well-being?

Links between environment and mental health are proven and profound (Maller et al., 2006). When we create biophilic cities we are supporting natural ecosystems as well as human health and well-being. A critical factor in the development of healing green space for human health and well-being is to provide food sources for local wildlife. Nectar-rich flowers, fruit and leaves create points of sensory interest for people, and are an important additional food source of forage plants for the pollinators (Urban Bees, 2013). Biophilic cities are full of trees. As we evolved on the plains of Africa, trees were an important vantage point, a place where we could look down on the world around us and evaluate our situation.

Tree houses

No discussion of the design implications of biophilia would be complete without consideration of the role of the tree house. Symbolically, the desire to be at the top is seen in the recent resurgence of interest in tree houses. Tree houses for adults, as

OPPOSITE PAGE: **Figure 8.5** New York City, USA: the Highline Park, like the original Promenade Plantée in Paris, is a good example of healing urban regeneration. The park offers a green reprieve in the midst of the central city.

Source: Jenny Brown.

LEFT: **Figure 8.6** Accessible green roof with beehives adds to urban biodiversity on the office roof, and is a powerful tool in workplace productivity, health and safety. The practice of mindfulness occurs best in a calm nature space. This healing roof garden benefits staff with increased calmness, improved focus and attention, enhanced self-awareness, effective conflict resolution, and the development of positive relationships and reduced stress.

Source: Image Shack.

sensory-rich places of pleasure and delight, are emerging in both East and West as a market trend amongst affluent executives. Although popular since ancient times, I believe the revived interest is due to two things: first as a natural response to stress, and second to our innate biophilia. 'Somewhere among the primeval genes that persist in us, are those that recall the arboreal life of our forebears. They persist in the indefinable feelings of identity, adventure, even of sanctuary, which so many experience in a tree house' (Pearn, 2013). Professor Pearn is a pediatrician by profession, someone who works long hours in a stress-filled, senior position, but he does not 'suffer' from stress. He has found balance between his work and private life. He has a tree house in his garden that 'offers real sanctuary and hospitality'.

Figure 8.7 Adult tree houses are popular with stressed executives, offering a therapeutic nature connection and safe retreat.

Source: Photo: Paul Munro.

Design that enables people to find a balance is a recurring theme throughout this book. Where best to make that provision is a question that will be decided by market forces. For example, rather than ground level cafe or arts and culture facilities around a traditional park, we could design adult-sized tree houses in public parks with facilities as part of the treehouse. Innovative ideas like this could improve the livability rating of some cities and make them become more attractive investment centres. Equally, planning regulations that allow bespoke tree houses in private gardens may benefit executives and their families, and also other community groups.

Design for healthy living

Urban designers have an opportunity to work with community leaders, developers and local politicians to create livable cities where people want to live, work and invest. Design for healthy living, to de-stress the stressed executive, is not just about providing healing green space. Gardens need to be incorporated into urban centres alongside other salutogenic design interventions such as the addition of internal communication routes within buildings that allow for social interaction. Simple things like open stairways can reduce social isolation and promote an active lifestyle. When assessing the impacts of design on health and well-being it is useful to consider the role of convenience. How often are the stairs visible, clean, well-lit, attractive spaces? A study by Harvard University alumni showed that high rise buildings that encourage users to take the elevator or lift deny them the opportunity enjoy a 20 per cent lower risk of heart attack than their peers who don't climb twenty floors of stairs a week (Sesso et al., 2000). How often do you walk into a building foyer and get directed straight to a bank of lifts? As designers and manufacturers strive to provide more ease and convenience to mitigate our stressed and harried lifestyle, the reverse is often the unintended result.

Health risks lie not only with a stressed and inactive lifestyle. Social isolation is a leading cause of depression. In many cities across the world, little sunshine penetrates the 'concrete jungle' of the central business district. The resulting unattractive, grey environment does little to encourage anyone working there to leave the building to meet a friend or go for a walk in their lunch break. If the outdoor air quality looks or smells poor, the fact that invisible indoor air pollution is generally a greater health risk may be overlooked (EPA, 2012). Similarly, if there is nowhere attractive to go and nothing to do close to their workplace, if it is difficult to get from the office to the local park on foot, why would already time-poor individuals look to nature for a solution to rising workplace stress levels?

Stressed executives need environmental supports such as

1 convenient, attractive spaces to connect with nature, close to the office;
2 design options such as open stairways and active transport routes from home to office that facilitate an active healthy lifestyle;
3 convivial, enclosed and open public spaces where colleagues and friends can meet informally, away from the office.

Cultural ecology tells us that space is a manifestation of social relationships. The reverse is also true. Human behaviour adapts and is modified in relation to multiple and variable factors, one of which is environmental design. To promote healthy social integration and connectedness it is important that spatial planning of urban environments is adapted using the three points above to support such behaviours. In cultures where social connections are naturally strong we find salutogenic urban planning and public space given priority. In southern Europe, public squares, pocket parks, streetside cafes, comfortable public seating and adult play areas (boules, chess, and fitness equipment) are a regular part of the urban fabric. Although sometimes criticised for being overstated, environmental design plays a large part in developing and maintaining healthy lifestyles. As a result, design determinism is frequently given as a reason for urban renewal (Franck, 1984).

Using design to incentivise health

With the increasing social costs of depression, heart disease, stroke and cancers impacting ability to meet personal goals and aspirations, we need environmental interventions that promote and support health and well-being. What is often missing from government, corporate health and other well-intentioned programmes is an incentive to get healthy. It is not enough to say 'do this or something bad will happen to you', however much people know it to be true. We live in a world of bonus payments and incentives, so it stands to reason that if we incentivise health and well-being we will improve results. There are a range of motivational tools available. Broadly put, we need to make getting and being outdoors, and using self-propulsion to move about, a more attractive option than the status quo. Internally, some buildings have playful slides for people to move down a floor or two, and open stairways to connect levels within the building. Some municipalities mandate that buildings be set within an attractive, green urban context to attract people outside in their lunch break, or promote walkable cities, with greened walkways and cycleways. Growing numbers of organisations also promote work-from-home options. Wherever the executives are working it is important that their environment is designed to be welcoming, accessible and attractive.

However much we work with incentives for one cultural group, we must be mindful that they may not work for all. For some communities it is from a sense of pride that they choose to drive their children even short distances to school and themselves to work, rather than cycling, walking or taking the bus. For some, it is considered important to show off a high status car as visible proof that they are successful in their career. In the case of such barriers to reception, to it is important to get alongside community leaders, professional associations and discover what the touch points are for them. Only then can we develop effective environments for the health and well-being of all.

How we develop and manage our parks and green space, whether informal, abandoned wild space within the city limits or more formal gardens, determines in large part whether people will access them. If we think back to Chapter 6 where we talked about Giancarlo de Carlo's comment that postmodern architecture has largely forgotten *why* we are working on design and development schemes and instead is focused on how to create symbolic spaces, we remember why we need to advocate for and design to provide gardens and green space that are engaging and accessible within an easy walk of where people work, live and play. To de-stress the stressed executive, to mitigate the costly non-communicable diseases that come from an inactive lifestyle, improve the broader health and well-being of all who work in the city centre and hence promote social cohesion, we need cities where people can interact with nature. We need accessible, attractive gardens, within five minutes' easy walking distance of all parts of the central business district, where people can feel part of the bigger picture, of the ecosystem in which we play a part.

The landscape architect Patrick Geddes believed we should all learn through practical experience, that we should grow fruit and vegetables and also that we should be led to learning through the delight and wonder of the natural world. Unfortunately many cities have been allowed to develop as hard spaces with few opportunities to interact or engage with nature, and little opportunity to grow food. This has important implications for the health, and productivity, of the men and women who work in the city, since experience of the outdoors and green and natural spaces offers vital support for physical, mental and social development (Hansen, 1998; TPL, 2010).

Residential garden design

At home there is a freedom to create the environment we wish to live in. Residential gardens have the opportunity to support the mental and physical health of their owners and families after working hours on a daily basis. As mentioned, executives tend to be time poor but cash rich. They work hard, so if they are to find balance in their lives they need somewhere convenient to relax. A home garden can be developed to support the health and well-being of the busy executive. Easy access from house to outdoors is essential. Whether on a rooftop, balcony or sprawling suburban space, accessible healing gardens can be developed with well-placed planted beds, some comfortable seating and an attractive view.

Residential gardens can offer a quiet space for intimate family al fresco meals. Sensory features within the garden can include mirrors to reflect light (as shown in Figure 8.10) pergolas for shade, varied textural planting and edible fruits and herbs within easy picking reach of the house. To de-stress the senior executive it is important to balance the healing features of the monastic garden style with the client's maintenance objectives and garden size. Spaces can multi-task, especially when space-saving techniques such as espalier[1] and dwarf root stock[2] fruit trees are used.

Public open space

Regardless of the size of the space it is vital that it be welcoming. Social isolation is one of the biggest social determinants of ill health. For the busy executive it is important to have a nature-rich space nearby the office to sit outside to eat lunch, meet friends for coffee. Going for a walk and sitting a moment to watch the birds will potentially attract a like-minded passer-by to pause and chat a moment. Likewise, playing in the local park is a great way to meet other local people and develop friendship networks outside of immediate school and work contacts.

Whether alone, or with friends, exercise in a beautiful natural environment is good for us. People may not recognise the degree to which their lives are compromised by

Figure 8.8
Sensory-rich water
feature and topiary
frames the view in
Hawkes Bay,
New Zealand.

a lack of quality green experience until it is provided. Royalty and captains of industry have, for centuries, enjoyed beautiful gardens and woodland as part of their prescription for success. The Natural England health advisor, Dr W. M. Bird, says:

> Prescriptions for nature experiences may sound a far-fetched treatment for mild to moderate depression, but they are as efficacious and cost effective as anti-depressants. We know the adrenaline rush of fitness junkies, but less strenuous exercise, simply being outside in a beautiful space, can produce powerful endorphins. Anecdotal reports state that: 'Suddenly it is as if a cloud has lifted and I feel invigorated, re energised, renewed.'
>
> (Bird, 2009)

Case study 18: Floyd (not his real name)

He fitted all the criteria of the stressed executive. As chief executive officer of a major organisation, he spent long hours in the office and rarely had time for family or friends. He desired a garden where he could relax at the end of a hard day. Floyd's design brief stated that he wanted 'a chance to reconnect with nature'. In that he actually used those words he was a step ahead of many clients who know they want a garden to relax in but often do not realise exactly what is missing from their lives and so cannot articulate their design brief beyond the basic. We often find sharing photos of resorts and health spas helps to gauge tastes and interests, as while they are in the city many people cannot think beyond the hard lines of the city environment. Floyd had set ideas about how he wanted to connect with nature. He wanted some grass where he could walk barefoot, some trees so he could sit in their shade, something tasty to pick and eat, and a water feature to attract beneficial wildlife. The designer, Shelley, worked with him to define the spaces that would make the most difference. In essence what Floyd was looking for was the monastic garden experience, as described in Chapter 1, there in his suburban West Coast home. Shelley says:

As we worked through the design process I wanted him to have a small pond, but Floyd was adamant he wanted a free standing water feature. It was important I supported Floyd's decision. For a garden to be a healing space its owner cannot look out on it on a daily basis and think 'if only . . .'
I knew I had to let go of part of my design objectives and give Floyd a water feature that met his taste. Too often we are called in by a stressed executive who first time round did not have the time or energy to discuss their requirements fully, who has spent a lot of money on a design only to say 'We hate it, the designer didn't listen. Will you please give us the healing space we need?' Garden designs must not add to the stress of the household! It is important to listen and observe the clients, to get to know their daily routine, likes and dislikes, before handing them a finished design.

Figure 8.9 Accessible flow from indoors to the garden facilitates a healing nature connection, calms and de-stresses in Wairarapa, New Zealand.

Figure 8.10 A shaded courtyard uses a mirror to visually enlarge the space in Wellington, New Zealand.

Indoor public spaces can be modified to benefit public health. Simple additions such as seats near potted trees in railway stations and airports provide an opportunity for social interaction. They also reduce stress, filter airborne pollutants, soften the acoustic and cost very little. Executives who travel frequently cite airports they most like to spend time in as Seoul's Incheon and Singapore's Changi, because they are not only efficient places but they feel good, due to their extensive indoor gardens and outdoor landscaping (WAA, 2013). In the same way as the airports have achieved success, local shops also benefit from seats and trees outdoors. Some local authorities and residents wrongly believe anti-social behaviour will result from such provision. In fact the opposite is true. Geriatric and paediatric mental health show particular benefit. This then spills over into the rest of the community. We can use our position of influence locally to ensure schools, healthcare facilities and homes provide balanced, quiet and active outdoor space, accessible green space, with opportunities to grow, pick and eat foods. We can build resilient communities, but we must design nature in.

Ease of access and the attraction of the space make the difference between 'valued and well-used' and a missed opportunity. When we talk of design for health and well-being we are at the fundamental level of design for mental health. Executives expect to enjoy good health. They also expect good value from management and investment decisions. Proving the worth of cost-effective development of healing gardens is vital to their acceptance. (Chapter 9 provides that business case.)

What else can we do?

When presenting to senior architects, health practitioners, landscape and urban planners, themselves stressed executives, each group generally asks 'How can we assist health and well-being with our small scale, often modest budget projects? Does it actually matter what we do?'

The short answer is yes, human health is impacted one individual at a time by salutogenic design. Through residential and urban design we can develop our towns' and cities' green infrastructure as healing gardens to support wildlife and people. As stated previously, without ecological health there can be no human health. When we create salutogenic environments, whether at home or in the workplace, we create opportunities for healthy, active lifestyles. Why we need to develop robust ecologies amidst sensory-rich spaces in and around people's homes is vital knowledge for today's busy executive.

In Chapter 2 we established the health benefits of green views and nature experience; here we examine how to incorporate them into the daily lives of the stressed executive. We need to provide somewhere to go, to relax, rest and recharge at the end of a busy day. When people work hard in demanding positions they need to balance their lives with easy access to high quality, low maintenance, nature experiences. Figure 8.11 shows a small suburban potager garden. Vegetables and herbs can be grown within the formal structure of the beds, adjacent to the house.

The author of *Green Nature Human Nature* describes the positive effect of nature in our lives. Charles A. Lewis states that in densely populated areas, where plants may be destroyed, neglected or carefully nurtured in discreet oases, green nature brings life to city steel, concrete and asphalt (Lewis, 1996). How many times have we heard of the soulless nature of corporate life? To what exactly do they refer? A sole trader architect working on residential design is a step removed from the life of corporate and civic leaders. Working from a well-lit design studio it can be hard to imagine the artificially lit life of the senior executive who is frequently a slave to the shareholders, a slave to the pursuit of the bonus, a slave to societal expectation. The reality is often different to what we may expect.

To put it in terms we can perhaps imagine, a young landscape architect who interned with us told us of her office in Guangzhou, China:

Figure 8.11
Sensory-rich planting and paving
provides a low-maintenance
green view from indoors, and a
welcoming calm space outdoors
in London.

There are 2,000 people working for the firm, working 12 hour days, 5 days a week. We produce major development plans under pressure, are expected to perform miracles of modern sustainable design and within rapid turn-around times, with penalties if we do not supply. Each designer has a potted plant on their desk. It is ours to nurture and is our link to nature in a high stress work environment. The plants help maintain good air quality, purify the air to allow improved concentration, and also ease the stress levels in the office.

'The plants made the job possible,' said Huiyi. 'Without them it is harder to work, it is less enjoyable and we are not as productive.'

Gardens, even in container form, offer a connection to the earth, a connection to something greater than us, our boss, the annual report. Residential gardens, appropriately designed, as with the bonsai plants in the office setting, provide a touch point to nature, a chance to step back from the maddening world.

Case study 19: William, a senior pharmaceuticals executive

William has worked for many of the world's large corporates. He is married, has two children and travels long-haul regularly. Weekends off are rare and precious things. Like most execs William is short on time. While outwardly glamorous, his life is a mad dash to the airport, the office, home to family, to the board meeting and on again. In his spare time William likes to potter in the garden. He grows some vegetables and fruit. The gardener keeps some flowers within orderly beds in the front garden to provide year round interest. William says his garden, out the back, gives him something to come home to, to watch the progress of the seasons, and helps keep him grounded. His partner is busy with her own career so initially figured she had little time for gardening, but she enjoys keeping the family healthy. Growing fresh fruit and vegetables is a great way to do that. They did some research and decided to have their garden made over, into a predominantly hard-paved space with easily maintainable growing space that they could enjoy whatever time of day or year William was home.

The lower part of the garden was turned into a fenced tennis court, with a choice of nets to enable the court to be used for tennis by the family and their friends, for informal soccer games after school, and basketball as the children got older. The court has sufficient space around it for spectators to be

Figure 8.12 Placement of pots and seating provides a sense of enclosure in this executive home in Wellington, New Zealand.

able to lie out in the sun or sit in the shade, with a small seating area to one side. Climbing plants such as passion fruit, grapes, goji berries and kiwi fruit, are trained along parts of the court fence to provide privacy. All were chosen to do double duty and not only look good but also provide tasty fruit. Apples and pears are espaliered along another section of fence. To one side of the court small raised beds allow for nutrients from a wormery and rich mulch from home composting to be used in productive areas. A range of salad greens, tomatoes and small root crops the family like to eat are grown. With the thick mulch and varieties chosen the garden is easy care and requires no more attention than occasional weeding and some additional water in hot weather. It is all located within twenty steps of the back door of the house. Providing ready access was a key part of the success of the garden. Many people make the mistake of placing fruit and vegetables at the bottom of the garden, where they can easily become out of sight and out of mind. For William and his family it was important to have an active and productive area that looked good, was visible from the kitchen/family end of the house and was physically close by.

When William had a nervous breakdown a couple of years ago it was decided that the garden at home was not enough to alleviate the stress of his executive lifestyle. He needed physical distance as well as mental distance from his work. He bought a small farm, three hours from the city, where he can really get away from it all. They built a house and developed another garden. Here the garden had to be completely low maintenance. Large trees provide the backdrop. Oaks impregnated with truffle fungus have been planted along the drive. Olives for eating and for oil have been planted along the earth banks of the swimming pool terrace. Raised beds of seasonal vegetables allow fresh food to be picked and eaten regardless of when the family manages to get away from the city.

William's children have recently left home so they are contemplating moving to an apartment. He acknowledges that it will be important to have a large terrace or balcony area in their new home where he can sit outside with friends and family and be able to grow a few favourite edible plants to soften the city environment. His depression is a thing of the past and he and his doctors put his recovery down to time spent de-stressing in the garden at home and on the farm.

William was fortunate. He had both the awareness of the influence of environment, as well as the means to create change. In Chapter 1 we talked about monastic gardens feeding mind, body and soul. The spiritual aspect of modern healing gardens is significant. When considering preventative and supportive environments for health and well-being, what we call salutogenic design, it is important to remember we are not necessarily talking of a manicured landscape that requires precise and extensive maintenance, but rather something fundamentally more basic. If stress and depression are a problem for individuals not supported by formal faith, an attractive large tree, perhaps an adult tree house or a simple swing and comfortable space to provide perspective and give some distance from the busy world, a place to observe nature, can be all that is required.

Notes

1   Espalier is a space-saving technique developed in France, by which full size trees are trained and grown flat against a wall or along wires.

Figure 8.13
Attractive outdoor
dining area, set
within sensory-rich
soft landscaping.

Figure 8.14 Timber
decking around tree,
outdoor fireplace and
upholstered seating
create a relaxing, low
maintenance social
environment.

2   Dwarf root stock trees are fully fruiting trees grafted onto a smaller variety such as quince, so at maturity the height of the tree is 2m (6ft) maximum, depending on the variety of root stock.

References

Abbott, A. (2012). Stress and the city: urban decay. *Nature Journal of Science*, 490:162–164.

Bird, W. M. (2009, June). Dr. Health advisor to Natural England. Interviewed by the author.

Defra (2011). *Value of green space report*. London: Defra.

EPA (2012, 10 March). The inside story: a guide to indoor air quality. Retrieved 26 Decemeber 2013, from *United States Environmental Protection Agency*: www.epa.gov/iaq/pubs/insidestory.html

Franck, K. A. (1984). Exorcising the ghost of physical determinism. *Environment and Behaviour*, 16(4):411–435.

Hansen, L. (1998). Where we play and who we are. Retrieved July 2013, from *Illinois Parks and Recreation*: www.illinois-prks.com

Lewis, C. A. (1996). *Green nature human nature: the meaning of plants in our lives*. Urbana and Chicago: University of Illinois Press.

Maller, C., Townsend, M., Pryor, A., Brown, P. and St Leger, L. (2006). Healthy nature healthy people: 'contact with nature' as an upstream health promotion intervention for populations. *Health Promotion International*, 21(1):45–54.

Pearn, J. (2013). A tree house. *Journal of Paediatrics and Child Health*, 49:E361–E364. doi: 10.1111/jpc.12228.

Sesso, H. D., Paffenbarger, R. S. Jr and Lee, I. M. (2000, 29 August). Physical activity and coronary heart disease. *PubMed, National Center for Biotechnology Information*, 102(9):975–980. www.ncbi.nlm.nih.gov/pubmed/10961960

Source Wire (2012, 20 November). British designers to present at Ellerslie International Flower Show, Christchurch, New Zealand, 2013. Retrieved 26 December 2013, from *Source Wire News Distribution*: www.sourcewire.com/news/75480/british-designers-to-present-two-conceptual-gardens-to-ellerslie-international

Sullivan, E. M., Annest, J. L., Feijun, L., Simon, T. R. and Dahlberg, L. L. (2013, 3 May). Suicide among adults aged 35–64 years: United States 1999–2010. Retrieved 3 October 2013, from *CDC*: www.cdc.gov/mmwr/preview/mmwrhtml/mm6217a1.htm?s_cid=mm6217a1_w

TPL (2010). *The economic benefits of Denver's park and recreation system*. Denver, CO: The Trust for Public Land.

Urban Bees (2013). Urban Bees dedicated to urban beekeeping. Retrieved 2013, from *Urban Bees*: www.urbanbees.co.uk

WAA (2013). The world's top 100 airports 2013. Retrieved 2013, from *World Airport Awards*: www.worldairportawards.com/Awards_2013/top100.htm

Zhu, X., Lu, Z., Yu, C-Y., Lee, C. and Mann, G. (2013). Walkable communities: impacts on residents' physical and social health. *World Health Design*, July: 68–75.

CHAPTER 9

Cost–benefits of greening the urban environment through healing gardens

It's all about the money. It shouldn't be. But it is. Unless we quantify the benefits of landscape people only see the costs. Since the economic boom times of the 1980s we have disconnected from the natural environment. In pursuit of active profit we have forgotten and/or largely ignored the passive benefits of nature. Now that the costs of manufactured solutions to health, welfare and education problems have increased to unsustainable levels, people are ready to explore cost-effective alternatives.

It is easy to quantify the potential cost of getting your tax return wrong. The cost could come from tax audits, fines, late payment penalty charges. As a result we are happy to spend $200/hour or more to receive financial advice. It is harder to quantify the cost of getting your city's design wrong because of the vast number of potential flow on impacts and diversity of parties capturing the benefits. If you quantify costs avoided or benefits achieved, for example from

- higher in-bound investment in a city or district,
- increased tourism,
- improved learning results in a school,
- fewer sick days in an office or factory,
- reduced hospital admissions (improved health outcomes),
- increased property occupancy rates and rental returns,

we would see significantly higher levels of investment in greenspace.

(Brown, 2013)

The cost of taking a salutogenic design approach is an investment in the health and well-being of the community and ultimately the sustainability of the local economy. The diverse impacts and flow on effects are potentially huge. When we evaluate the efficacy of healing gardens we must be mindful of those downstream effects.

Imagine a situation where Mum or Dad comes home from work. The day included a walk from the office to the park for lunch under the shade of the deliciously fragrant, big lime trees. They feel relaxed and take time to show an interest in their children and read them a bedtime story. The children's results improve in school. As a result Mum or Dad are less stressed and therefore less likely to overeat, drink to excess, develop diabetes, coronary heart disease or a range of stress-related illnesses. These are quantifiable benefits from the addition of healing green space in the city.

'Cost-effective design and development works with nature – creating community environments that respect, conserve, and enhance natural processes' (Ignatieva, 2008). Aside from leaving land to naturally regenerate, assuming a local seed-source, there will always be a cost associated with actively greening the urban environment. What we aim to show here is that that cost is outweighed by the benefits accrued to the community.

Cost–benefit analysis

In any discussion of the cost–benefits of a salutogenic approach to urban and landscape design, it is important to place a value on healing gardens for their ability to curb and combat the spiralling costs associated with non-communicable disease. It is important to note that the value will change, as for any particular location the economics will vary. This is due to factors such as the size and health of the population, materials and labour costs, and the existing ecology of the area. At this stage we need to develop an understanding of relative costs and benefits.

When talking of comparative costs it is helpful to first appreciate the scope of cost–benefit analysis (CBA) and cost-effectiveness analysis (CEA). From the early 1800s, the focus of CBA was on supply-side efficiencies and the supply of private goods from public projects, such as meeting water quality standards. As people began to shift their emphasis to the benefits of water quality and quantity, including the recreational benefits of water, it created problems for CBA and the analysis was broadened. In the 1970s and 1980s researchers started to recognise non-use benefits of environmental assets. Wildlife, human health, air quality and aesthetics were gradually brought into the CEA/CBA study framework. A green view became a valued asset, as did clean air and viable urban wildlife populations. Formal CBA techniques have been required in support of US environmental legislation since the 1970s (Hanley and Spash, 1993). While it is easy to dismiss economics as someone else's concern, the reality is that without a robust understanding of the advantages that a proposed development will provide, measured against the costs of providing or not providing that asset, we are unlikely to progress with many green infra-structure projects.

The process of analysing a project or a new policy at the planning stage allows us to step back and consider *why* we are embarking on the project. What are we hoping the development will achieve? Will it add value to a community? The environment? The local economy? Will it look good politically? Sometimes the analysis may not be a formal CBA, but rather be an important way to frame a project. By way of example, when a new play strategy for Scotland was recently being developed the working group was asked to consider such questions as:

- What do policy makers hope to gain from it, politically and programmatically?
- How do they expect it will change or support existing play provision/site management/urban design?
- Does 'play provision' extend to active ageing?
- To what extent are the health/education/forestry sectors involved?
- Are there to be any desired outcomes or key performance indicators associated with the strategy?
- What are the cost implications of going ahead versus not going ahead?
- Who do we expect will benefit?

ABOVE: Figure 9.1a Detail of periscope hung from trees.

RIGHT: Figure 9.1b Periscope hung from trees in public space as an interactive art installation encourages nature and social connections.

The questions allow people to think beyond the immediacy of children and play to the benefits to society. As the Defra report, *UK National Ecosystem Assessment: Understanding Nature's Value to Society* (Watson and Albon, 2011) found, the very broad impacts of access to green space include healthy, socially adept and environ- mentally connected children and young people. As part of the evaluation of the project we then balance benefits with an assessment of the costs. When we talk of the costs of healing gardens, play spaces and communal green space we need to consider what makes up those costs: operating expenditure versus capital expenditure.

Operating expenditure versus capital expenditure

Operating expenditure is the cost over the lifetime of the asset to run or maintain it; in this case, the cost of maintaining a garden. Capital expenditure is the cost to develop the asset, including design, build and project-management related expenses. Many projects have limited capital budgets but relatively extensive operating budgets.

'Operating expenditure' versus 'capital expenditure' is a well-known funding dilemma. Project funders can be reluctant to swap budget between cost or profit centres. That statement implies of course that money is available to be reallocated, either from current or future year budgets. Chapter 13 discusses the options when funding is an issue. Sometimes it does not take a reallocation of cost, just a change of mindset.

Case study 20: Rugby House, Wellington city, New Zealand

Surrounded by cafes and small specialist shops, the large, sun-filled public forecourt area in front of the building was a well-used recreational space for office workers during coffee breaks and at lunch time. Raised lawn areas, shade trees, colourful amenity planting, low walls that afforded seating or lying out full stretch in the noonday sun created a haven in the city. The lawn and planter beds required regular tending, and the grass became worn through its popularity. The building's operating expenditure included a budget for forecourt maintenance. When the building was recently renovated, the forecourt area was also subjected to a makeover. The capital expenditure for the project was fixed, as was the thinking of the project team. Unfortunately the former largely soft, green oasis in the city has become a sea of concrete hardscape, surrounded by a palisade of young birch trees. The feeling has changed. Where once low planting beds provided a sense of enclosure while giving an open feel to the space, now the new planting is more like a stark fence, with a subtle 'keep out' subtext. Although now low maintenance, the previously popular public space is hardly used, so benefits accruing to the wider community and to the workers from the building from the (former healing) garden are marginal.

The capital expenditure required to develop a soft salutogenic environment is the same or often less than required for a hard space. The hard style of 'contemporary' design adds further costs downstream as it contributes to the need for pathogenic healthcare. Operating expenditure may be higher for the salutogenic environment, but as with most successful prevention programmes, benefits are widely felt over a long timeframe.

Multi-benefit Model

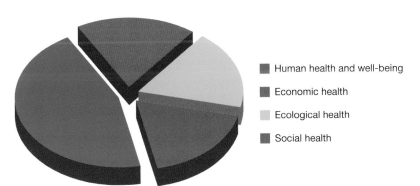

■ Human health and well-being

■ Economic health

■ Ecological health

■ Social health

Figure 9.2 The multi-benefit model shows the relationship between human health and well-being and social, ecological and economic health.

Salutogenic benefits are calculated by an analysis of the state of the community/residents/environment today versus projected likely advances made in the health and well-being of that community in the future. Benefits would expect to be seen in mental health, physical health, school results, and crime. Other 'soft' results, such as perceived stress within the community, are also anticipated.

Example 1. Sprott House care home in New Zealand. The management of the secure dementia unit wanted to reduce costs of care and improve the residents' quality of life. They chose to manage the environment rather than use medication to manage the individual's behaviour. The multi-layered and textured healing garden space we developed also required minor adaptations of the buildings. Sheltered porches were added to access points, allowing doors to be left open in warm weather; flowering and fruiting shade trees were positioned in the courtyard so the glass 'fish bowl' sitting room became a comfortable place without the need for air conditioning; private areas within the gardens allowed residents somewhere to go with visiting family or to retain their dignity when they needed calming. Therapeutic garden spaces allowed residents to engage in meaningful lives, growing fruit and vegetables, and doing small chores such as sweeping, digging and raking. Their success was shared with other residents and visiting friends and family with 'dine out' days in the garden. The predominantly hard paved outdoor space that was there cost almost nothing in terms of operating expenditure budget, but provided little benefit either. The new gardens will be maintained by residents, the occupational therapists, and family and friends, with annual donations of seasonal plants secured through a local corporate social responsibility programme. Cost: ~$120,000. Benefit expected: $50,000 year on year savings.

Example 2. In 2012 we were invited to develop healing gardens for a kindergarten in Chicago. The design brief was a bit different in that our design was required to break three generations out of a cycle of drugs and violence. The gardens had to be a place where the children could relax and feel safe, would connect with nature and develop essential social skills. The space also had to provide an informal educational opportunity for parents and carers. The local community lived in bleak housing dominated by hardscapes, and had almost completely disconnected from nature. With minimal funding, the preschool needed to get maximum value from its investment. With their vision for a healing garden they were well placed to start with the young and allow the ripple effect to spread through the community, one family group at a time. With our design, given heightened levels of stress within the community, it was important to create a feeling of safety. The outside area was securely fenced but to ensure the feeling was of sanctuary and not one of imprisonment, the boundary was obscured by bio-diverse planting. When developing the interior of the leafy oasis, we decided to use low edible shrubs such as currants and clear stemmed trees to provide sight lines across the garden. Winding paths and engaging spaces such as sand boxes, water play, scented and colourful planting prompted a sense of discovery. Therapeutic gardens to the front of the centre allow adult community members to come into the space for their own education and healing, and to learn to grow and harvest quality food, with classes in literacy and cooking amongst other life skills. It is too early to tell if the scheme will be a long term success, but measureable benefits are seen in the addition to urban green space that has been

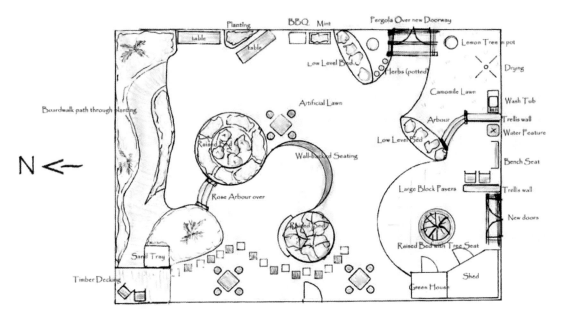

Greenstone Design - Landscape for health & well being
January 2013
Scale 1:75 @ A3 Revised CONCEPT PLAN
Title: Sprott House Sensory Garden

welcomed by the local bird population. Butterflies are attracted to summer flower beds, and human health and well-being is improving, seen in reduced child absence days, and reduced violence in the playground. Cost: ~$30,000. Benefit: ongoing.

Example 3. We were contacted by a charity running a residential school for disabled children in Ghana who required a stimulating outdoor classroom. Superstitions still hold power in rural communities and it is believed by many villagers that physical and mental disability is caused by being possessed by demons. This has led to problems for the charity, as no one has wanted the school in their village in case demons escaped and infected healthy people. The school takes in young children to adolescents and teaches them life skills so they can live independently one day. The emphasis is on individual dignity and building the children up to allow and enable them to live meaningful lives. Our design had to showcase and celebrate the success of the therapeutic programme such that disability was demystified. It also had to protect vulnerable children from interference from the villagers. An enabling, salutogenic design approach was important to prevent these children from being cast out from society on a permanent basis. The land was divided into zones, with a public area and a private area. In essence we needed to create two outdoor classrooms such that as their skills and confidence progressed the students could work in the public classroom where passing villagers could observe from a distance. We added companion planting to attract birds and beneficial insects, while deterring pests, trees, water and sand play to ensure that the outdoor classroom stimulated the children's biophilic senses. The sensory classroom was designed around a minimal budget using local and recycled materials to boost the children's cognitive function,

Figure 9.3 Concept sketch of dementia garden for Sprott House, a secure dementia unit. Designed to reduce costs of care through reduced need for medication, as a supportive space for therapeutic horticulture programmes, the design replicates a home garden, with looping paths, gentle contouring, accessible growing areas, abundant wildlife-attractive planting, colourful walls and raised beds to create privacy for individuals and family groups. Designed by Greenstone Design New Zealand.

improve mood and memory and make them receptive to new experiences. Secure, richly planted, playful sensory gardens provided a changing, stimulating environment where children could play, test their boundaries, explore and discover. The children were kept safe while the project respected local beliefs and acknowledged the perceived need for security for villagers. Cost: ~£20,000. Benefit: incalculable.

Example 4. The city of Berlin, Germany, in the aftermath of reunification was broken socially. It was decided that an urban greening response would be the most cost-effective way to tackle broad, interlinked environmental, social and economic issues. Abundant street and neighbourhood tree plantings, green (living) walls, natural playgrounds, cycleways, parklands in disused railway yards, city farms, community gardens and edible plantings within public spaces were all employed as part of the solution. The result is the greenest city in Europe, with a booming tourist industry, healthy children, high employment, a thriving creative and artistic sector, and safe public spaces that are well used throughout the week. The investment cost has not been quantified against benefits derived across health, education, welfare and business sectors, but the salutogenic results are evident on every street corner. Cost: ~€100 million. Benefits: many millions more.

Example 5. Raglan, a social (public) housing provider in Bournemouth, England, had frequent problems with vandalism and anti-social behaviour. When the buildings were renovated management decided to tackle the situation outdoors. We were asked to work with the residents to develop a landscape treatment that would

Figure 9.4 Cost-effective natural play space in Berlin, Germany. As trees and shrubs grow, the play value of the area is enhanced with minimal maintenance required.

become the healing focus for the building's community. Co-design[1] is a powerful way to ensure community buy-in of a development. To be successful it requires an unhurried attitude such that all viewpoints can be aired and considered. The land to the rear of the site sloped down to a degraded waterway. Immediately adjacent to the buildings was a mix of sunny, flat land and areas shaded by the buildings. The project involved working with all stakeholders, in this case the residents, schools, the local authorities and the Environment Agency. It was important for everybody to understand the issues and potential of the project. The design needed to soften the day-to-day living environment of the residents, and create a healing experience through direct connection with nature. It was important to restore the stream as a biophilic element so that it became both a haven for wildlife and a safe, playable amenity feature. The children had swimming lessons in school so learnt to respect and not to fear the water and how to be safe around it. Social workers and community play workers and school field trips to the stream taught them what lived there and what to look for in times of drought and flood, and gave the children and adolescents a connection with nature, knowledge and experience they could share with their community. Natural play spaces were developed around communal areas with espaliered fruit trees trained up sunny walls to provide fresh food. Shade trees and culturally relevant planting beds of edibles make the communal space engaging and attractive, year round. Older residents are made comfortable to come outside to sit in the sun, potter in the gardens, chat with neighbours and watch the children play. When salutogenic design is effective vandalism and anti-social behaviour decrease as stress levels drop, the environment is valued, and residents have a heightened sense of self-worth. This carries over into the wider community of schools and the local town. The capital costs for a project such as this are relatively small. Ongoing operating costs are likewise small from the housing manager's point of view. Benefits to the broader community fall across health, education and welfare budgets. Cost: ~£100,000. Benefit: ongoing.

When we talk about cost–benefits of greening our cities, we must consider the cost–benefits of including the green space against reducing or maintaining current levels of healing spaces. Levels of stress and depression in the community are often poorly understood and at best, underestimated. Stress and stress-related illnesses, burnout syndrome, insomnia and fatigue, depression, feelings of panic, etc., take a growing part of the budget for medical services across many cultures. Costs have increased dramatically. Their impact has been evaluated for the effect on society through workplace productivity, lifestyle choices (as relating to the incidence of obesity, rickets, diabetes, heart and lung disease, and cancers) and educational impacts (Stokols, 1992). Some research has also been done on the effect of depression on early onset dementias (Jorm, 2000). Kaplan's restorative environments theory (Kaplan, 1983) has been tested and supported by further research. A Swedish study found statistically significant relationships between the use of urban open green spaces and self-reported experiences of stress – regardless of the informant's age, sex and socio-economic status. The results suggest that the more often a person visits healing urban green spaces, the less often they will report stress-related illnesses. The same pattern is shown when time spent per week in urban open green spaces is measured (Stigsdotter and Grahn, 2003). We know the current costs of residential care and pharmaceutical and medical health treatments for these conditions. We know the cost of incarcerating criminals. We know the cost to support children with additional needs in school. With rising levels of stress, the proportion of people in our communities requiring costly support is increasing, and rapidly. Imagine the scenario, the cost to society, if we do nothing to alleviate that pressure.

Cost-effectiveness analysis considers the overall worth of a development. To achieve maximum value, complex social and environmental issues are best addressed using a multi-disciplinary design approach. Design inquiry is increasingly being used to create intentional system changes in society and culture. Intellectually the scope of design has grown from a narrow focus on the function and aesthetics of a space towards an ecosystems services approach.

'Systems thinking focuses on understanding the relationships between constituent elements and the resulting qualities of an emergent whole as it interacts in any given situation with larger contexts and environments' (Salustri, 2010). Integrated systems thinking allows us to approach design challenges from a joined-up thinking perspective, to provide optimum cost effectiveness.

Cost-effectiveness analysis also measures the benefits in terms of green infrastructure gains. As mentioned in Chapter 4, low impact urban design and development (LIUDD) is a sustainable living concept that promotes urban sustainability and health through effective management of stormwater, waste, energy, transport and ecosystem services. Greening the urban environment through ecological planting is thus a vital aid to the health and well-being of ecosystems and citizens. As such any measurement of the total benefit of healing gardens requires an awareness of ecological as well as cultural issues and factors.

To redress the domination of artificial human environments over natural systems, and a lack of awareness and understanding of the significance of natural ecosystems and ecosystem services within urban environments, especially for human well-being, we need to add green infrastructure, more healing green space. Meurk states in the *Urban Greening Manual: How to Put Nature into Our Neighbourhoods*, that

> Biodiversity or nature heritage contributes to an enduring sense of place or identity – a key element of nationhood. City-dwellers must see nature where they live if the highly threatened habitats and species of lowlands and coasts are to become identified with, and thereby secure. We hope here to demonstrate the surprising potential of, and methods for, enhancing natural biodiversity in urban environments. Natural heritage may then rightly share the stage with valid cultural layers.
>
> (Ignatieva et al., 2008)

Gathering the evidence for evidence-based design: making a case that guarantees healing gardens are included in the final scheme

In previous chapters we have discussed how strained health, education and welfare budgets are protected when public mental health is strong and physical health is supported and maintained through a healthy, active, lifestyle. However, while increasing numbers of health, disability, housing and education professionals recognise the potential of greening the urban environment, at the same time financially constrained developers and contractors seek to stretch their profit margins in every possible way. Although design schemes may be approved through the planning process on account of the included environmental provision, these same design elements are often later removed from the final development as 'the (capital) budget has overrun and we just cannot afford the gardens/playground/varied planting at this time'. In these instances the landscape or environmental components of the scheme are seen as optional, nice-to-have-if-we-can-afford-it design features. As integral to effecting societal change, I would argue that we cannot afford not to have them (Haas, 2012).

Through this text we wish to show that not only are gardens an essential part of the urban fabric, they are also cost effective. To invest in green space is to invest in the social, environmental and economic health of the community. However, all landscape interventions are not created equal. 'Social issues are too often ignored or misunderstood by architects, landscape architects, developers, and urban planners', according to Dr Denese Neu: 'failures with green space, redevelopment of blighted areas, etc. are due to a "fix the space, fix the people mentality"' (Neu, 2013). Healing garden interventions need to be mindful of the reasons why they are being created to ensure best practice outcomes.

As previously stated, healing gardens can take many forms. In Chapter 4 we talked about the value of street trees. Roadside plantings in Portland, Oregon, USA add almost ten times more to home values than the cost of maintaining the trees – $45 million compared with $4.6 million (Thomas, 2010). People enjoy living in the

Figure 9.5
Opportunistic play on the street in Beijing, China. Urban design can facilitate healthy, casual outdoor social opportunities through attention to space provision within residential neighbourhoods.

Source: Sue Dutton.

area, and are attracted by the green views to the front of their homes. Benefits to the mental and physical health of the residents derived from the trees have not yet been calculated in monetary terms. No longitudinal study has been made by the real estate agents who noted the increased property values. But as with earlier examples, quantifiable benefits accrue from the 'daily dose' of nature. The cost is borne by the City, but the benefits come back directly in increased tax income, as well as indirectly through reduced costs. It is fair to say that when we green the urban environment we gain far more than we spend.

The value proposition also comes from using healing landscapes as effective early management of major threats to public health. Design inquiry is increasingly being adopted in a growing number of disciplines as a path toward innovative progress on real issues. Sustainable urban planners and designers have the ability to address the top six health concerns of deprivation, obesity, low physical activity, poor mental and physical health and climate change through quality experiences of nature (Marmot, 2003).

A salutogenic perspective can be a marketing tool for developments, offering real benefit to investors. Through salutogenic landscape design we aim to enhance the environment and thereby provide an ambulance at the top of the cliff. To continue the analogy, if we wait for someone to fall, the chances are that their injuries will impact their family, their ability to work, their employer and the wider community. It will cost all of these people financially and emotionally. If we move away from short term thinking to take a broader perspective it becomes apparent that we can easily, and inexpensively, make a landscape-led difference in our communities.

Developing the business case

When it all comes down to the money it is important to be able to quantify costs and benefits. A business case is a balanced examination of the health-in-all-policies approach to green space development. Healing gardens are of interest to corporates looking to improve staff health and output efficiency, private housing and eco-resort developers in need of a marketing edge, health and education officials looking to reduce costs of service delivery. It is relatively easy to cite the evidence and detail the benefits of biophilic design. However, it is relatively difficult to develop the business case for healing gardens in that the benefits are not generally borne by the same people who pay the cost of developing the gardens. We need to calculate social costs and social benefits, in addition to the usual capital budgets. Whole-of-life business models are a useful analogy.

Example: cost–benefits to healthcare environments

In reviewing the literature on the benefits of creating biophilic urban centres and using environmental design both as an early intervention and to prevent lifestyle-related diseases, I believe it is important we promote and use our expertise. As science recognises the value of the natural environment and in particular a nature connection, we will see increasing need for design, guidance, appraisal and stakeholder engagement to ensure cost-effective, sustainable environmental design. Salutogenic design that promotes health and well-being across all sectors of society,

Case study 21: new pediatric hospital, Helsinki, Finland

In July 2013 I interviewed the director of paediatric rheumatology at the Helsinki University Hospital. He was on the team to design the new children's hospital, which would be a specialist children's hospital with 95 per cent of the patients under the age of 1 year. A senior practitioner, Dr Lahdrenne, was also interested in exploring how environmental design could achieve cost savings for the hospital. We discussed the importance of nature, healing environments and play.

Q   *What is the importance of play in the hospital setting?*
A   Play as an opportunity to explore and manipulate the environment is vital for children of all ages, even babies. In my job I stick needles into children's joints. It is less expensive for the hospital if I do not use anaesthetics. The patient recovers from the procedure faster, which again means less costly hospital stays. In order to be able to safely stick a needle into a baby or young child it is important to be in a playful environment. When approached in the correct manner and in an appropriately designed environment, you can do almost anything with the child.

Q   *What is the essence of a successful work environment for you?*
A   One where nature is accessible or at least visible from the treatment space. Gardens can be a wonderfully healing addition to a healthcare setting. Children respond to nature and are calmed by it.

Q   *When designing the new children's hospital what will you aim to achieve from the environment?*
A   We need to provide a cost-effective healthcare service. Budgets are shrinking so we need to get maximum benefit from every dollar spent. By integrating our operating and capital expenditure budgets we save overall. We will be aiming to have accessible play gardens adjacent to every treatment room. In that way our operating costs will be reduced, and by a greater amount than what we will spend on capital expenditures up front.

(Lahdrenne, 2013)

increases in-bound investment and improves the livability of our cities, is infinitely valuable.

Cost-effective landscape treatments, soft landscapes that balance the harsh modern architectural aesthetic, are effective for their impact on the triple bottom line: society, the economy and the environment all benefit. Healing gardens have an important role to play to safeguard the sustainable future of our towns and cities. Vulnerable children, adults struggling to support their families and careers, the elderly and people living with disability, and the stressed executives – all cost the healthcare system. The introduction of healing gardens across the public realm offers cost–benefits across all groups, such that the accumulated benefits outweigh the costs.

To fully identify the multiple and diverse benefits of healing, sensory and thera-peutic gardens will take several longitudinal studies, set within a multi-disciplinary postgraduate research programme. It will also take a project overseer who can imagine the potential such that the breadth or scope of the study fully encompasses that potential. For now we can only make the case as strongly as possible and leave it to the funders to determine whether we were sufficiently convincing.

However much we know landscape in general and healing gardens in particular to be a useful tool, we must acknowledge that complete cost–benefit data sets have not yet been gathered. Longitudinal studies are required to show what we know from short term qualitative and quantitative studies. For now it is important to share what we do know.

Note

1   Co-design refers to the methodology whereby the designer works directly with the stakeholders to ensure they are an active part of the design stage.

References

Brown, C. (2013, 9 October). MBA, CA, AICS, BCA. Interviewed by the author.
Haas, T. (2012). *Sustainable urbanism and beyond*. New York: Rizzoli Interntional Publications.
Hanley, N. and Spash, C. (1993). *Cost–benefit analysis and the environment*. Cheltenham and Northampton, MA: Edward Elgar.
Ignatieva, M. E. (2008). *How to put nature into our neighbourhoods*. Lincoln, New Zealand: Manaaki Whenua Press/Landcare Research.
Ignatieva, M. E., Meurk, C., van Roon, M., Simcock, R. and Stewart, G. (2008). *Urban greening manual: how to put nature into our neighbourhoods – application of low impact urban design and development (LIUDD) principles, with a biodiversity focus, for New Zealand developers and homeowners*. Lincoln, New Zealand: Landcare Research New Zealand Ltd/Manaaki Whenua Press .
Jorm, A. (2000). Is depression a risk factor for dementia or cognitive decline? *Journal of Gerontology*, 46:219–227.
Kaplan, S. (1983). A model of person–environment compatibility. *Environment and Behaviour*, 15(3):311–332.
Lahdrenne, P., Dr. (2013, 12 July). Interviewed by the author.
Marmot, R. W. (2003). *Social determinants of health: the solid facts*. Copenhagen: WHO Europe Centre for Urban Health.
Neu, D. (2013). Ph.D. Letter to the author.
Salustri, F. (2010). Special issue on integrating systems thinking and design action. *International Journal of Design*, October. http://designcalls.wordpress.com/2010/03/01/intl-j-of-design-special-issue-on-integrating-systems-thinking-and-design-action/
Stigsdotter, U. A. and Grahn, P. (2003). Landscape planning and stress. *Urban Forestry and Urban Greening*, 2(1):1–18.
Stokols, D. (1992). Establishing and maintaining healthy environments: towards a social ecology of health promotion. *Journal of the American Psychological Association*, 47(1):6–22.
Thomas, L. (2010). Calculating the green in green: what's an urban tree worth? *Science Findings*, September: 1–4.
Watson, R. and Albon, S. (2011). *UK National Ecosystem Assessment: Understanding Nature's Value to Society*. Report. Retrieved December 2013, from Defra archive: www.csd.org.uk/uploadedfiles/files/value_of_green_space_report.pdf

PART III

DESIGNING HEALING GARDENS USING AN INCLUSIVE, SALUTOGENIC APPROACH

CHAPTER 10

The salutogenic design process

A design process that aims to achieve cost-effective health and well-being outcomes requires an in-depth engagement between client, stakeholders and design team. It is slow paced and considered, offering a sustainable solution. In project terms the design component can be more expensive but robust early design-phase work results in overall savings in project build and ongoing maintenance costs.

As stated previously, there can be no human health and well-being without ecological health. The two are intrinsically linked. A salutogenic design process is mindful of this. Social, economic and environmental values are upheld throughout the life of the project, offering sustainability as a respected consequence. The development of healing gardens thus results from a collaborative process based both on evidence derived from study of previous successful developments and deep community consultation.

Developing the design brief

Landscape and urban design for health and well-being is a new concept for many people. Therefore designers may need to be able to educate the client and actively work with them to develop the design brief. Evidence-based design requires examination not only of what people have done before but why they have done it. To provide landscape-led, cost-effective health promotion interventions across our towns and cities we need to know the client's motivations for design. To understand their motivations requires a close relationship with clients and stakeholders. An informed design brief will flow from this connection.

An outcomes-focused approach promotes a robust dialogue between funder and stakeholders. Less green nature means reduced mental well-being, or at least less opportunity to recover from mental stress (Pretty et al., 2005). As Ambra Burls notes in her paper 'People and green spaces: promoting public health and mental well-being through ecotherapy', this evidence does not, however, seem to have greatly influenced town and country planners; nor has it predisposed the establishment of public health policies that are inclusive of nature (Burls, 2007). Inclusive design needs to welcome and support everyone, regardless of ability, culture, age, sex, or religion. If the planned outcome is a healthy, resilient community, this will inform the specific design elements appropriate to that development.

Integrated design thinking affords a collaborative approach. When used in conjunction with a formal Health Impact Assessment, the potential health impacts of a design can be measured as a ripple effect through a community. Human centred design (HCD) allows designers to get away from ego and self-expression and recall why we are designing and hence who we are designing for – the people, the individual users. We don't use empathy or concept mapping but rather map the effect of, for example, an integrated healthcare facility set within walking and cycling routes. The map extends to an inclusive, outdoor communal space with edible healing gardens and natural play, and indoor parenting, budgeting and other courses as locally relevant. Using the same example, this is mapped as occurring alongside nutrition and health checks on school and work attendance, anti-social behaviour, incidence of self-reported stress, obesity, STDs and other preventable lifestyle-related diseases.

The design brief needs to identify and address principle health concerns. It is important that both client and designer are aware of the potential for flow-on effects from the development into the wider community. For example, although the design may provide for young children, the needs of their parents and carers must be considered equally in order for the children to be able to access the area. Flexible, inclusive spaces therefore often provide best value for money.

As we have seen in previous chapters, social isolation kills. If a client asks for a landscape intervention that will 'design out' anti-social behaviour, stress or depression we need to know how to go about that. While salutogenic designs promote an active healthy lifestyle, abundant places to stop, sit and talk are equally important. The brief needs to take note of this. For example, seating options for people using walking frames, mobility scooters, wheelchairs and unassisted walkers must be provided, and arranged in such a way as to facilitate conversation between 2–4 people. To get around the problem of deciding how many seats to provide and how to best arrange them, some cities such as Paris and Berlin have successfully trialled the use of moveable lightweight garden chairs in public space. In areas where such free standing chairs have been offered there has been little theft as the community values the opportunity to create its own space. Small groups of friends and acquaintances can create their own seating groups, allowing for more or less people to congregate within a space. Areas set aside for seating have been bordered by biodiverse planting, to provide a sensory-rich environment with shade, scent and flowers and to delineate the space.

For young parents   we can break down social isolation and boost parenting skills through informal networking, by providing space to meet casually, where their children are safe. To develop an effective brief we need to be able to talk with the stakeholders. These traditionally hard-to-reach groups do not go to parenting classes or post-natal exercise groups, so we need to go to wherever they go.

Indigenous, refugee, immigrant and other minority communities   are frequently under stress and their health, well-being and social and educational outcomes of their children can suffer as a result. To mitigate this we can provide gardens and green space for these groups in schools, social housing and communal areas that reference their traditional customs, home country, or cultural norms. Where culturally men and women are separated or chaperoned it is important to provide space with planting as privacy screening. While needing to be appropriate for the local area, planting can be specified to provide familiar fruit, such as fig trees for Middle Eastern people, banana palms for Polynesian, African and Southeast Asian people (and yes, varieties of bananas now grow in areas of the previously cool climates of New Zealand, the UK and northern states of the USA). In developing the brief it is vital that before planting choices are made community engagement encourages co-design of the space, so the people 'own' their public space.

Disabled members of the community and especially those living with mental health issues   require spaces that allow them to choose whether to actively engage or to remain separate from and observe the busy goings-on around them. To enable this choice we need to think in terms of providing secondary paths and some adjacent quiet, smaller seating spaces. Connected calm spaces ringed with planting offer a soft reprieve for those stressed by close contact.

Tree seats tend to look outwards from the tree. When we place the seats to the outer edge of the space, looking inwards to a specimen tree, we offer a different perspective. Wherever we place seating, so that it feels secure we need to ensure it has a 'back'. That 'back' can be a planted screen or a solid wall. For veterans and others suffering post-traumatic stress, solid seat backs and clear sight lines forwards offer a sense of safety and security, allowing the individual to relax and de-stress. As always it pays to put yourself into the place of the people you are designing for. By knowing your client, the individual people who make up the community, you will be better placed to design an effective environment.

Understanding the brief – what do clients really mean when they ask for a healing, sensory or therapeutic garden?

With the recent political upsurge in interest in the rising cost of obesity, funds have been made available for projects to promote healthy active lifestyles. In the UK, schools and playgrounds have had makeovers. In the USA the grey to green, asphalt to ecosytems movement is gaining ground as schools notice that students are less sociable, less willing to negotiate and are more aggressive in their play. Around the world a lot of play equipment has been sold but there have been questionable gains in healing green space as rubber play matting, prescriptive play items and steel fencing predominate. For too long designers and developers have been prepared to 'take the money and not ask questions'. At the same time clients have been unaware of the harm their decisions have perpetuated.

I believe we have a responsibility to use resources wisely, including and especially public money. A comprehensive understanding of the design brief is essential to ensure the cost effectiveness of a development. In order to gain maximum benefit from the design process we need to ask and answer as many questions as possible. In this way we will ensure we create environments that genuinely enhance human health and well-being.

As we start to interpret a brief we need to look at wider community issues, environmental issues, and local economic issues. When we look at the big picture we can better gauge where our project sits within that broad framework. In that way we are able to provide a truly cost-efficient solution for our client. We can no longer afford to work and think in isolation. Each project we work on has implications for the wider community, public health, the environment and the economy. When we recognise and communicate the true potential of landscape the significance of the project increases. Collaborative relationships within the project fuel engagement and enthusiasm. With a healing garden project everyone involved benefits.

When people ask for a healing, sensory or therapeutic garden they may initially be just 'ticking a box'. Increasingly, authorities are requiring green space to be included into the built environment. This is our opportunity to sell the benefits of a salutogenic design approach.

Design for health and well-being can be emotional. Previously dispassionate professionals can become passionately involved as they recognise themselves, a grandparent, friend or neighbour in the needs mix. Having a personal interest in the design outcome can be a good thing. Design is built around a fashion-based industry so it is easy to forget the personal focus of the healing function of the space we are creating.

When people ask for a healing garden they will likely be imagining a space with calming colours and attractively scented blooms. Rose arbours are favoured as providing height in the garden, as well as offering a sense of mystery as the view is partially shielded by the structure and the planting. Instantly we need to be thinking in terms of creating a personal space, a 'garden' rather than a wide landscape. A large scale landscape can be made up of smaller gardens linked together. The concept of the 'garden room' works well in this setting. The healing function of the space must be remembered, however, so that fashion and ego are not allowed to take over.

If people ask for a sensory garden it is likely they envisage sound, smell and touch, the classic garden-for-the-blind. Rustling grasses, smelly and spiky gardens are traditionally created with flat beds of lavender interspersed with clumps of grasses. Given our senses are more complex, and broad sensory impairment affects many more people today, a good sensory garden will include contouring for height and views, light and shade, warm and cool, light and dark, taste, and texture underfoot as well as at hand and eye height. A good sensory garden attracts wildlife. Birds, butterflies, bees and other beneficial insects create movement and sound, and add seasonal variation. Outdoor music, with chimes, drums and resonating spaces, can also be included.

Clients generally seek therapeutic gardens in healthcare settings. Raised beds for ease of access for those of limited mobility are traditionally seen as the mainstay of a therapeutic garden space. A good therapy garden will offer, in addition to accessible raised beds, open space for outdoor group activities such as tai chi and dance classes. It will also offer multiple places of protection. Our biophilic natures are enhanced when we are feeling-impaired, so we seek spaces that protect our backs and offer a safe vantage point or outlook over the surrounding area. Groups offer strength and safety in numbers, so communal spaces are also important.

We know that when we adopt salutogenic design principles the resulting spaces become a synthesis of each of the healing, sensory and therapeutic garden typologies. In this text, what we call a healing garden is in fact a green space that includes all three aspects to a greater or lesser degree. Regardless of definitions, it is important to use both client and funder's ideas as a catalyst for discussion around the broad scope of the project before moving on to discuss design concepts. With understanding of the public and individual health and well-being potential of green space, we can advise the client to make informed budget decisions.

Case study 22: the importance of an informed brief

A few years ago we had project at a school in London. They came to us wanting a natural play garden as they had a falling roll and desired a point of difference for their school. They had funds allocated for the project that needed to be spent by the end of the financial year, so were in a hurry to get started. We had just two weeks to work with the staff and children to gather their ideas for what they would like to do in the outdoor space, and get a feel for the local environment, numbers and preferred activities, where the sun rose and set. We worked overtime, produced a design concept, the client loved it, the project was costed and tenders were called to build the garden. By now six weeks had passed, with regular client meetings throughout that time. During that period, as the client became more educated as to the possibilities, they started to input little extras into the scheme.

Figure 10.1
This award-winning natural play garden in London offers edible planting, shade trees and multiple opportunities to explore, experiment, create and destroy, engage with nature, pretend, imagine and relate with others. Designed by Greenstone Design UK.

Figure 10.2
Textured paths with recycled railway sleepers make an interesting bike track for these preschool children. Designed by Greenstone Design UK.

As work began on site, additions continued to flood in. Informal discussions during site visits finally provided the opportunity to chat with the teachers we had lacked access to during the rushed formal design phase. As the staff's knowledge grew, so did their enthusiasm. Previously reluctant participants became firm supporters of the playground project. Some of the staff had thought that spending hard won funding on the outdoor space was a frippery, a waste of time and time and money given the long list of things they were short of indoors. What they hadn't realised was the effect we could make on educational and social outcomes indoors by developing the outdoor space. The teachers had not known, for example, that we could boost the children's writing skills by working on motor planning skills, using hand/eye coordination development opportunities with hand-over-hand activities on ladders in the playground. More items were added to the must-have list. Unfortunately, given the by now advanced stage of the build, many of the new ideas required expensive alterations to the existing works. The budget was stretched, time scales were strained. The atmosphere on site became tense and relations with contractors terse.

Ultimately an award-winning play garden was developed (described by the assessors RoSPA as amongst the best they had seen) but it took six months longer than scheduled and the civil engineering contractors who won the initial tender proved inadequate for the varied soft landscape-led scheme. There were many unnecessary sleepless nights, both for the school and our design team. The budget overran by £100,000. It was a classic example of a publicly funded project where people had the best intentions but ultimately public money was wasted.

The cost and time overruns were avoidable. We learnt that we need to stand firm before the client, even when facing funding deadlines. There are ways of securing time-critical funding that do not involve design commitments. We need to explain that good, sustainable design cannot be rushed. The client came to us wanting a natural play space that would make their centre stand out from the rest. They

Figure 10.3
School garden
food-growing area.
Designed by
Greenstone Design
UK.

Figure 10.4
Playable insect
sculpture affords
seating, balancing
and an elevated
viewpoint. Designed
by Greenstone
Design UK.

were operating in an area of social and financial hardship, where cultural and language barriers were a common cause of lack of uptake of educational, parenting and health-related initiatives. Their project was for a community in need as much as children in need.

For the full salutogenic potential of a project to be realised it takes time for everyone to be involved and input their ideas, feel valued and gain a sense of ownership of the scheme. It takes time to educate the stakeholders as to the full potential of the site, and of the overall development's likely impact on the wider community. Designers also learn from their clients. The biggest lesson is that good things take time. In a culture of instant gratification, that can be hard for both sides to understand.

Figure 10.5
Natural play requires natural elements. Here a tree house, boulders, logs, bark chip surfacing and 'jungle' style planting will mature to create an adventurous play zone in north London. Designed by Greenstone Design UK.

Figure 10.6
Community outreach programmes benefit from performance space within a garden. This school opens on weekends to the community to offer art, gardening, parenting and literacy as part of a community health initiative. North Islington, London. Designed by Greenstone Design UK.

Interpreting the brief

Budget will always feature in our response. While designers by nature like to design individual elements for each development, we can do a lot with off-the-shelf items and appropriate planting. Classic elements such as Lutyens-style bench seats became classics for good reason. Their rounded form, sculptural lines, and warm-to-the-touch timber make ideal accessories in a healing garden. Their materials neither radiate nor absorb heat excessively in the sun, making them useful year round. Their ability to take occasional use padding is an added bonus. When budget is tight why waste time and money recreating something readily available?

As with any design-based project, the client brief is the starting point. However, although clients may know what they think they want, as a salutogenic approach is new to many people we often find we need to educate the client and/or third party funders as to the project's full potential before we can reliably take their brief.

Although in an ideal world clients would come to us requesting a healing garden, reality says that we live and work in a competitive environment. We are more likely to be tendering for a low-cost amenity edge to a building project than we are likely to be invited to show our real talents. In this case careful interpretation of the brief and client education is vital. With a landscape-led intervention we frequently justify the expense of the healing garden development by contrasting the cost of traditional management of a health, justice or education problem, against the positive ripple effect of social costs out across a community of the garden. The cost of developing a utilitarian landscape may be small but the benefits are often little more than a short term aesthetic. By taking a salutogenic approach, we can offer health, social, economic and environmental benefits. Given that we can create the experience by creating the environment, we offer a cost-effective preventative and early treatment option.

Today community health concerns are increasingly centred on chronic lifestyle-related disease and safety. To counter this, public health practitioners, architects and city planners must collaborate with landscape specialists. Decisions civic leaders have made regarding land use, community design and transportation have affected local

Figure 10.7 The rounded form of the classic Lutyens bench seat is at once welcoming and comfortable. Such 'off the shelf' items are relatively inexpensive, durable and offer superior salutogenic qualities over contemporary, backless concrete and steel forms.

air quality, water quality and supply, traffic safety, physical activity, mental health, social interactions, and exposure to contaminated industrial sites (i.e. brownfields). Architects and engineers have made decisions affecting indoor air quality. These decisions are linked to some of the most intractable challenges of our time, including adult and childhood obesity, cancer, respiratory problems, inactive lifestyles, rapidly rising rates of depression and climate change.

> In the last several years, a growing body of scientific evidence has indicated that the air within homes and other buildings can be more seriously polluted than the outdoor air *in even the largest and most industrialized cities*. Other research indicates that people spend approximately 90 percent of their time indoors. Thus, for many people, the risks to health may be greater due to exposure to air pollution indoors than outdoors.
>
> (EPA, 2012)

As a way to mitigate the effects and impact of poor indoor air quality we need to work with communities to (a) design attractive environments that encourage people to spend more time outdoors, and (b) bring healing gardens to the people, wherever they may be. Whether at work, at school, in care, at home in high rise apartment blocks or detached family homes, healing green space can offer food for the mind, body and soul. This salutogenic advantage is only available to us, however, if the design elements are in balance. In Guangzhou, China, parks include open

Figure 10.8 Public space designed and managed to facilitate health and well-being, Guangzhou, China.

Source: Huiyi Liu.

space where people can come together spontaneously to exercise and play games. Practical paving is balanced by lush planting. The area is made more accessible by being close to toilet facilities and a cafe with covered seating options.

Consultation and community engagement

Design for health and well-being relies on community involvement. Perhaps more than any other style of design, salutogenic design requires effective engagement with all stakeholders. Workshops with focus groups may be time efficient but are often miss the valuable input of the disengaged. When we reach out to listen to the disgruntled and disenfranchised we can often address their needs within the scheme in a manner that produces a better result overall. We need to accept that effective engagement is time consuming, and budget accordingly.

Managing client expectations

Gardens have been presented on popular television makeover shows as being able to be developed in a day or a weekend. As a result there is a false perception amongst the public that people, designers and clients alike, 'just know' what they need to put where, that will meet everyone's needs, and that all specified design elements are instantly available to be delivered on site. One of the joys of working with healing gardens is that they ground people, from the design process through to completion. Good things take time.

When we take time at the outset to work with the client to explore the full potential of their site, appreciate their programme, talk to the end users, and get a

---

Case study 23: designing a natural playground

An international school contacted us to design a natural playground. Due to their location we decided for cost reasons to work through the first stage remotely. They had canvassed the views of staff and students through questionnaires, and explored ideas through art and geography classes. That took four months. We then developed concept drawings for their feedback. That took another month. When we went on site we met with the focus group of staff spearheading the project. They put forward their thoughts for inclusion into the developed design. At that stage it would be easy to think 'consultation done'. However, it was while walking around the site after the focus group meeting that I happened to meet the disgruntled staff members who were not interested in being part of the focus group. Their concerns were valid. One objection that was raised was 'why should the school waste a lot of money on a playground that is dark until 11 a.m. in winter?' Without this comment we would not have thought of lighting as a problem. Floodlights illuminate the space, so until then we had not considered the atmosphere created by the lighting. The objections of the disengaged inspired us to include fairy lights throughout the planting to create a magical play area, even in the depths of winter. The revised brief added another month to the design stage, but the result was well worth the wait. With large schemes it is easy to miss important details, little things that make a big difference. When designing a space to feel good in it is worth taking time to consult as widely as possible

feel for where the challenges lie, then we can develop a space that will truly provide value for money. The result will be an adaptable, flexible, sustainable space that can meet the client's needs today and into the future.

Community and stakeholder consultation

Whether designing a residential garden for a special needs user or a large landscaped public space, it is important to talk to the stakeholders, the people who will be directly and indirectly affected by the development. In a home or closed setting it is easy to identify who to talk to. In an open space setting, users will change over time so it is important to establish who the current users are and seek out those who will be, or who you would like to be, future users.

To ensure designs are inclusive it is important to go to the people, to talk to children and young people, their parents and carers, in playgrounds, parks and on the street. When researching a new design scheme I go out into the community and approach people with the opening line 'Hello, my name is Gayle and I am a playground, streetscape, bus station – insert whatever project you are working on – designer and I'm wondering what you like most about this space as it is? What would you change? What would it look and feel like in your ideal world, if money was no object?' People with learning disabilities have needs and rights as citizens too. It is important to gain their views. Sometimes they will have a carer with them who can interpret your questions for you. Sometimes you can patiently ask directly and be prepared for a long, slow but often well-considered answer.

Disability

When engaging with people living with disabilities it is helpful to research in advance of the first client meeting the health conditions of the people you will be designing for. Appendix 3 supplies a glossary of disability related terms.

In a residential or special educational setting, by the time a parent becomes a client they will have potentially dealt with enormous personal issues around having

Case study 24: Burwood Hospital, Christchurch, New Zealand

In 2012 I met with occupational therapists, medical and surgical consultants, and physiotherapists to discuss the development of a therapeutic horticulture programme for spinal injured, brain injured and stroke rehabilitation patients. I talked with patients about their previous lives and their hopes and plans for the future. Importantly I also talked to the hospital caretaker, the groundsman, who had sole charge of maintaining the 90-acre parkland site, assisted only by a team of volunteers. While the staff and patients had high hopes for what could be achieved, the spatial design of the programme needed to work with the caretaker's ability to maintain the space with a restricted budget. While it would have been exciting to develop a state of the art healing garden with high maintenance features requiring skilled labour for expert pruning, it would have quickly fallen into disrepair. It is vital to match the design brief to the reality of who will maintain the garden and the budget to achieve that.

a special needs family member. They need respect and to know that their views and needs will inform the inclusive design solution.

Where the client is someone on the administration team of a large hospital, school, or municipal authority, it is important to also talk to the people who will be actually using the space. There are stories told of the new hospital rooms designed to accommodate wider beds for obese people, but where the doors were left at the standard width because the porters who move the beds around were not consulted.

Before we think of the detail of what a salutogenic design approach can offer, we need to know who the end users will be, their hopes and dreams, their needs and aspirations. Healing gardens, by their nature, are designed to provide health and well-being benefits. There is a perception that, because of this, they must be for adults or children who are in some way 'unhealthy', or have learning disabilities, mental health problems and other special needs. While this is partially true, the scope is much wider. Intentionally therapeutic and intentionally personal, urban settings for social and nature connections offer a preventative health benefit for all people, regardless of age, culture or ability.

Older adults living with dementia, recovering from stroke or brain injury, or managing other disabilities; children living with ADHD, asthma, autism, cerebral palsy, cystic fibrosis, Down's syndrome, dyspraxia, epilepsy, obesity, spina bifida, hearing and sight impairments; along with other childhood and adult disabilities, all benefit from healing gardens, and all come from families in need of support and acceptance.

Healing gardens are most in need where the balance between hard and soft landscaping has been weighted towards the hard. When the built environment is dominant, where hard surfaces prevail, we have both an opportunity and a responsibility to redress the balance. To enjoy a feeling of health and well-being people need, and indeed intrinsically seek, a softer environment.

References

Burls, A. (2007). People and green spaces: promoting public health and mental well-being through ecotherapy. *Journal of Public Mental Health*, 6(3):24–39.

EPA (2012, 10 March). Inside story. Retrieved October 2013, from *United States Environmental Protection Agency*: www.epa.gov/iaq/pubs/insidestory.html

Pretty, J., Peacock, J., Sellens, M. and Griffin, M. (2005). The mental and physical health outcomes of green exercise. *International Journal of Environmental Health Research*, 15:319–337.

CHAPTER 11

Salutogenic design guidelines

Simple is best

> . . . very often it's the more stripped down, inexpensive schemes which work best – we have much to learn . . . about how to avoid overcomplicating schemes and creating additional costs through the over specification of materials, street furniture and lighting . . .
>
> Paul Quinn, regeneration manager, West Northamptonshire Development Corporation, UK (CABE, 2008)

Over specification has become almost endemic as landscape architects and designers struggle with inadequate budgets. It is based on the hope that after the almost inevitable project cost overruns some green features will be retained if the starting point is sufficiently grand. It is more cost efficient, however, to value landscape from the outset. If we are to create the best possible spaces for the communities we are working with, we need to value salutogenic landscapes alongside or even in front of the built environment as a significant and particularly cost-effective influence on human health and well-being.

There is so much more to creating a healing garden than just getting the plants right. Salutogenic design aims to

- prevent illness through promotion of an active healthy lifestyle using natural sensory rich environments;
- soften the built environment and work with it to create holistic environments that maximise potential of the site, the budget and community well-being;
- promote wellness and reduce rehabilitation times after trauma and infection; improve mobility, memory and mood; reduce aggression, stress and requirement for chemical pain relief; improve outcomes for diabetes, obesity, heart and lung disease, some cancers and depression; using attractive, engaging soft landscape treatments.

The salutogenic approach to health and well-being is effective because of biophilia. 'We respond particularly positively to grassland, trees, edible plants and friendly animals . . . Healing gardens then must include those elements . . . in order to achieve best value and maximum effect' (Ely and Pitman, 2012). Biophilic sensory stimulation is important to counter the effects of impairment associated with a variety of mental and physical health conditions such as stress, depression, behavioural disorders, autism, deaf-blind, ADHD, delayed healing, delayed development in children, and dementias. A degree of sensory impairment is common but generally unrecognised throughout the so-called healthy population due to excessive exposure to digital information. This sensory overload has been proven to be countered by outdoor nature experiences. Such experiences likewise cost-effectively improve mood and lower stress cortisol levels.

Salutogenic design reduces stress. Close collaboration is required between planning, building and landscape professionals so that the health and well-being potential of urban outdoor space is fully realised. There is enough complication in our lives without making green space complicated too. Therefore, a stripped down scheme that stresses neither the architect nor the user is to be preferred. If we think back to the sensory-rich, meditative simplicity of monastic gardens, we have a template for success. Inclusive healing gardens afford opportunities for rest and relaxation in a way the built environment cannot. In our overstressed modern world we need green space as a fundamental part of the urban landscape. There is a lot of old fashioned charm in a salutogenic space and less of the modern design statement.

Figure 11.1 The ultimate nature connection? The central stem of this tree has been pruned to provide a 'seat' within the tree.

Features of healing gardens designed using a salutogenic approach:

1 attractive environment to look at from indoors, as well as to be in outdoors – offers a reason to get outdoors;
2 functional, so that healthy, active, meaningful activities may be lead in the space;
3 practical, so that maintenance costs are minimised;
4 cost effective, designed as a beneficial therapeutic environment (to reduce costs of care/intervention in school/recidivist behaviours);
5 balanced, so that the overall space affords rest as well as activity.

Using nature's simplicity within healing garden design

Although nature is inherently complex, it is also refreshingly simple. Natural systems work to achieve a state of balance. Unfortunately, post-industrial society has all but erased that state of balance from our communities. Information overload has created stress in our communities as never seen before. As our lives have become filled with time saving devices we have found ourselves paradoxically time poor, and more importantly perhaps, disconnected from nature. Fundamental life lessons, cause and effect, risks and benefits are best experienced first-hand. 'Never have we been shown so much and seen so little' (Follet, 2013). When we watch nature documentaries and view pictures of forests our stress hormones are reduced. However, it is not until we have sat quietly and observed a real bird or real tree moving in the breeze that we connect with nature and receive her health giving properties (Selhub and Logan, 2012).

Like natural ecosystems, human systems work best when in a state of equilibrium. Without necessarily being consciously aware of it, we seek a balanced state and our, at times unhealthy, lifestyle choices show us far from that simple state of equilibrium. Healing gardens are uncomplicated spaces that we respond to on a deep, intuitive level. Whether designed as natural playgrounds in schools, light wells in hospitals, or urban rooftop retreats on city office blocks, it is important that we recognise the health-giving properties of nature, assign value to that and then seek opportunities to incorporate natural biophilic elements within our developments.

When designing healing landscapes, whether in city plazas or institutional gardens, it can be easy to forget or ignore the principles of good garden design. Texture, height variation, colour and scent are overlooked and the hard, mono-chromatic, monocultural, massed flat plantings ubiquitous in public housing, schools, hospitals and care homes are the result. If we refer back to the biophilic elements – grassland, trees, edible plants, a safe vantage point and friendly animals – we will achieve the textural balance necessary in a satisfying healing space.

Beauty and biophilia play a role in the salutogenic transformation we must make towards communities that promote health, are culturally rich and ecologically restorative. Without ecological health we cannot design for human health and well-being.

Case study 25: Abenteuerlicher Bauspielplatz Kolle 37

In Berlin, Germany, Abenteuerlicher Bauspielplatz Kolle 37 is a construction playground. Run by a group of social workers and counsellors as a kids-only space and funded by the city of Berlin and private donors, the adventure play area offers a safe place for children to create and destroy, work together and alone, to share and develop the vital 'soft skills' that are often missing from their lives. Children and young people at risk of crime, drugs and substance abuse between the ages of 6 and 16 years are able to access an adventure play garden. It evolved out of an idea in the late 1980s and came to fruition after the reunification of Germany when new funds were allocated to assist at-risk children. The playground is securely fenced with high, close-board timbers, but so densely planted with trees and shrubs as to obscure the boundaries. The playground is almost hidden within its multi-layered garden setting. Thirty years ago it was a bare site. Kolle 37 offers an uncomplicated garden setting where children and young people can find their balance. It is a sensory-rich refuge with abundant natural play materials, including:

- clay, including a kiln to fire objects;
- fire, to warm hands and feet, toast bread and potatoes, to gather around, sing songs and tell stories;
- water, for transporting to the sand box, for cooling off on hot days, for admiring droplets on leaves after rain, for puddles to splash in;
- sand, for creating and destroying, for feeling it run through fingers and gently rub against bare feet;
- building materials, for creating semi-permanent structures, houses, swings, slides;
- ironworks, including a small forge, to make real tools and implements;
- sticks, mud;
- child-made slides and swings, constructed from 'found' materials;
- ducks and chickens, to encourage care and responsibility, and to provide a non-judgemental audience for children to tell their stories to.

Manager Marcus Schmidt says

> staff at the Kolle have seen a change in the children and young people's behaviour over the past five years. When the adventure play centre was first opened the 6–16 year olds would arrive straight from school and run directly outside. Now we have 5 year olds pretending to be 6 and 17 year olds pretending to be 16. The centre is very popular, with the children and the authorities. Since the opening of the new building, and the addition of extra seating outside, now the children see it is a place to come and be quiet, to slow down. The kids pause to enjoy the leafy quiet of the space before going on to build stuff. Staff had wanted them to be busy, to 'do' something all the time. But now the staff acknowledge the kids need to calm down after school.
>
> (Schmidt, 2013)

Schmidt is a social worker and advocate for healing landscapes for children. In an unused corner of East Berlin the team has partnered with the Regional Social Educational Service of the Youth Office, the Senate Department for Urban Development, the Senate Department for Education, Youth and Sports, and Office of Environment and Conservation, amongst others, to create a haven for young people affected by crime, drugs, alcohol and domestic violence. It is significant that the Urban Development department sees the value in this sensory-rich play provision. Since the centre opened the neighbourhood has attracted new business, property values have increased, improved air quality has improved local health and the children can now access the educational and social supports they need.

Essential ingredients

Healing gardens must offer ten basic features in order to realise the mental and physical health benefits inherent in nature.

Light and shade, a view or outlook, comfortable seating, textural detail, water, accessible features, wildlife, cultural reference to create a sense of place, personal reference to create a sense of belonging, and human scale all need to be considered. These features rely on long term thinking and a mindset that values an investment in the fabric of a community. Gardens improve over time as trees grow and wildlife moves in. Short term thinking has led us to many of society's current difficulties. With healing gardens we are looking for both short- and long-term gains, in public health and well-being and also in the environment and the economy. In particular we seek to provide a living and working environment where people are able to derive health benefits from an active lifestyle, enjoyed outdoors in nature. In order to restore communities to health and well-being, a salutogenic approach requires us to address issues of sustainability and ecology. Using this multiple benefit model it is easy to find supporters of healing gardens.

Light and shade   is fundamental to a biophilic healing experience. When we are under artificial light there is a relatively uniform light in the room. Outdoors, trees and open space allow for sensations of affirming warmth from the sun and calming cool in shady spaces. Variations in light and shade allow sight impaired and other sensory impaired or developmentally delayed individuals to experience their environment more deeply, and bring colours to life. Moving from light to shade provides stimulation and affords way-finding for the partially sighted. Feature trees or planted pergolas, arbours or other structures add height to the garden and change light levels. To create a bio-diverse habitat is to create a garden offering a mixture of light and shade. While natural shade is the least expensive development option, plants take

Figure 11.2 The ten basic elements of a healing garden.

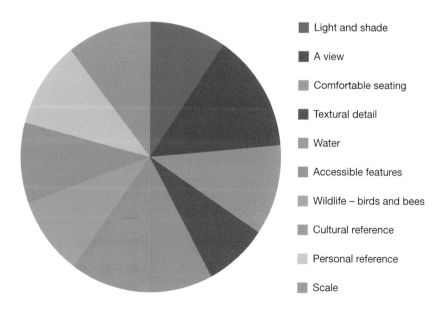

- Light and shade
- A view
- Comfortable seating
- Textural detail
- Water
- Accessible features
- Wildlife – birds and bees
- Cultural reference
- Personal reference
- Scale

time to grow. Structural, built, shade has its place but planted, natural shade has benefits of its own. Once grown, transpiration through the leaves further cools the air, negating the urban heat island effect. Views up through a gently moving tracery of leaves are hard to match within a manufactured environment.

In a healthcare setting design for light and shade is particularly important. Some medication and some health conditions make eyesight and skin sensitive to high glare and to high light levels generally. Personal temperature regulation is compromised through illness and ageing. The elderly and the ill feel hot faster than others, but conversely feel cold faster also. Providing an environment with a relatively constant temperature becomes the focus of clinicians and designers. However, in denying these people fresh air and the opportunity to feel hot or cold we deny them an entire sensory experience.

In a special needs sensory garden setting light and shade allows an added depth of experience. Children and adults living with sensory impairments or developmental delays benefit from time spent in a sensory-rich environment.

In a school playground sunlight not only lifts mood but provides children with vital vitamin D, and protection from rickets. Rickets was once a disease of poverty, maiming children through deformed bones. Alarmingly it is on the rise again as parents keep children indoors or cover them with sunscreen. Vitamin D is vital for positive mood and energy.

In a public playground maintenance is often used as the logic behind the development of featureless non-salutogenic landscapes. The degree of (dis)connection from nature within the local authorities tends to dictate design of public space. A perception that nature requires expensive time-equals-money maintenance means that too often a space is allocated, cleared of vegetation, a rubberised impact

Figure 11.3 Built shade in Marrakech, Morocco.

attenuating surface (IAS) and some equipment is installed, and the children told to 'play nicely'. However, just as children living with disability benefit from a diverse range of sensory inputs, so too do non-disabled children.

Climate change requires more natural shade to be provided in public space. Trees have the added advantage of improving biodiversity, absorbing CO_2 and filtering storm water runoff.

A view or safe vantage point   allows observation of and a connection with the wider world. A distant view from an elevated position is uplifting. In an enclosed setting the view is inwards and upwards to the sky, so sight lines must account for this. An ability to observe a space from a safe vantage point is especially important for people on the autistic spectrum, but the biophilic benefits of a view are universal.

Opening windows in this hospital shown in Figure 11.5 affords a view and fresh air from a heavily planted courtyard space to waft into the building, cooling and scenting the air on the upper floors. Downstairs, lightweight doors allow even frail patients' access directly into the courtyard space. When accessible doors are provided, patients can benefit from the opportunity to explore the meandering path and sit with family or friends in one of the secluded seating spaces. In this way patients are encouraged to be independent and confident. With trees come wildlife and the opportunity for further staff and patient interest and interaction. Depression

Figure 11.4 A sculptural form planted with bougainvillea provides a shaded walkway through South Bank Park, Brisbane, Australia.

Figure 11.5 This bird's next is best viewed from upper floor windows in this hospital courtyard garden, affording healing nature connections for patients.

and feelings of oppression are more common in environments lacking natural daylight and a view to green space. In locations where space is at a premium, roof gardens can offer a space for informal meetings, somewhere to 'walk off problems', somewhere to pause during the day to think, breathe in fresh air and admire the greenery. In some office roof gardens workers can even tend their own crops in the lunch hour.

In densely populated areas where space is limited, a roof garden is ideal. Roof gardens can be extensive, intensive or simply a space greened with plants as shown here. They serve to combat the urban heat island effect by cooling the air through evapotranspiration, as well as by providing natural shade. Throughout the Arab world and around the Mediterranean local architecture evolved as a response to the climate. With global climate change, designers in other climate zones have much to learn from the architectural history of North Africa, the Middle East and southern Europe. In hot climates where too much sunlight can be a problem, it is important to provide a range of cooling, shaded options. In traditional architecture such options came from nature with courtyard and roof gardens. Planted with herbs and fruit trees, the air is fragranced and the mood soothed.

Seating   is important in every healing garden space.

With the push towards an active lifestyle it would be easy to neglect our equal need for calm, quiet contemplative spaces in the sensory overload of the modern world.

With increasing levels of mental disability alongside an ageing population, public need for security and ease of access is increased. Comfortably sloped seat backs and smooth edged arms allow people to relax.

In schools, principals, directors and head teachers take the health of their students seriously. As a result some have mistakenly removed seating from playgrounds in the hope that students will run around more and become healthier. The

Case study 26: House of Fraser department store, Guildford, England

Internationally, the marketplace has become more competitive, and retail sales are declining as demand for low cost internet shopping increases. To address this and in order to entice customers into premises, it is essential that the staff are happy and the environment attractive. The experience must offer the individual a point of difference, something they cannot easily find elsewhere or online.

Store management decided to create a point of difference from the outset. Knowing that nature evokes a feeling of well-being and a sense of luxury in our harried world, the original building design included natural light and opportunities for fresh air. Central to the circulation space, a large window spanning three floors allows natural light to penetrate deep into the building. A view of the surrounding city was afforded by the roof garden shown below. It is part of an indoor–outdoor al fresco dining area. Business turnover in the store increased after installation of the garden as people from around the area sought out this vantage point as a soothing oasis in the city. From a return on investment point of view, the roof garden paid for itself within three years. Given that the restaurant is on the top floor, customers need to pass a tempting range of goods to reach their goal.

The spa experience, creating a feeling of health and well-being is the focus, and has crept into the market. While initially a purely financially motivated move, this new focus could be leveraged to have a profound effect on salutogenic urban design. When retailers proactively work with the community to boost the health and well-being of their customers by providing a healthy environment in which to spend their time and money, social, economic and environmental gains can be seen.

Figure 11.6 Guildford, UK: a rooftop water garden on a department store attracts customers up through the floors, and so past the tempting merchandise, as they access this healing oasis in the city.

Figure 11.7
Residential roof
gardens afford healing
outdoor space where
there is little at ground
level.

Figure 11.8 Residential roof garden by night.

Figure 11.9 Magnolia petals on blue resin-bound, recycled glass path soften this healthcare centre courtyard.

opposite tends to occur as children cannot find the simple balance they seek and tend to play aggressively on the hard space.

> We want to create a more natural playground to counter the undesirable behaviours shown in the current space. By adding seating and softening the play we hope to reconnect the children with their imaginations, sense of curiosity, exploration and adventure. We hope their social skills will improve and attention span increase and that these benefits will flow through to the classroom and onwards into society.
>
> (Griffin, 2013)

Figure 11.10 Seating around the edge of a sunken sand pit also acts as a step-up out of the space. Designed by Greenstone Design UK.

Figure 11.11 Swing seat under a treehouse. Designed by Greenstone Design UK.

Figure 11.12 A talk-tube, crawl space under a bridge, fruit trees, living willow playhouse, tree seat, and varied textures and materials on the surface treatments create a sensory-rich healing garden space in this school. Designed by Greenstone Design UK.

Figure 11.13 Boulders for balance and a trapeze swing help develop essential proprioception skills in this school's natural play garden. Designed by Greenstone Design UK.

Figure 11.14 This classic outward-facing tree seat will become a special secret space when the willow matures and branches are allowed to grow low in this children's centre in London. Designed by Greenstone Design UK.

In public spaces wherever people gather, outside schools, local shops, community centres, at 30–50m intervals on established walking routes, it is important to provide seating. Sometimes the seat can be as an affordance, a widened step or cap on a low wall where young or old in need of a rest can pause. In other locations a formal park bench or higher seat may be more appropriate to the setting.

The riverside park setting shown in Figure 11.15 shows an historic tree felled due to storm damage. Rather than going to waste the timber was passed to a local craftsperson who recycled it into very comfortable seating.

Texture and surfacing   With attention to sensory detail comes an awareness of the surfaces and materials we use. Norwegian landscape architect Frode Svane uses timber, sand and stone to create sensory-rich paths through parkland (Figure 11.17). These paths provide the uneven surfaces found naturally in forests and on coastlines. For childhood development of balance and proprioception skills it is vital they learn to walk and negotiate uneven surfaces before the age of 7 years. Natural play areas thus need to be texturally rich, to include irregular logs, boulders, tree roots and stepping stones to account for this. In an urban parkland setting, if the stepping stones, cobbles or river pebble path are edged by a handrail they can promote core strength, balance and confidence in older people or anyone living with a disability.

Biophilic cities need to consider how and where to provide opportunities for people to reconnect with nature. Varied surfacing in neighbourhood parks, outside shopping centres and health hubs, shows that the city values the health of its citizens and is interested in providing some variation and relief from the manufactured built environment norms

LEFT: **Figure 11.15** Recycled, carved tree trimmings form a sensory-rich sculptural seat.

ABOVE: **Figure 11.16** Rustic bench seat with warming wall behind.

Surfacing choices are also important for sustainable urban drainage. Permeable materials such as self-binding aggregates, resin-bound recycled glass, rubber and CDs provide a firm footing. In Figure 11.19 granite sets create a channel for collected rainwater to flow. The school has chosen to store rainwater collected off the roof and make it available via a timer switch at the top of the channel. Pebbles and larger rocks create disturbance and turbulence in the water flow, adding sound and visual interest to the post rain playable event.

Street and path slopes and levels are an important part of design for health and well-being. Healing landscapes need to occur throughout the public realm if we are to embrace active, inclusive design. While uneven surfaces can be a positive design element in certain locations, for general accessibility it is important that smooth, level, non-trip surfaces are provided.

Excessive camber or cross fall is often put on paving, either because the contractor is too lazy to properly bench the path, or mistakenly for drainage. A path's camber is defined by the centre of the surface being higher than both path edges, which allows surface water to run off to either side of the path. Cross fall is where the path slopes away to one side. People with gait difficulties and wheeled users

Figure 11.17 Barefoot walkway with sensory log rounds.

Source: Frode Svane.

Case study 27: show garden, Ellerslie International Flower Show

In 2012 I designed a show garden for the Ellerslie International Flower Show as a therapeutic sensory garden; a low maintenance space where busy people could relax, unwind, and reconnect with nature. Filled with tasty edible plants, wildlife-attracting blooms, a safe water feature, comfortable upholstered seating under a pergola, bench-style garden seating under fruit trees, some grass, paths and a patio space, it was a winning garden even before the judges saw it. As the thousands of show visitors streamed past it was interesting to see people engage with the space. During the week of the show two women who were recovering from strokes and three congenitally disabled people felt moved to get out of their mobility scooters and walk on the subtly textured resin-bound pavers. Their carers were alarmed at the risk their charges took, but the 'non-walkers' said they just knew they would be able to walk on the natural textured surface. One commented that the 'smooth but bumpy' texture provided the feedback she needed for her to be able to feel her feet. Other show visitors commented that they couldn't identify exactly what it was they loved but that they just 'felt good' in the garden.

Figure 11.18 Resin-bound aggregate provides tactile permeable paving.

Figure 11.19 Interactive, attractive, playable drainage channel in a school in Berlin, Germany.

such as cyclists, baby buggy or wheelchair users prefer a camber to a crossfall, as they can travel along the centre of the path without needing to correct gait or steering. Minimal slope is required for drainage: only 2 degrees.

Texture is used in reflexology parks in Canada, Malaysia, Korea, Japan and elsewhere in a very controlled way to create wellness gardens (Aminuddin, 2010). On a barefoot path at Bad Sobernheim in Germany, reflexology stimulates the whole body through the transition over grass, clay, sand, stones and bark chips . The 3.5-km route along the Nahe river starts with shoe lockers, includes shallow water wading points, bridges, kiosks, seats and tables, and ends with a footwash.

Water   Essential to all life, water can be incorporated as a temporary or permanent, standing or moving feature. A key biophilic element, water needs to be part of our urban existence. Barrel ponds (Figure 11.20) are inexpensive self-contained habitats that quickly acquire their own balance, requiring little maintenance other than water top-ups during hot weather. Rills cool the air and provide safe water interest, as at the National Botanic Garden, Wales (Figure 11.21). Shallow reflecting pools bring a contemplative feeling, as on the roof garden in Figure 11.22.

Accessibility   Put simply, everyone needs to be able to safely get outside, and once there to be able to enjoy the experience. In settings where weak, frail or vulnerable people may spend time, such as hospitals, rehab centres, senior living, care homes, preschools and social housing, door furniture needs to allow independent movement. If it is too heavy, has signage stating 'fire exit: keep closed', is painted a dark colour, does not open fully back against the wall to allow safe egress, or opens in an unexpected way, it will not be used.

When creating healing gardens it is important that young and old, able bodied and disabled, can access them.

Figure 11.20 Inexpensive, self-contained freshwater pond in a barrel, requiring minimal intervention.

Figure 11.21 Rill water channel provides safe water play.

Figure 11.22 Roof
gardens, terraces, decks
and courtyards benefit
from containerised
water features, as in
this water lily bowl.

Case study 28: Sprott House, Wellington, NZ

As mentioned in Chapter 9, Sprott House dementia care unit prides itself on managing the environment rather than the people who live there. Medication is kept to a minimum and the environment indoors and out is specifically designed to be enabling. The dementia unit was designed as an addition to the existing residential development. Project architects worked with staff to discover staff and resident movement patterns, specific needs and occupational therapy programmes. The result is a light airy space, set around two courtyards. Unfortunately, sliding glass doors were used in the day room area. Residents can safely and independently walk outside when the doors are left open, but if someone feels cold and closes the door, residents left outside do not recognise a sliding door as a door and quickly become upset, banging on the glass walls, searching for a way in. This in turn stresses residents indoors and a staff member has to be diverted to let the 'lost' resident back in. In another part of the unit self-closing external doors are too heavy for frail residents to push open, again requiring a staff member to be diverted to assist.

Wildlife   One of the biophilic elements we respond to is a positive experience with wildlife. Bird song, gentle visitations from butterflies, the antics of squirrels searching for food, a trail of worker ants, are all a positive distraction from the stresses of the modern world. They engage and fill us with wonder. Healing gardens need to be bio-diverse spaces to attract a healthy animal community.

Cultural reference   A healing garden provides a sense of place. This is central to the ability to fix individuals in time and space, to provide a reference point. With

Case study 29: Wapping Women's Centre children's daycare garden, London

The Wapping Women's Centre provides valuable support services for the largely Bangladeshi local community. The women come to the UK often as brides from rural areas of Bangladesh, and are frequently illiterate and without any family support. We needed to make them feel safe and 'at home' at the Centre. In an area previously stark and overlooked, we designed a soft space where mothers (and their children) could safely explore their new home. We planted a palm, fig trees to provide a cultural reference during Ramadan for their Iftar[1] feast, alongside English strawberries and salad greens around the edge of the natural play garden.

ABOVE: Figure 11.23 London: inadequate children's play provision in social housing area characterised by anti-social behaviour, poor child health, low attention and high levels of arousal (See King et al., 1983).

RIGHT: Figure 11.24 Concept sketch to improve play provision in the social housing area. The design aims to create a nature-rich space that reduces arousal, and improves health and well-being through mindful spaces, freshly grown and harvested food, and with culturally responsive planting. Designed by Greenstone Design UK.

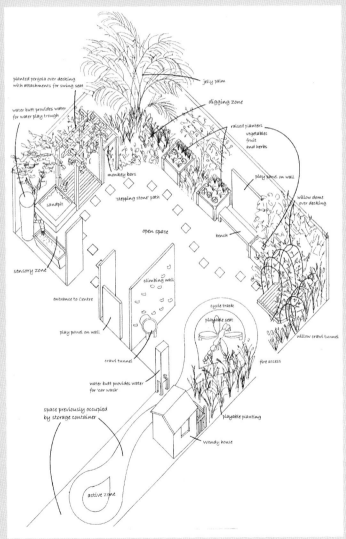

rising levels of migration due to conflict and climate change it will be increasingly important to supply green space that offers cultural indicators. Art, sculpture and native planting that connects people to the area is important in public healing gardens.

Personal reference   With ever increasing population densities in urban centres around the world, it is important to be able to claim an area of green space as one's own. To be able to create a path through planting, to trim, pick flowers and eat some fruit allows local people to feel it is their garden. In 'Taming the wild', landscape architect Dr Mattias Qviström notes

> the ready-made plan with specific sections and areas for certain activities was particularly provoking . . . , even though the planners emphasized that it (the plan for Gyllins Garden) was only an illustration. An upset woman argued '[In your plans] I see something which is ready-played where I want to be able to walk in my own footsteps. You have decided that there one should do this and there one should do that.' An elderly man continued; 'I would like to support these arguments. If you want to be on your own and philosophize, you go to Gyllin's.'

> (Qviström, 2012)

Scale   An urban healing landscape is of human scale. That is, it is sized so that people do not feel dwarfed by the environment. Supercities demand dense and tall developments. To be healthy, the vertical plane must be balanced by accessible green space. Deck gardens and ground level gardens are central to the development as an aid to mental health. It is important to balance vast public plazas with areas of small seating areas, trees, grass and low planting around the space.

Form and function

When we desire healing green space we must be aware of both the form and function of the space. To promote health across the urban public realm we need to provide for social and nature connections, wherever people spend time. Healing gardens are the spaces we create to meet that need. To create a garden we need to be able to think like a gardener, whatever the setting. To be a gardener is to under-stand the complex interrelationships between plants, animals, soil, sun and water, to understand how we, as humans, will use and respond to the garden.

In nature there is constant change as each element in the ecosystem strives to capture its niche, to find equilibrium. When we seek to create gardens that promote human health and well-being we need to be mindful of the natural systems at play. When we work with nature required inputs become less and the outputs (health-promoting social and nature connections) become more. The gardens require less drainage, less water, less weeding, less pruning, and less replacement of plants. In short, nature does its work and the garden costs less to maintain.

Simplicity in our designs does not equate to being boring; it requires us to create a subtle harmony between the built and natural environment. That harmonic state is often described in terms of feng shui. The principles of feng shui are based on 5,000 years of ancient wisdom, expressed as the Taoist belief that all things in this universe are interconnected. Energy flows, both positive and negative, must be in balance. We find a space *feels* right when texture, scale and proportion are in equilibrium. A sense of harmony is achievable by anyone when presented with an appropriate environment. Native American people, like many other indigenous peoples, believe in this connectedness.

To design and develop a garden that honours those connections is to provide for healing green space, within and around our homes, our schools and our workplaces. Salutogenically designed apartment blocks need to have outdoor communal spaces where people can meet friends and neighbours safely and in comfort, with nature close by to soften the hardscape and gently remind people of what it is to be a human and a part of the ecosystem that is our city, our town, our home.

Public space

To be a healing, nurturing environment, which reduces stress and is accessible for all, public space needs to be welcoming. In our home we offer seats and tables and some refreshment to our guests. In a public park, outside a supermarket or a theatre, outside a medical centre or a school, an office block or a factory our towns and cities need to be similarly welcoming. Gardens soften the environment and balance the hard edges of the buildings and roadways. As with all good gardens, seating is essential. A low table facilitates chatting over a drink; a high table allows a picnic. As we saw in Chapter 7, to allow a space to be accessible for all, we need to provide quiet space as well as open space. The stress of being with so many people can be overwhelming, so to offer a quiet seating area just outside a supermarket allows people to take a break from the stressful experience as required.

Slow cities

Form and functional requirements of an ageing population are seen in increased need for accessible public space. Slow cities embody the concept of inclusion and accessibility. To keep the ageing population active and healthy we need engaging places for our community to go, and easy access to get there independently. As we age we naturally slow our pace of life, decision making and response times. If it is physically or mentally difficult to leave home, older people may choose not to. For the overall health of the community we must provide easy opportunities for the ageing community to get out in the fresh air, take some exercise and meet people. Urban design tip: it is important to provide accessible car parking spaces close to larger parks, arts, community and shopping areas. These are in addition to the traditional 'disabled parking spaces' as 'enabling parking spaces'. Currently our community is concentrated in the areas they can get to. Multi-level car parking buildings, while convenient for urban planners, can be a nightmare for older people. Busy pedestrian zones can likewise be intimidating. It is good to slow down the traffic with mixed tree-shaded and sunny seating placed at regular 50m intervals.

When we design urban environments to suit our ageing community we de-stress the urban environment for all. Many of the design considerations for the ageing community are similar for those living with stress and other mental health issues, People may need somewhere to rest after an arduous navigation of the supermarket, or indeed an excursion to any destination. People need to feel safe, so heavily cambered paving must be eliminated as it puts pressure on hips and knees and can cause people to feel they will fall, with one leg resting higher than the other. Clear sight lines are important, ensuring navigation and way-finding is easy. However, we must be mindful that for most people a therapeutic space is sensory-rich. Wide avenues and flat grass may offer good way-finding but they can be fast moving spaces. Routes that offer possibilities for hidden areas to branch off the main path allow for mixed needs and greater sensory interest. People need somewhere to meet their friends comfortably.

Countries with a good record for care of their elderly population such as France, Italy, China and Japan have seats outside of neighbourhood stores, parks and gardens that are within easy walking distance of home.

We need to provide places for people to connect with others, and with the natural world. In areas where the local park may not be a safe option then we need to provide alternatives.

To be fully accessible

Barrier free design requires the spaces we create to connect to neighbouring buildings, transport links, parks, services and open space. We need to work with our colleagues in engineering, in architecture, in project management and property development. If we do not, the result is a waste of time and money, which causes further stress to those who we are aiming to provide for. An example of a lack of joined up thinking is evident in a five-star hotel in Hong Kong. The hotel is known for its cutting edge, accessible design. Rooms have wide door openings; well-placed hand rails allow for easy transfer from wheelchairs, hearing loops are in place, oxygen supplies are available for guests. There is a choice of large open and smaller intimate public spaces within the hotel. Garden courtyards and quiet fountains add to the atmosphere of accessible, relaxed luxury. But there is one fundamental flaw in the overall design. As someone with mobility problems arrives, there is no way to gain independent entry into the hotel. This otherwise wonderful example of barrier free design has beautiful curving steps lead up into the hotel from both sides of the arrival area. There is no alternative access. What on paper looked so good suddenly causes dignity to be lost and the guest must ask to be lifted into the hotel. Once they are in, all is well, they just cannot get in or out by themselves.

When we are commissioned to provide a therapeutic healing environment, gardens are a key part of the package. However, gardens on their own will do as little as the hotel with wide internal doorways and no ramp access. If the people we are providing the healing gardens for do not have any experience of nature we may need to first introduce them to the idea of gardens as a positive experience. They need to know how to access the garden from an intellectual point of view, before they will bother to consider the physical reality of moving their body into the space.

To design a salutogenic environment, one which aids the health and well-being of all, we need to be mindful that we are making a functional environment, one that is integrated into the wider setting. We cannot simply look at our area of concern, design that piece and say 'job done'. To ensure optimal use of funding, to ensure the satisfaction of clients and stakeholders, not to mention to make best use of our design talent, we need to talk to the neighbours and other interest groups. When we invite feedback and peer review, we gain a broader understanding of local issues and concerns. Fears, while real to the person experiencing them, are often based on a misconception. If we address those fears we can both educate and accommodate to mitigate them.

Supercities and slums

With countries across Asia, the Americas and Europe tending towards more supercities, and increased urbanisation occurring everywhere, the number of people living vertically is set to increase. Concomitantly with this increase in population density is an increased risk of disease. Young and old relocated to city high rise blocks are likely to suffer most; both from social disconnection and a disconnection from nature. Simple affordances for reconnecting socially and with nature can be incorporated anywhere, from the favelas of Rio de Janeiro to within the world's tallest building, the Burj Khalifa of Dubai. The Burj Khalifa's website states that 'Exclusive sky lobbies on levels 43, 76 and 123 include state-of-the-art fitness facilities, indoor/outdoor swimming pools, jacuzzis and a recreation room for gatherings and events' (Emaar Properties, 2013).

For supercities of the future to be healthy, livable places it is vital that they offer high quality green space, opportunities for social and nature connections, an active healthy lifestyle, and a quality diet. Rather than just the minimal outdoor communal areas provided at the Burj Khalifa, one solution is to install balconies of at least 15m^2 per apartment and open-air planted, communal deck space on every tenth floor. Nature connections and natural play opportunities are as important for people in high rise settings as they are for those living in detached ground-level homes. As we have seen, people living with a disability benefit from the sensory stimulation of nature, so even if their care home is situated fifteen floors above ground it is important residents can access living plants, fresh air and natural daylight.

In the slums of Rio and Johannesburg, nature connections could be inexpensively designed in. Fruit trees planted on corners of alleyways would offer the chance to see a bird, pick and eat fruit, and meet friends in the shade. When we design shared space for a new town in China or communal space for a Native American community in the Dakotas, a school in Turkey or a playground in Russia, we need to remember that simple, inexpensive, predominantly soft landscape treatments aid community health and well-being.

> A 10% increase in greenspace buys an equivalent 5 years in life expectancy.
>
> (European Environment Agency, 2012)

Planted roofs and walls offer a new planting opportunity to extend above the ground plane. Singapore aims to become the greenest city state on the planet. The ancient hanging gardens of Babylon may soon be rivalled by the emerging gardens spilling from roofs, terraces, balconies and walls of skyscrapers and low rise buildings across the island.

As Singapore has found, although a lush jungle landscape surrounding the city is an asset, we need to do more. Dr I. Hanski and fellow researchers at the University of Helsinki studied the relationship between contact with the natural environment and incidence of allergies and asthma. 'Urbanisation can be seen as a lost opportunity for many people to interact with the natural environment and its biodiversity, including the microbial communities', he reports, and further:

> While it is not possible to reverse the global trend of urbanisation, there are a number of options. Apart from reserving natural areas outside of urban areas, I think it is important to develop city planning that includes green spaces, green belts and green infrastructure.
>
> (Hanski, 2012)

Green or living roofs are one easy way to bring nature into the built environment. Green roofs perform a vital role in helping city office blocks, hospitals, schools and homes to adapt to the effects of climate change. Providing natural insulation, they reduce the need for artificial cooling in hot weather and heating in cooler months, attenuate flow or capture rainwater runoff, as well as providing a range of habitats for urban wildlife. By greening the built environment they offer a softer experience, aiding human health and well-being at the same time. Although still a new concept in some countries, by 2001, 43 per cent of German cities provided incentives for green roof installation (Sheffield, 2011).

There are many myths about green or living roofs. However, any roof with a slope of less than 10 degrees can enjoy a living green covering. Roofs of greater angles can be planted but will require specialist advice. Simple lightweight green roofs weigh between 60 and 150 kg/m^2 (13.0–30.0lb/ft^2). It is important to consider the weight of rainwater or snow on the roof as well. However, most roofs can handle the increased loading. Not only does the planting filter and slow rainwater runoff flows, it attracts beneficial wildlife, bringing life to an otherwise sterile environment.

Natural play

Natural play gardens are a good example of a functional space where form is vital to its success. They are play spaces that employ planting, water courses, bridges and stepping stones, mud, sand, rocks and logs in a playful way, in an urban area. Sometimes it is referred to as play using loose parts, as many items are not fixed in place but can be manipulated and moved. Adults can perceive such areas as 'messy'. Children do not see the mess but rather focus on the opportunity such freedom to manoeuvre, manipulate, create and destroy allows. In the 'good old days' we were allowed to play out and create our own fun in wild spaces around our neighbourhoods. Our young bodies were well muscled, we were aerobically fit and we allowed our personalities, the weather and our friends to guide us as to how best to enjoy the day. Childhood depression rates were low and childhood obesity almost unheard of. We played hard, went to school and worked hard, came home to eat and sleep and enjoyed a repeat performance the next day. It cost our parents nothing except perhaps extra laundry detergent and the community only as much as the price of the land we roamed.

Article 31 of the UN Convention on the Rights of the Child, which requires all countries that are signatories to uphold children's rights, states that every child has the right to relax, play and take part in a wide range of cultural and artistic activities (UNICEF, 2013). Other articles refer to the rights of disabled people, the elderly and the infirm. Fundamental human rights require us to provide access to healing green space. Natural play opportunities are a basic expression of the provision. To be effective, natural play areas need to stimulate the biophilic senses. They aim to recreate the grasslands, forests, woods and gulleys, the rivers and streams we, our parents and grandparents grew up with. They offer simple fun like rope swings and tyres by way of 'props' or equipment and rely on nature to provide the rest.

Natural play is about examining, exploring, dreaming and pretending, taking risks and developing the confidence to try something new. Damming small streams or building sandcastles, and watching what happens as nature sweeps all away, gives children a sense of nature's power and majesty. It puts human life into perspective. As nature is a little untidy and blows piles of leaves into corners, drops birds' nests and occasionally fledglings out of trees, so too are natural play areas a little untidy. That requires us as the designers and practitioners to overcome our adult desire for neat, close cropped grass, ordered rows of planting, and bland, easy-care zones devoid of life to create, and allow children to create, a space of sensory delight. We must suspend our maintenance schedules to allow a more flexible approach that removes hazards, but allows nature to provide the fun. We must provide appropriate, playable planting. Plants that stimulate the senses, attract wildlife, and hence boost local biodiversity are listed in Appendix 1.

Manufacturers have attempted to capitalise on the resurgent interest in natural play. To recreate the experience of dragging a stick along a sandy beach, some have created brightly coloured plastic coated panels where your finger can trace a shape. Others have designed fake rock climbing walls. Large plastic logs, designed to look like the real thing only smoother, replace real fallen trees. Others have taken real logs but chemically treated and/or machined them to be so smooth as to defy any living creature to get a hold on them. On a cruise ship or within a theme park there is a place for such manufactured nature, as the whole environment falls within a manufactured space. However, in public green space, in residential care facilities and within school grounds we need to provide the biggest and best impact possible. We need to meet our obligations under UNCRC's Article 31 and provide for the health and well-being of our children. Natural loose parts play costs little but makes a big impact on children's creativity, freedom of expression, self-confidence, mood and hence mental health.

To encourage and promote natural play we need to change a generation of thinking. We also need to be mindful of the stress that any change inevitably causes. Parents and elected officials have acted in good faith, using the information to hand at the time. They have also based their decisions on their *perception* of the risks and dangers of various options. Now the science has changed. The *risk benefits* are emphasised in face of the known harm that comes from allowing children to disconnect from nature. The wisdom of old, the 'get out and have fun, and enjoy your childhood' ideology is being re-employed. Where children have been offered opportunities to reconnect with nature they have embraced them wholeheartedly.

Like any systemic change, it takes time for new ideas to become embedded, and for full understanding to filter through all levels of decision makers. We must be aware that for this new idea of natural play to work the stakeholders' belief system must change to allow it. Around the world parent and school bodies are embracing the concepts of natural play and biophilia; but it is patchy. In 2010 when we were brought into a school in Hampshire, England, to create a natural play area within and around an outdoor classroom/outdoor science discovery area, we did not anticipate the head teacher being afraid of snakes to the point where she would not go outside into the school playground. While we worked with the school board, enthusiastic staff and students, the development ultimately failed when the head vetoed the expenditure because she and some of the parents did not feel it was safe. Change management is a specialised area, and we must be aware of the need to handle client groups and individuals gently.

In early 2013 we went into a school on the Kapiti coast of New Zealand to create an outdoor learning and natural play area. Before we could start the design process we had to run workshops for the parents. Their perception was that play was not important and that the children needed more time desk learning to succeed in the modern, competitive world. They were afraid that if their children were not at their desks they would not be learning. We talked through statistics from Learning through Landscapes to show the benefits of time spent outdoors, and the accelerated indoor learning it induces, until they were convinced.

The survey of 700 schools and early years settings, commissioned by the UK national school grounds charity Learning through Landscapes (2003) proved that schools which invested in and improved their playground design experience significant tangible benefits, such as

- enhanced pupil behaviour (73 per cent of respondents),
- a reduction in bullying (64 per cent of respondents),
- improved attitudes towards learning (65 per cent of respondents),
- better social interaction (84 per cent of respondents),
- increased community/parental involvement (66 per cent of respondents).

Parental expectation and perception of risk is a large area requiring education. Parks managers also benefit from instruction on the benefits of natural play. At one workshop a local parks and playground manager took issue with the idea of playable planting in a playground. He wanted pyracantha (firethorn) as the only plant, on the basis that it 'ticked the boxes for year-round interest being evergreen, having berries and attracting birds, and the sharp needles would keep the kids away!' It turned out he didn't much like children as they got in the way of him being 'able to do his job', as he saw it, of keeping the area clean and tidy.

Stakeholders and user groups are slowly undergoing a change. Parents are catching up but many still believe we need to wrap children in cotton wool lest they come to any harm outdoors. This is in stark contrast to the fact that by keeping their children seemingly safe indoors in front of a screen, or in ballet class or extension maths, they are in fact doing known harm, in addition to denying their child their rights as under Article 31 of UNCRC. Parents are also guilty of putting pressure on schools to cut play time in a quest to get their children to achieve better results by spending more time at their desks. This false assumption that formal instruction time = success is behind many children's inactive lifestyles, stress, weight problems and unhealthy diets.

As awareness of the benefits of natural play have grown, design specifiers and play procurement managers have bought from a catalogue of 'natural play' equipment just as they did with the old-style manufactured climbing frames. Horticulturalists with knowledge of species with suitable low branches for climbing are hard to find, so it is easier to simply purchase something that says it is part of a natural play range and tick 'job done'. As the play workers and landscape designers knew no better, alternatives to manufactured nature were rarely offered.

Much has been written about the restricted range of today's children. Parents have become fearful and their children have absorbed that fear. For parents the perceived risk is that their child may be kidnapped if allowed to play outdoors freely. Their other fear is that their child will fall behind if not found an appropriate extra-curricular activity. Children, with their unsophisticated logic, have taken their parent's fears to mean that the outdoors generally and time spent playing specifically must somehow be bad for you, and therefore it is safer to stay indoors, or go to football where the coach will take care of you.

So, to allay parents' fears and to placate the parks manager who wants a tidy playground we need to provide an area sufficiently attractive to both parent and child, which offers the parks person an environment to be proud of. Easier said than done? Not really.

In Kew Gardens, England, the narrow boardwalk invites exploration (Figure 11.25). Simple and inexpensive to construct, such a boardwalk offers an alternative access to another part of the garden. This example is inclusive in that any age can use it, and for non-ambulatory explorers there is an alternative means to get to the other side, via the perimeter path.

Other examples of natural play include the green-roofed sandpit seen in an early years playground. While the children can happily play in any manufactured sand pit, this example shows a sand pit that has been set within a pebble 'beach' with boulder stepping stones, also used as casual seats. The planting on the roof is designed to attract bees, butterflies and other pollinating insects. Local biodiversity is augmented as the children have something to catch their eye and ear as it flies past their sand castles.

ABOVE LEFT: **Figure 11.25** Boardwalk balancing beam in Kew Gardens, London.

ABOVE RIGHT: **Figure 11.26** Green roof on the sand pit attracts butterflies and other beneficial insects, while protecting children from sun and rain. Designed by Greenstone Design UK.

By using a mixture of natural and manufactured play elements you can achieve a 'best of both worlds' scenario. Natural play elements offer advantages over manufactured items by being a little irregular. As much as we plan, prepare, hope and dream, life is unpredictable. I say this as a mother of identical twins, as someone who has spent twenty-five years working and living in most climate zones around the world, as someone with a spinal cord injury after breaking my back while horse trekking in Ireland. None of those events was expected and an early life lived with abundant free play, field trips and outdoor learning opportunities has allowed me, I am sure, to be adaptable and flexible as an adult. Learning through Landscapes agrees. Their 2001 study showed that after increased time spent outdoors, results in reading, maths and science accelerated and the children are happy, healthy and have fun! The inaugural conference of the International School Grounds Movement held in San Francisco, California in 2011 brought together educators, designers and environmentalists from around the world aiming to give children their childhood, outdoors. The movement for natural play and outdoor learning is growing as a direct response to the challenges facing our time.

A wise school principal once told me that the only thing in life that is constant is change. When we design natural play and learning environments we provide opportunities for children, and their families, to (re)connect with nature. Natural play is ideal preparation for accepting and understanding that change is an essential part of life. Nature changes with the seasons, the clouds move by the minute, the sun moves by the hour. Animals come and go. Leafs bud, unfurl and fall. Annual plants grow, flower then set seed to die and reappear somewhere else next year.

Appendix 1 shows a selection of plants suitable for natural play areas. They each offer more than just their greenery and are suitable for planting in public space. Some offer edible fruit, some offer a low branching habit ideal for climbing, some attract birds, bees and butterflies. All change with the seasons, offering a glimpse of life unscheduled by humans. While all new plantings benefit from early care in terms of watering or support, the examples shown here are relatively robust and require little by way of long term maintenance.

Jungle planting

Healing gardens are uncomplicated spaces. Simplicity has to do with scale. A single bush may look 'architectural' and work as a sculptural piece of art, but when grouped together such lush planting can disguise harsh boundaries, add a sense of mystery, and invite exploration and imagination. In a natural play area, robust, flexible-stemmed evergreen shrubs can evoke the feeling of a 'jungle'. Vines planted around a 'rough' area with uneven surfacing (boulders, bark mulch and leaf litter), soften an urban play space. The softer environment calms and refocuses attention, for adults and children alike. At a project in London our client had care of delinquent 3–5 year olds, many of whom who had never walked on grass, tasted fresh fruit off the vine or seen the beauty of nature up close. After installation of the richly planted natural play garden the children's behaviour improved, staff absence decreased, children's attendance improved, parent/carer involvement increased and the centre's neighbours reported increased wildlife in their gardens and increased property values.

Lawns, wildflower meadows and herb gardens

Of the biophilic elements, grass is a vital part of a healing landscape. Lawns are notoriously high maintenance, however, requiring regular weeding, watering and mowing. Low maintenance options such as no-mow herb lawns can be useful within healing garden schemes.

Wildflower meadows offer a timeless appeal. They are another low maintenance option, requiring only an annual mow. Ground preparation requirements are minimal. Poor soil quality is best. In low budget areas on urban regeneration sites, around the periphery of schools, prisons and healthcare facilities wildflower meadows attract honey bees and butterflies, are colourful, and sufficiently resilient that they can withstand being walked through occasionally and the flowers picked. There, are two main choices to be made – perennial or annuals. The procedure for annuals (i.e. plants last for one year) is as follows:

- The ground has to be prepared and the seeds re-sown every year. This involves rotovating the ground, making sure it is weed-free, applying fertiliser and re-sowing. An advantage is that you can use a different mix from year to year.
- The seed mix is sown in spring and the first flowers will show in late May or early June at the earliest.
- The flowers will last until about late November depending on the weather.
- There is no need to do anything once the seeds are sown – just watch the meadow develop.
- Annuals are more brightly coloured than perennials.

Perennials (i.e. plants that remain for several years, depending on the species) tend to be less brightly coloured but still very attractive. Points to consider are:

- The plants will start flowering earlier and finish later than the annual mix, so there is less of a gap – probably more like 3–4 months.

- More work is needed in the first 18–24 months; to get the meadow established requires a system of timed cuts and weed checks.
- Once established, the perennial wildflower meadow just needs to be cut once or twice a year – there is no annual preparation of soil and re-sowing.
- There is an ongoing requirement to check for weeds, which is not the case for the annual. This should diminish as the meadow gets more established.
- The length of the 'empty' season (although this could be mitigated using bulbs).
- The choice of colour.
- The type of maintenance overhead – either all concentrated in the winter and spring (annual), or more spread through the year once established (perennial).

When restricted to passive exposure, the subtle nature of a herb garden isn't appealing to older people, who typically have poorer vision. Where residents can actively engage with an edible garden, can tend, pick and eat the plants, strong memory prompts have been reported. Dr W. Bird, of Natural England, found that Alzheimer's patients who did not know who or where they were, when offered time in a wellness design oriented herb garden could relax and explore the garden, taste a fresh mint leaf and then safely cook a roast lamb dinner. Natural deep memory prompts are significant and opportunities for their increased provision need to be made (Bird, 2009).

Case study 30: Japanese gardens and Alzheimer's patients

Japanese gardens relieve stress and calm people who sit in them, according to researchers from Rutgers University who observed the effects of Japanese gardens on Alzheimer's patients in a care facility. Residents were surveyed for their response to various garden styles. The facility has a series of courtyards with thirty-two gardens, and residents were asked which they preferred to sit in. The Japanese gardens scored highest. The herb gardens scored lowest. Japanese gardens significantly reduced stress. This was confirmed with a heart-rate test comparing the Japanese garden, the herb garden, and an unstructured space with a single tree (Braun, 2010).

Car parks – for supermarkets, hospitals, industrial estates, shopping malls

It is difficult to imagine a setting less like a healing garden than a car park. Car parks have tended to be bleak places, predominantly hard paved, occasionally with token planting. Pre-climate change planning policies allowed unshaded, impermeable concrete, tarmac and asphalt paving to add to the urban heat island effect, and create overland flow of storm water. Car parks need to be inexpensive to build and maintain as they offer little value to the developer, other than providing a necessary service. However, simple things like shade trees can make a big difference to their usability. Clear-stem deciduous trees can replace low planting for the same price. Drainage grates around trees can slow and filter storm water runoff. To facilitate health and well-being we need to make getting out of our cars and onto our feet attractive. Inclusive, greened car parks are thus an important feature of salutogenic urban design.

Green roofs, decks and roof terraces, 'sky lobbies' and slums

Healing gardens can be developed almost anywhere. In fact, the more spaces we green, the better. On office blocks and on residential developments, balcony gardens allow a personal reference point. As the visitors to Gyllin's garden enjoyed, people with even small amounts of space can enhance their environment, connect with nature and tend plants. When designing balcony spaces it is important to consider water requirements. If the garden area is completely under cover it will only receive wind-blown rainfall. On a balcony of any size greater than $4m^2$, floor drainage, rainwater harvesting and/or an outdoor tap (faucet) encourages gardening.

Floor materials can be slatted timber, tiles or a durable waterproof membrane that is not harmed if it gets wet, or soil spilt on it.

Built-in planters along the edge of balconies add security, green the facade of buildings and aid biodiversity

Other features

Orientation and height of buildings to ensure shade lines fall away from key functional outdoor use areas; rainwater harvesting to ensure water is always available to nourish plants and animals; and sustainable urban drainage systems to ensure excess water is filtered, transported and discharged appropriately, are all back-end features of a healthy, healing environment. A back-to-basics, sense-and-sensibility approach informs salutogenic design guidelines.

Note

1   Iftar is the meal eaten after sunset during the fasting month of Ramadan in the Islamic calendar.

References

Aminuddin, M. (2010). Port Dickson wellness zone healing path. Retrieved December 2013, from *Landscape Surrounds You*: http://mlina74.blogspot.co.nz/2013/06/port-dickson-wellness-zone-healing-path.html

Bird, W., Dr. (2009, 22 July). Interviewed by the author.

Braun, D. (2010, 15 February). Japanese gardens calm Alzheimer's patients. Retrieved June 2013, from *National Geographic*: http://newswatch.nationalgeographic.com/2010/02/15/japanese_gardens_cal_alzheimer_patients/?goback=.gde_4287 769_member_215692487

CABE (2008, January). Archived content. Retrieved February 2013, from *Commission for Architecture in the Built Environment*: http://webarchive.nationalarchives.gov.uk/20110118095356/http:/www.cabe.org.uk/public-space/scholarships/2008

Ely, M. and Pitman, S. (2012). Green infrastructure. Life support for human habitats: the compelling evidence for incorporating nature into urban environments, November 2012. A review of research and literature prepared for the Green Infrastructure Project, Botanic Gardens of Adelaide, Department of Environment, Water and Natural Resources.

Emaar Properties (2013). Homes and offices: the residence. Retrieved 27 November 2013, from *Burj Khalifa*: www.burjkhalifa.ae/en/HomesOffices/TheResidence. aspx

European Environment Agency (2012, 6 January). Health benefits of greenspace. Retrieved June 2013, from *European Environment Agency*: www.eea.europa.eu/ articles/forests-health-and-climate-change/key-facts/health-benefits-of-green-spaces

Follet, M. (2013, 28 September). Interviewed by the author.

Griffin, M. I. (2013, 5 August). Headmaster, King's School. Interviewed by the author.

Hanski, I. (2012). *Environmental biodiversity, human microbiota, and allergy are interrelated.* Washington, DC: National Academy of Sciences.

King, M. G., Burrows, G. D. and Stanley, G. V. (1983, November). Measurement of stress and arousal: Validation of the stress/arousal adjective checklist. *British Journal of Psychology* 74(4):473–479.

Learning through Landscapes (2003). National School Grounds Survey 2003. Available at www.ltl.org.uk/childhood/research.php

Qviström, M. (2012). Taming the wild. In A. J. Keenan, *Urban wildscapes* (p. 195). New York: Routledge.

Schmidt, M. (2013). Manager, Abenteuerlicher Bauspielplatz Kolle 37, Berlin. Interviewed by the author.

Selhub, E. M. and Logan, A. C. (2012). *Your brain on nature: the science of nature's influence on your health, happiness and vitality.* Missisauga, Toronto: John Wiley and Sons.

Sheffield, G. (2011). Green roof guidelines. Retrieved June 2013, from *Green Roof Guide*: www.greenroofguide.co.uk/what-are-green-roofs/

UNICEF (2013, 1 February). Fact sheet: a summary of the rights under the convention. Retrieved from *Rights Overview*: www.unicef.org/crc/files/Rights_overview.pdf and http://ipaworld.org/general-comment-on-31/un-general-comment/un-stands-up-for-childrens-right-to-play-arts-and-leisure-in-a-landmark-moment-for-children/

CHAPTER 12

Inclusive design

Key design elements

As Hippocrates said, healing is a matter of time but also of opportunity. In this chapter we explore landscape and urban design elements that afford the best opportunity to heal. Inclusive urban design draws together government ideals, political expediency, economic reality and social demands with ecological necessity. This joined-up thinking, outcomes-based approach is fundamental to a salutogenic approach. Key elements of design for health and well-being acknowledge our need to connect with people and nature, to create resilient communities, economies and ecologies. We are part of something intricate and interconnected. The environments we create need to be mindful of the big picture while being supportive spaces for those individuals (humans, plants and animals) who live in or visit the place.

If we are to understand design for health and well-being, we must first understand the concept of inclusion. Inclusive design differs from accessible design in that it enables people of differing ages and abilities to be together and feel equally valued. Accessible design tends to focus on codes of compliance for access – ramps, handrails and signage. In Rio de Janeiro, Brazil, some interesting work is being done by researchers at the Instituto Helena Antipoff–IHA. Professor Renata Mattos Eyer de Araujo at the Pontifícia Universidade Católica asks

> To what extent are the physical barriers the fruit of emotional barriers? To consider this type of issue we need to examine accessibility to collective spaces and, before this, question the accessibility to our hearts when recognising and accepting differences.

> If we are internally capable of recognising and welcoming individual aspects, accepting differences, with the flexibility that is inherent to life, we are capable of developing inclusive thinking. Following that we are capable of designing objects from the exchanging and sharing relations that man is capable of and that determine his actions in relation to the environment. Thus we build the form from building ourselves.
> (Mattos Eyer de Araujo, 2002)

Salutogenic healing, sensory and therapeutic gardens are by their nature inclusive and accessible. They acknowledge difference and cater for it within a soft landscape-led spatial treatment. Healing gardens offer collective and individual appeal as they reconnect children and adults with nature. Designed to promote health and well-being as well as to speed recovery, the garden design permits and encourages access and everyone feels comfortable in the space. For inclusion to be a reality rather than a vague aspiration, however, we need a system of design for a population with special needs that is universally appealing. That universal appeal is at the heart of inclusive, accessible design.

In contemplating *why* we are designing inclusive landscapes and urban centres for health and well-being, we need to be able to both recognise and accept difference. Imagine for a moment a new hospital. Designed to sit within extensive grounds so that healing garden spaces can be developed off wards, it was envisaged that staff, patients and their families would benefit from access to nature. The staff courtyard was designed with looping paths through colourful garden beds, comfortable seating on natural timber decking, soft, rounded planting and a shade tree. Patients' courtyards have a free standing pergola over the seating area, and offer backless bench seating so staff can be seated and swivel to monitor patients' progress in any direction. The seating is laid out in rows and fixed into hard paving. Straight line paths run along the edges of the space to take patients to a dead end, and then around a right angled corner to the next dead end. The staff love their courtyard. They go outside in their breaks and after five minutes feel rested and rejuvenated, so go back to work at their productive best. Spinal, stroke, brain injury and dementia patients go outside as part of their rehabilitation. They also love their outdoor space. It is a welcome relief to breathe fresh air and feel the sun and breeze on their face after hours indoors. However, they do not benefit from their therapeutic programme as much as expected and the results are put down to a failure of nature to work her wonders. Under the guise of being 'practical' the sensory experience provided in the patients' courtyard fails to deliver the desired outcomes. The fact that patients' gardens are equally in need of softening was overlooked. The designer stopped being creative when confronted with difference.

Should someone miss out on an experience because they cannot access it in the expected way? Inclusive design costs no more to design, build or maintain, yet the misconception persists. 'Practical' does not equal 'hard'. The inclusive designer knows that difference in mental, visual, or physical perception does not affect our deepest biophilic sense, and so works to provide a range of low maintenance, natural sensory experiences.

If we go back to the hospital courtyard example, although there is a need for staff to feel calm, rested and therefore productive in the workplace, there is an equal need for patients to feel calm, rested and rejuvenated so that they heal faster and can get back to their normal lives. Cost savings from reduced requirement for medication, reduced length of stay, faster return to society with flow-on positive impacts on family and community, outweigh costs of development. Soft landscape interventions can be used as a cost-effective tool when they adhere to the principles of inclusive design.

'Currently landscape is there to make the hole in the ground where the building sits look less ugly. There is generally no budget set aside so it becomes a question of "what can we do with no money?"' (McKellar, 2013). This is both our challenge and our opportunity. The growing body of evidence shows it is time landscape is valued

Figure 12.1 The rare beauty of nature.

for its potential as a cost-effective tool within any environment that seeks to enhance the health and well-being of the people who live, work, play, go to school, or recuperate there. The short answer to the question McKellar identifies is, 'We get creative.'

In the emerging field of salutogenic landscape and urban design, no one individual holds the sum of all knowledge. I therefore urge readers to continue to research and explore as many viewpoints and literature reviews as possible. In the USA, Clare Cooper Marcus and Naomi Sachs have written an excellent book on healing gardens in healthcare environments. In the UK, Play England has produced an invaluable guide on natural playground design. Landscape-led natural play areas, with abundant edible, playable planting, can become a wonderful healing resource. To date there is no text on healing environments specific to social/public housing, that I am aware of. Aged care is mentioned in senior strategies in Canada, Australia, Germany, Taiwan and Japan, but there is as yet no universal design guide. Clients in the sectors of public health, aged-care, community, police, justice, education, leisure, heritage, and housing will all benefit from a salutogenic approach.

Back to basics

When creating landscapes and urban designs for health and well-being we need to first evaluate the project from the high level master planning stage down to the detail, the small scale, in terms of creating an experience. Salutogenic design relies on creating spaces that stimulate our biophilic senses. Public and private spaces need to feel good to be in, to be easy to get around in, and to be welcoming to all ages and abilities.

To be a healing space the design must focus on introducing opportunities to reconnect with nature, using the basic principles of garden design. It can be a difficult thought transition for practitioners used to contributing to the landscape component of large development schemes. This is not the place for swathes of impermeable paving, pre-cast concrete plinth seating, hard square edges and monocultural planting schemes. Successful healing gardens rely on an in-depth knowledge not just of plants but importantly, how built and landscape elements interface and combine to create a biophilic sensory experience.

The importance of colour

Inclusive landscape and urban design uses colour in planting and surface treatments to bring people together, to stimulate, to soothe and to calm. Introducing and emulating nature's colours across the public realm brings a city to life. Colour makes a city more liveable, and attractive to local people, visitors and investors alike.

While conducting a peer review of a large new hospital project, one architect told me he had just discovered that green can be a useful colour as it is calming. True. Colour psychology informs a vital part of every successful sensory experience. For example, as green is calming, terracotta, reds and oranges are stimulating, and are particularly good at encouraging conversation. It is important to know your users, however. Colour-blind people are confused by green and red, so hues close to those colours, such as blue and orange, have a similar effect on mood, without causing the same confusion in colour blind people.

In communal spaces such as waiting rooms and break out zones, a terracotta coloured feature wall indoors or out in an adjacent courtyard, when combined with appropriately coloured and rounded leaf planting, can de-stress by prompting shared experience.

Another architect told me of his plan to incorporate a variety of medicinal plants in planting beds outside patient room windows. While no doubt a laudable acknowledgement of medical history, given the restricted budget, rare herbs that can be seen but not touched or tasted may not be the best use of funds.

Figure 12.2 Red flowers stimulate social engagement.

Figure 12.3 Medicinal herbs in a physic garden reference Waverley Abbey, as part of historic gardens at the Museum of Farnham. Designed by Greenstone Design UK.

The practice of garden design is generally associated with residential settings. Home gardens are generally gentler, more colourful than public spaces. They function, as McKellar said, to soften the building, but also as a haven from the outside world. Home gardens offer the opportunity for an active lifestyle connected with nature, with health and well-being benefits included, for free. As increasing numbers of people live in high rise apartments, fewer people have access to home gardens such as their grandparents may have had. Garden designers work closely with the end user to create a space that is both personal and nurturing. Occasionally it will also shout 'Look at me. See how successful I am.' With larger development projects some of that close client relationship is lost. Third party funding often means the end user – the patient, social/public housing resident or school student – has only a token part in the design process. In these situations it is important to talk to as many patients, residents and students as possible, to put yourself in their shoes.

Therapeutic horticulture settings

In any discussion of inclusive design it is important to make provision for those who are deemed to need support. To be truly inclusive, we also need to consider the people outside of the system, who are also affected by stress and depression, and who would benefit from working in a garden. Therapeutic horticulture, as a structured therapy programme, is often delivered in a controlled setting. In public space, where there is no stigma attached to simply joining in, horticulture programmes can attract people perhaps on the margins. Community gardens afford an ideal opportunity for people not served by formal therapy programmes to try gardening. Although a conscious desire to tend soil and plants, or even to be in a garden, is not universal, the benefits derived from such activities are. Therapeutic horticulture requires a flexible, inclusive garden setting that will accommodate non-gardeners and gardeners alike.

As the UK veterans' charity Help for Heroes found, some hardened soldiers were not interested in the therapeutic horticulture activity of propagating seeds as part of their rehabilitation from post-traumatic stress disorder. But the therapists knew they would benefit from being outside so engaged them in heavy manual labour. The veterans loved getting outside to rake compost and dig garden beds. Gardening is not just about growing the plants. Health benefits also come from all the activities associated with gardening. It is up to the therapist to match the activity with the patient/client.

Some landscape architects choose to call themselves garden designers, to differentiate themselves from those who design public realm, highway embankments and other 'look but don't touch' environments. I believe the distinction is telling on those practitioners who have moved away from creating environments that support people, towards monoliths that support consumption.

When we think like a gardener we create spaces for people and nature. For example, planted highway embankments are important visual amenity features and filter noise and air pollutants. They can be monocultural, monotonal and devoid of wildlife, or, when designed as a garden and with appropriate planting they can offer texture, colour and seasonal variation while pollutants from road runoff can be filtered. They can also create valuable additional habitats for local and migrating species. Roadside plantings, as with street trees, can be an important part of a green view and an overall salutogenic urban environment. Regardless of our professional title, when we think in terms of creating gardens our mindset necessarily shifts; we think of who will benefit from the garden, regardless of the scale of the development scheme.

Healing gardens, as we have seen in previous chapters, can be formed on roofs and up walls, as well as on the ground. In schools, prisons, around social housing and in hospitals, a green view can significantly de-stress and improve the mood of both young and old. As shown in Figure 12.4, low maintenance, colourful, living walls and roof gardens can be a powerful part of the healing garden experience, even if only able to be viewed from a distance.

To create a healing environment, in addition to thinking about garden design we also need to consider interior architecture in terms of transition zones (positioning and size of windows and external doors, and how they relate to internal visual and physical access points), interior design and colour psychology. To gain maximum value from the landscape intervention the interior needs to support what is going on outside, and the garden space likewise needs to work with the interior of the building (Figure 12.5).

As we saw in Chapter 1, if we think back to the early healing Buddhist, monastic and Islamic gardens, covered walkways or cloisters offered enticing views out to green lawns and gardens.

Figure 12.4 Living green wall and industrial-style roof garden aids biodiversity, cools the air, acts as insulation for the building, and improves sustainability ratings of the building while promoting human health and well-being.

within the wall of the cloister, there is a wide level ground . . . with . . . many different fruit-trees . . . It is close to the infirmary, and is very comforting to the brothers, providing a wide promenade for those who want to walk, and a pleasant resting-place for those who prefer to rest.

(Hobhouse, 2004)

Porches over doorways allow doors to be left open, allowing fresh air in and people out. Where the client requires maximum health benefit from the development some questions will inevitably have to be asked of the project architects. For example, if a hospital or school building is planned to have window shades, could the money be better spent on shade trees planted around the periphery of the building? Shade trees offer many more benefits than the shade of steel or timber louvres. Trees' root systems absorb excess runoff from the surrounding land, decreasing the load on stormwater drainage systems. The leaves move in the breeze, offering positive visual sensory stimulation. If the tree is a flowering variety there may be perfumed blossom, attracting a variety of happy pollinators such as bees and birds, again offering positive visual distraction. When the building offers opening

Figure 12.5 The colourful pots, wall and planting visible through the doorway attract you outside, encouraging you to engage with nature.

windows, sounds of song birds and rustling leaves can filter indoors. Shade trees offer a visual amenity while at the same time boosting the ecological health of the local environment. Through the planting of shade trees rather than building shade systems, it becomes a healthy place for humans too.

Dr Pekka Lahdenne, chief of the Outpatient Department and associate professor of paediatrics at the Children's Hospital, Helsinki University Central Hospital, says:

as a rheumatologist I have to do some nasty things to the children, painful things. It is best to have a playful, sensory rich environment to treat the children in, a room where there are positive visual distractions inside and outside the room. Then the children don't notice the pain so much, the parents remain calm and the procedure is much faster and much more successful.

(Lahdenne, 2013)

A good garden is an ideal positive distraction. It has planting of varied heights, hidden corners, focal points to tease the eye, and paths that entice you to explore. The sensory path shown in Figure 12.6 is textured with pebbles. While a traditional mosaic can be expensive and time consuming to install, paths such as this can be a wonderful volunteer community engagement activity. There are 'hot coloured' borders with perhaps a table and seating, and cooler, coloured bedding areas with a solitary seat for quiet contemplation. Low maintenance sensory planting can be left to self-seed, as shown in the gravel garden (Figure 12.7), where fine-textured gravel allows for wheeled access with a satisfying crunch as it is passed over. Drought-tolerant perennials and annuals such as these aquilegia, topiary buxus sp. and geraniums can grow happily with little attention.

Healing areas for quiet contemplation are kept deliberately simple (Figure 12.8). Here seating is arranged with sufficient space for private conversations between garden visitors. Garden beds are planted for year-round interest, with seasonal, flowering scented roses, lilies and shade trees adding to the sensory experience.

Shade and sunshine are important to the garden, and to the style of plants grown in each micro-climate within the garden. A connection with nature, feeling the rain on your face or a breeze in your hair, wildlife, seats, views, scents and sounds are a key part of the rich experience that is time spent in a well-designed garden. Often, however, when designing public space, social housing, healthcare or municipal gardens, those vital salutogenic attributes can be forgotten.

In a healing garden, individual garden areas have character and identity. A water feature of some sort is an essential element of a sensory garden. The tiled pool with basin shown in Figure 12.9 can be installed indoors or out. Colours of the tiles can

LEFT: **Figure 12.6** Reflexology path using carefully placed mosaic creates a texturally rich walkway through the garden.

ABOVE: **Figure 12.7** Low maintenance, self-seeding sensory planting.

RIGHT: Figure 12.8
Quiet contemplative seating area at the Royal Horticultural Society's Wisley Gardens, Surrey, UK.

BELOW: Figure 12.9
Water feature within a healing courtyard garden space.

be chosen to match the surrounding garden or interior. When a pumped water feature is too expensive, a simple barrel pond becomes an effective means of bringing a space to life, and attracting interesting wildlife such as dragonflies and goldfish. Mosquitoes are not a problem as the fish will eat any larvae that may appear. Colourful water lilies and reeds shade the water and create the habitat for pond dwelling animals (Figure 12.10).

In the public realm, architects, planners and designers are concerned with placemaking. Healing gardens are a central part of developing that sense of place. Both a sense of place and an ability to identify with that place are important for mental health. Of equal interest, with cities competing with each other for corporate patronage, it is important to create a strong, positive civic brand. Civic planting can help build that brand, with street trees and healing gardens. If the city's colours are black and gold, planting beds in the town square can reference those colours and support the city brand.

When there is just room for a single planting bed it is important that it takes its cue from the surroundings. If the area is shaded by nearby buildings, ferns and other shade-loving plants create an exotic feel, and will attract self-colonising shade-loving plants and animals.

Figure 12.10 Colourful water lilies and reeds shade the water and create the habitat for pond-dwelling animals.

Design for the young and the young at heart

A healing garden lifts the spirit and brings a smile to the passer-by as a sample of the wonders of nature. As mentioned in Chapter 3, children, older people and those living with or recovering from disability or ill health find solace in a healing environment. They are encouraged to become or remain active and independent.

We all need access to natural play areas. Inclusive spaces do not distinguish between age or ability. It is here that the young and young-at-heart develop or maintain their innate curiosity, test their limits, stretch brain, muscle and confidence as they experiment. Pleasantly shaded by deciduous trees in summer, and with small shrubs to provide interest and something to hide behind, abundant 'loose parts' – sand, spades, logs, sawn timber and wheeled toys – allow children to create and destroy, imagine and explore. Children learn through observation, trial and error, and gain confidence, storing positive memories for later years.

In contrast, the playground in Farnham, England shown in Figure 12.12 follows the traditional 'KFC' approach of kit, fence and carpet. Recently renovated as part of a government investment programme designed to improve the health and well-being of inactive and overweight children, the design shows questionable salutogenic benefit for money spent. The kit is all manufactured play equipment with prescribed entry and access points. The fence acts as a barrier to free play. The 'carpet' is an inert safety surface with no play value. There is no natural shade and no edible planting to entice children to eat a healthy fresh fruit snack on the way past. Interestingly, the photo was taken just after the children came out from school for the day. I was shielded from view so as not to deter any would-be playground visitors. However, none of the 300 plus children on this particular route home felt attracted to stop and play. If we design and develop playgrounds with the aim of building resilience through bringing the community together and keeping children

Figure 12.12 The contrasting, manufactured, 'KFC' approach to play area design – some kit or equipment, some fencing and a safety play carpet – offers little for the imagination, little excitement and little opportunity for interaction.

Figure 12.11 Natural play area with artificial stream and pebble 'beach'.

and young people healthy and active, surely it is important we create an engaging design that works for the particular community?

Playful healing gardens are not just for children and young people. Older people need to maintain their mental health and physical fitness too. Playful opportunities for adults are an excellent way to maintain an active lifestyle. In Figure 12.13 the author is shown swinging on a recycled timber pallet, hung from two wide canvas straps attached to an old metal pipe. The slight give in the canvas gave a very satisfying spring to the swinging experience! Taken in the construction playground Kolle 37 in Berlin, the swing is one of numerous all-age play opportunities available around the city.

Healing gardens can be messy places. Sometimes play requires adults to suspend their love of order and tidiness and to allow children to use their fertile imaginations, make a mess and get a little dirty (Davis et al., 2009). The girls in the salutogenic play garden shown in Figure 12.14 are moulding new island communities, baking mud pies and arranging flowers. There is even a 'pizza oven' (not shown) in the rear of the communal garden area. Some programmes, such as the UK-based Eco Schools, promote the reconnection of children with nature through environmental and sustainable education programmes. School grounds need to be designed and managed to facilitate such programmes. Shelters within gardens allow year-round use. When set within sensory planting they offer additional salutogenic benefits, as shown in Figure 12.15. The planting can make an excellent playable resource. Flexible-stemmed shrubs and small trees such as Portuguese laurel (*prunus lusitanica*), make excellent trees for climbing.

Playful, healing gardens also benefit from sound. Outdoor music allows young and old to express their mood through xylophones, drums, 'rain makers' and various stringed instruments (Figure 12.16). However, in some therapeutic and rehab spaces

LEFT: **Figure 12.13** Berlin, Germany: the author enjoying a home-made pallet swing suspended from canvas straps, hung from a recycled metal pole.

Source: Teresa Martins.

ABOVE: **Figure 12.14** Messy play in a sand and mud kitchen, Berlin, Germany.

it may be contra-indicated to have music, so check with staff and user groups before adding music to a healing garden.

As designers we are actively involved with the children throughout the design process. Where it is hard to find them in public (in some socially deprived neighbourhoods where parents/carers are not involved or suspicious of 'community events') we seek them out in local schools and create design projects in conjunction with the teachers to tease out what they really want, and then by extension what the teachers would like to have on their doorstep as a resource, as somewhere to take the kids on walkable 'reward' field excursions. It's amazing how you can construct a maths lesson around the theme 'How high can you go?'

The narrative is about providing a kids' space, for kids by kids, which works for adults too. We have to justify our decision (to adults) to 'just', for example, provide a pile of dirt, so we create meaning around that to satisfy the criticism that inevitably comes if we don't specify 'recognisable play equipment'. Child's play is messy.

Healing gardens for mental health: barrier free design

Affording opportunities to heal, as Hippocrates said, is as important as allowing time. Too often we put literal and figurative barriers in the way and deny people the opportunity to access healing spaces. Barrier free design is a term that is used interchangeably with universal design. Concepts of inclusion and accessibility are combined such that we create no barriers to access an experience. With the recent announcement that depression is now the second largest cause of disability globally (Ferrari et al., 2013; Medscape, 2013) it is important that we recognise and

Figure 12.15 Biophilic shelter in this healing garden promotes deep connections between people and nature.

Figure 12.16 Outdoor
music is an important
interactive component
in a sensory garden.

mitigate barriers to access, potential mental health stressors in the public and private realm.

Bev McAlpine, our occupational therapist at Greenstone Design UK, has worked with dementia, psychotic, neurotic and depressed clients for twenty-two years. Working with the national UK gardening charity Thrive, she has designed and delivered social and therapeutic horticulture programmes in a wide variety of settings. Each setting requires the same basic design elements to facilitate the therapeutic activities. Here we examine the key elements required in a sensory garden for clients with mental health issues.

Background: Clients may experience poor self-esteem, lack of self-acknowledgement and feelings of inadequacy which can lead to anxiety, stress, depression, anger and sadness.

The garden should aim to:

1 Reinforce sense of self, e.g. through providing different textures underfoot (grounded theory).
2 Reinforce sense of achievement, e.g. through creativity using loose natural materials.
3 Reinforce a safe atmosphere, e.g. entrances, safe spaces, privacy, seats with full backs.

4 Promote an atmosphere of self-acknowledgement/self-acceptance, e.g. climbing up, looking out, communicating, discussions.

5 Promote sense of competence, e.g. through an activity using natural materials.

6 Be a permissive space, e.g. provide enjoyment through being able to pick flowers, pick vegetables, plant a seed.

7 Be stimulating, e.g. facilitate activity that evokes symbolic thoughts, i.e. caring for something living, completing a simple gardening task – provide suitable raised beds, tables and seating.

8 Promote calm by providing water features, stimulating auditory and visual receptors.

9 Create space which reflects strength and tranquillity through appropriate seating, bright flowers, strong smells, variety.

10 Provide swings, bridges, gates, steps . . . options for physical change along the route.

When we design a landscape for universal appeal we design out social isolation. Social isolation is a leading cause of stress, depression and consequent physical ill health. By softening the built environment using landscape-led interventions such as permeable surfacings and planting, we can design for positive mental health.

It is relatively easy to design a therapeutic space as a standalone garden. While more difficult perhaps conceptually, barrier free or universal design across the public realm in practice is no different. Joined-up thinking is a term used to describe an acknowledgement of the multifunctional, multifaceted nature of interconnectedness. A holistic design approach provides a benefit greater than the sum of its parts. Using the above design guidelines and an embedded understanding of salutogenesis, it is possible to create an inclusive experience for people living with mental health issues on a town or city scale.

Design for an ageing community

In an ageing community we can expect more of the disabilities that come naturally. Inclusive urban design requires that city streets, shopping precincts, parks and public space acknowledge this. As bodies age and wear, increasing numbers of people will have sight, hearing and mobility impairments. Dementia is already increasing in prevalence across communities. In 2002, 13.9 per cent of the American population was estimated to be living with a form of dementia. By 2022 it is estimated that it will affect 80 million people in the USA (Plassman et al., 2007). It has been suggested that Alzheimer's, the most common form of dementia, is linked to chronic stress (Alzheimer's Society, 2012). Depression is also being studied for its links to Alzheimer's (Greenwald et al., 1997). Nature connections and healing gardens have been found to reduce stress and relieve depression; so to alleviate future costs of dementia care we need to introduce salutogenic landscapes across towns and cities.

Residential care

The key to health and well-being starts with a home that best meets our needs. When we design for older people we need to move our thinking away from standard facility-based care home design and design to create a welcoming space. The business model of an isolated care home has all but gone.

> The care home is an isolated island in a community sea. It risks further isolation by remaining an over 80s catchment. In a world gravitating back to community by desire and efficiency via financial structure, the opportunity is emerging for multi-generational health and wellness hubs. True integration is to have a care home setting inside a multigenerational health hub, not in a purpose built leper colony.
>
> (Crawley, 2013)

Today people want to live comfortably and safely within the community, in a place their friends and family can visit, with somewhere to go and something to do on site to keep residents and visitors alike stimulated and entertained. A central TV lounge and individual rooms looking out to some flat planting beds is no longer enough. People are living longer and in better health. The style of gardens we provide needs to offer all the features of a healing garden, with seating, paths, light and shade, colour, sound and water. The spaces need to allow people to participate, to trim and prune, make compost and spread it on the gardens and offer accessible areas for less mobile people to have their own growing areas and pursue their own horticultural interests. If we think in terms of what we would like, and would like our parents and grandparents to be able to enjoy, using the principles of monastic garden design we will create a salutogenic healing garden.

Case study 31: Patricia

Patricia is an 89-year-old woman who currently lives alone in her own two-bedroom apartment. She was concerned for her future and asked me:

> What am I going to do if my mobility fails, if I can't look after myself? How do you design a care home where you don't age 10 years just by walking in the door? At the moment I live alone in my own home. A subsidised bus takes me to my pilates class and University of the Third Age lectures. Every morning I go out to collect the newspaper. I take holidays to my younger sister's house. I take a taxi out to have lunch with friends, or they come to visit me. If I'm in a 'home' I won't have any reason to go out. They give you everything you need, there, on site. You don't need to make any decisions, so you just sit in a chair and fade away.

Patricia makes a good point. She values her independence but realises at some stage she will need care. When we design care home environments we need to be mindful of Patricia's concerns. We need to allow for individualised care, while designing a cost-effective, easy nursing environment. Can visitors come and enjoy private time with the resident? What incentives to go outdoors can be designed in? Can the resident go outdoors to post a letter, buy a newspaper? Is there a sunny, secluded space in the garden where family members can come together? Does the garden feel institutionalised or does it feel like a homely garden?

Although Patricia has lived in a home with a garden all her life she is fearful of what the new environment might look like. For people who have lived in high rise apartments all their lives it can be challenging to be surrounded by gardens and opportunities for gardening when they move into care. When people lack nature experience as a recent reference point, gardens need to be designed with more formality in certain parts. When planting is structured and ordered people learn which birds and insects visit which plants, and develop preferences. Over time they can express their preferences in less formal areas of the garden where they can plant and plan their own spaces. When we work collaboratively, with the end user as well as the client and funder, we can achieve a sustainable result – balancing social, economic and environmental benefit.

Social, public and affordable housing

At a lecture entitled 'Anatomy of a healing garden' by Canadian garden therapist Paul Allison, the surgeon introducing the talk observed that 'surgery and drugs don't help loneliness, depression and boredom. Gardens and gardening can.'

Housing for people in need is provided precisely because they have additional needs. These differences can set them apart from the wider community, with social isolation as the result. Loneliness, depression and boredom can be precursors to a range of mental and physical health problems, anti-social behaviours such as vandalism and hooliganism, and poor lifestyle choices such as overeating, binge drinking and drug abuse. Away from work, school and community supports, our homes are the principle setting, prompt and prop for our lifestyle. To ensure lifestyles are healthy, residents need to be able to connect socially and with nature. Their housing needs to make provision for sunny spaces to sit comfortably with neighbours, just outside the front door. Inclusive gardens must offer safe, engaging spaces where children can play. The development must ensure there is something to do and space for pets and hobbies. Loneliness, depression and boredom are rife within many housing areas. Human Centred Design (HCD), like Patient Centred Care, and Education of the Whole Child, are contemporary notions that encourage us to consider the people, the individuals we are working for. It is appalling that anyone should need to be reminded. If, as part of the early design phase, we consider *why* these people need housing, value the people as individuals and work with them to establish their needs and desires, we will ensure the environment is healthy.

Housing is a prime sector in need of a green space boost. It is important that the community own the development, though. Co-design ensures that the designer works not just through a stakeholder engagement process but actually empowers and enables the stakeholders, in this case the future residents of the new housing development, to share their design ideas, model them, own them. If the 'experts' come in from on high and 'give' the community something which is not valued then it will be a wasted effort. Vandalism is frequently seen in areas where meaningful engagement has not taken place. Sustainable results from healthy, resilient, ecologically balanced communities ensure a positive return on investment. Welfare, education support and social care costs decrease while tax income increases as businesses are attracted to invest in the area and workers are healthy, enabled and motivated.

Iterative design, where an idea is trialled, tested and evaluated, is being espoused as a new way forward. However, since the global financial crisis, the need for cost-efficient development is more important than ever. Given current economics, can we really afford the try-it-and-see approach, to experiment on people? Without disregarding the potential for progress and innovation, we have been housing, schooling and caring for people for enough years to know what works and what does not. If we step back from the modern marketing machine and listen to our hearts and the people we are providing for, we know what will be appropriate within the local cultural context. Traditions develop over time in the same way as species evolve. The best ideas are retained as local knowledge within the community. The only situation where iterative design is economically prudent and socially acceptable is where small groups of residents understand they are part of an experiment. Ideally, learnings from one project are built into the next. However the reality is often different and instead the same mistakes are perpetuated.

As we said in Chapter 11, simple is often best. It is easy to design a healthcare facility or a healthy workplace as a standalone facility, but more difficult to integrate that design thinking across the urban public realm. HCD and iterative design only take us so far. It requires a multi-disciplinary approach and an awareness of the advantages of the universal design concepts to create valuable, supportive and healthy environments of maximum impact for minimum expenditure. Inclusive, universal design allows and promotes a focus on preventative healthcare. As we have seen, the positive health impacts of a salutogenic approach are well documented.

It is vital that housing affords connections with neighbours, friends and family, and with nature. For stressed indigenous and immigrant communities, the need for social and nature connections can be even more pronounced than for the local population.

Case study 32: housing for at-risk families in Auckland, New Zealand

In Auckland state housing is provided for at-risk families based on a determined level of need. Many of the residents are refugees, indigenous Māori or immigrants from Pāsifika (principally Tonga, Samoa, the Cook Islands, Fiji, Tokelau, Tuvalu and Niue). The islanders' cultures are distinct and proud. The story is told of the social worker who introduced a recently arrived Pāsifika family to their new home. They toured the detached house and she showed off sleeping, living and bathroom facilities, before ending in the kitchen. The social worker concluded the tour with the comment '. . . and this is the oven where you cook'. Some hours later emergency services were called to the address to put out a fire that had been lit inside the oven. No thought had been given to who the likely residents would be and their traditional outdoor communal cooking practices in the design of the housing, nor had the social worker considered cultural difference in her briefing. Healing gardens are not just about texturally rich, fragrant flower beds or edible community gardens. When designed as a culturally appropriate, integral part of a housing development healing gardens can help acclimatise migrants into their new community, retain their connections with nature, and stave off depression, loneliness and the boredom that comes from sitting inside not knowing who to talk to. In housing developments with immigrants as likely residents, culturally appropriate planting is also a simple tool to ease the culture shock that comes from immigration. The Pāsifika staple root crop, taro, may be more appropriate than the usual *griselinia littoralis* (kapuka) hedging. Similarly, *ficus carica* (fig) is culturally more appropriate for refugee communities from the Middle East than *malus sp.* (crab apple)

Outdoor cooking facilities afford the opportunity for native peoples and immigrants to enjoy traditional communal activities. Where the climate is not naturally conducive, covered sheltered areas can be provided.

Local food supplies

As part of housing provision it is useful to provide space for local food growing. A healthy diet is integral to a healthy life. When tasty food is available, grown by residents for residents and free for the picking, it is easier than walking to the takeaway store. Convenience is everything as we design for well-being. To create a change in mindset that values a new, healthy lifestyle, it has to be the attractive, easy option.

It is important that the gardens multi-task, so they are not kept apart from the people, but become normalised within their daily movements. As seen in early monastic and Islamic gardens, food growing can be added to seating areas as edible borders. Fruit trees ought not to be banished to some distant corner or placed in a stand-alone orchard, but need to line walkways, set corners to aid way-finding and be espaliered up sunny walls. When grown beside paths they will provide summer shade and a rich sensory experience as the tree flowers, is perhaps fragrant, carpets the ground with petals, attracts pollinators and birds, sets fruit, and changes leaf colour if deciduous. When mature, many fruit trees offer easy climbing opportunities for the young and young at heart. As seen in Chapter 11, a view or vantage point is one of the top ten biophilic elements. Affording tree climbing opportunities around a housing development is a good way to gain maximum salutogenic value from the garden.

When we design for health and well-being we are, in effect, designing 'feelgood' gardens. Like the ancient tea gardens of Japan, feelgood gardens are true sensory gardens where you are encouraged to pause, pick and eat, to watch your food grow, to nurture it. Key elements of healing gardens, sensory gardens and therapeutic gardens include fruit bushes and trees, herbs, vegetables and edible flowers.

Young babies, those with developmental delays and people living with some sensory impairment put things in their mouth to make sense of them. Our mouths have the most receptors of anywhere on the body, so it stands to reason that if we do not recognise something, we would pick up (touch), smell (as it enters our mouth) and taste the item. Healing sensory gardens therefore need to offer edible plants. In settings where management is not comfortable with the idea of edible plantings, it is important that non-toxic plants are chosen.

Tools

Additional tools and equipment can bring a garden to life and increase its value through the seasons.

Webcams are great tools in sensory gardens. We use them in schools, care homes, community centres, hospital day rooms, almost anywhere we have a 'captive' indoor audience we want to engage with nature outdoors. Webcams allow people to view the interior of a nest box, for example, or to watch the nocturnal habits of a visiting owl. We don't use the webcams to replace an outdoor experience but to supplement it.

Barbeques and fire pits give an additional social element to a garden. Outdoor cooking is part of many cultures. Fire and warmth are biophilic elements that are very attractive and when located adjacent to seating areas promote social connections. Fire pits in schools are becoming popular as a way to de-stress children at risk of under-achievement due to ill health, family violence or disability. Sitting around a fire prompts deep memory experiences. Gas barbeques are more heat efficient and clean burning than wood or charcoal.

Adapted ergonomic garden tools allow arthritic and stroke-damaged hands and mobility impaired bodies to participate in active gardening. Tools need to be stored in an accessible location, close to where they will be used. In this way independence is promoted and self-confidence gained.

References

Alzheimer's Society (2012). Stress link to Alzheimer's goes under the spotlight. http://alzheimers.org.uk/site/scripts/news_article.php?newsID=1243

Cooper Marcus, C. and Sachs, N. A. (2013). *Therapeutic landscapes: an evidence-based approach to designing healing gardens and restorative outdoor spaces*. New York: Wiley.

Crawley, Esmonde (2013). *New business model to replace care homes*. Report. London: Over 50s Housing.

Davis, L., White, A. and Knight, J. (2009). *Nature play: maintenance guide*. London: National Children's Bureau.

Ferrari, A. J., Charlson, F. J., Norman, R. E., Patten, S. B., Freedman, G., Murray, C. J., Vos, T. and Whiteford, H. A. (2013). *Burden of depressive disorders by country, sex, age, and year: findings from the Global Burden of Disease Study 2010*. San Francisco: PLOS.

Greenwald, B. S., Kramer-Ginsberg, E., Bogerts, B., Ashtari, M., Aupperle, P., Wu, H., Allen, L., Zeman, D. and Patel, M. (1997). Qualitative magnetic resonance imaging findings in geriatric depression. Possible link between later-onset depression and Alzheimer's disease? *Journal of Psychological Medicine*, 27:421–431.

Hobhouse, P. (2004). *Plants in garden history*. London: Pavilion.

Lahdenne, P. (2013, 13 July). Dr. Interviewed by the author.

Mattos Eyer de Araujo, R. (2002). *Accessible school furniture and appropriate technology*. Rio de Janeiro: Pontifícia Universidade Católica.

McKellar, E. (2013, 13 September 13). Principal Architect. Interviewed by the author.

Medscape (2013, 6 November). Depression now world's second leading cause of disability. Retrieved 6 November 2013, from *MedScape Multi Speciality*: www.medscape.com/viewarticle/813896

Plassman, B. L., Langa, K. M., Fisher, G. G., Heeringa, S. G., Weir, D. R., Ofstedal, M. B., Burke, J. R., Hurd, M. D., Potter, G. G., Rodgers, W. L., Steffens, D. C., Willis, R. J. and Wallace, R. B. (2007). Prevalence of dementia in the United States: the aging, demographics, and memory study. *Journal of Neuroepidemiology*, 29(1–2):125–132.

PART IV

ADDITIONAL RESOURCES

CHAPTER 13

Funding sources for public sensory, therapeutic and healing gardens

In this chapter, traditional top-down funding streams are challenged to think in terms of broad linkages. Whether as designers, funders, procurement managers and clients, awareness of the big picture is vital. Why pipe water underground when you can create a health-giving, playable, above-ground water channel for storm water, as in Figure 13.1, in a school in Berlin?

> It is not as simplistic as finding funding. An attitudinal shift is required; a fundamental ground swell that directs the line of enquiry, the measurements of success, goals and aspirations. Currently measurement criteria don't include a sense of well-being. We are working on ways to measure and calculate what previously has been intangible. How do you measure that sense of satisfaction when a previously dying duckling, starts eating from your hand? How do you measure the joy when winter withdraws and the bright colours of spring appear? How do you measure the comfort that comes from sitting in green space with the sun on your face? Do we measure this by serum Vitamin D levels, or days off school, increased productivity at work or Likert scales? What we do know deeply and intuitively is that whilst technology aids and assists us, it is the natural world that feeds and sustains our soul.
>
> (Parkinson, 2013)

So long as people think it is easier to take a pill than to eat responsibly and enjoy fresh air, funding will favour pharmaceuticals. Likewise, if school communities believe they will achieve better results by spending longer hours in the classroom rather than playing and learning in the field, outdoor play areas will be sold and funding will favour remedial programmes. As Dr Parkinson says, an attitudinal shift is required.

Fortunately attitudes are shifting. An integrated salutogenic approach is already changing the way we do business. New funding sources are evolving as individuals, innovators and early adopters vent their frustration at government inaction. Bottom-up, community-based initiatives are seizing the healing potential of nature, without waiting for public funding. Internationally, a groundswell of interest in the healing properties of green space has begun.

While the development of community-based green space programmes is a positive sign, it is important to have the support of government agencies.

Figure 13.1 This safe, playable dry river bed is part of a practical stormwater system in a school in Berlin, Germany.

Case study 33: Mr J

In Sydney, Australia, I recently met a young man incensed that his 80-year-old father, Mr J, had so little by way of pension income that he had decided to grow his own food on the sunny roadside verge outside his home. He lived in a socially and economically deprived area beset with typical lifestyle-related concerns across health, education and diet. The well tended vegetables and small fruit bushes he grew beautified the area, and provided a public education opportunity to passing children interested to see someone tending and eating the plants. Any surplus was distributed freely around the community. Mr J was connected to nature and his community in a very public way. He benefited from the social connections, and his son reported that since planting the verge he was happier and felt he had a purpose in life once more. While he worked in the garden Mr J kept active and enjoyed the opportunity to interact with people, and the local people appreciated occasional free food and the improved aesthetic. Previously the verge was overgrown with weeds and long grass. The roadside healing garden space was entirely self-funded, using seed swaps and local compost and recycled materials as water-saving mulches. Despite the broad community benefits derived from the garden, the local council took exception to Mr J's initiative. The garden was on their land. They sprayed the plants with herbicide, poisoning the soil and their relationship with their tax-paying community. They could not see the big picture connections between the individual's need for a nature and social connection and their reduced budget requirements for ground maintenance, health, education or welfare support.

Sensory, healing and therapeutic gardens can be found on verges, around social (public) housing, in schools, in care homes, senior and assisted living settings, around hospitals, airports, bus and railway stations, parks and city buildings. Some of the land will be government owned, some will be privately owned. Regardless of ownership or management of the land, the general public benefits from the addition of inclusive, physically accessible green space; which becomes the core feature of any funding application. Public benefit is guaranteed as even when people cannot directly access the garden they profit from a green view. This feature is important during the design phase in considering sight lines from adjacent buildings, and in proving benefit to planning authorities (who are not necessarily working with the funders). While neighbours may not be willing to contribute financially to the development of the green view, they will profit from it so may be useful in building a business case for the development.

Healing gardens need to be developed across our urban centres, on both public and private land. So, in addition to community-based initiatives we will examine the features that interest government funding, including increased revenues from taxes, political dividends from popular initiatives, and the triple bottom line of saving budgets, people and the environment from harm.

The economics and the politics of healing gardens

For all their potential gains, governments have been slow to realise their role as a facilitator, overseer or regulatory guide. Green space was traditionally considered good for the public and in economic terms, a 'public good'. Hence the public, represented by their elected officials in parliament, city and town hall, was generally responsible for ensuring its provision.

Definition: A public good is defined as a commodity or service that is provided without profit to all members of a society. The product is supplied such that one individual can consume or benefit from it without reducing its availability to another individual and from which no one is excluded. Flood protection and healing gardens are equally classified as public goods. A public good can be provided either by the government or by a private individual or organisation.

Definition: Social goods, in contrast, are defined as offering a service that benefits the largest number of people in the largest possible way. Some classic examples of social goods are clean air, clean water and literacy; in addition, many economic proponents include access to services such as healthcare in their definition of the social or 'common good'.

(Investpedia, 2013)

Healing gardens cross the boundary to fit the definition of both public and social goods. While being doubly advantageous, it is also a problem. The modern world is one of specialists and compartmentalised thinking. While this has promoted advances in some areas, significant regression and degradation of services and environment have occurred in others. If something does not fit a certain category it is often ignored as 'outside the scope of enquiry'. Confusion over where green space sits within the economic framework has led to piecemeal development, inadequate regulatory frameworks, and, significantly, a burgeoning burden of disease. However, society's healthcare needs are just the tip of the funding crisis that surrounds the growing numbers of adults and children affected by non-communicable diseases.

Silo thinking within the design fraternity, and in education, housing, welfare, justice, environment and commerce has meant opportunities from recent discoveries in health and environmental psychology have been slow to filter through. Funds have been wasted and opportunities lost as valuable integrated systems thinking, multi-sectoral initiatives, policy frameworks and value-engineered innovation are affected by the lack of joined-up thinking. Albert Einstein is credited with saying that insanity is doing the same thing over and over and expecting different results. What does this have to do with the funding of public landscape and urban design as a cost-effective tool for health and well-being? Politics can both create and destroy innovation and initiative, regardless of the sense and sensibility of the scheme. The WHO called for an innovative solution to the rising tide of stress and depression and we have found it. Healing gardens are an ingenious addition to the social, economic and environmental health toolbox. That the tool is so flexible and adaptable is one of its prime features and selling points. Using natural play and sensory, therapeutic and healing gardens for all ages, stages and abilities allows us to tap into resources and funding streams across multiple sectors.

In the same way as politics can obliterate even commercially astute environmental interventions, lobbyists can both help and harm support for healing gardens. Powerful campaigners who feel threatened by change may discount and try to discredit the benefits of cost-effective soft landscape-led initiatives. It is important to allay fears and support individuals and groups through the necessary transition phase. Healing gardens will not replace manufactured playgrounds, classroom-based education, or hospital-based healthcare, but can make them more cost effective. In an age of value for money solutions to complex problems, funding of public green space is vital. Public funding is needed to supplement and support community-led initiatives. It is time to redress the imbalance seen across the health of three generations by rapid urbanisation, consumerisation and digitisation.

Concurrently with the identified disconnection from nature, three themes arise:

1 The population is ageing, which brings opportunities and additional costs.
2 The working population is under stress and suffering from lifestyle-related diseases at unprecedented rates.
3 Children are under pressure to perform and out-compete their peers.

Social determinants of health and well-being are a key policy focus for governments seeking to improve population health and curb burgeoning healthcare

Figure 13.2 Playing in the dry river bed.

budgets. As seen with recent storm events, governments face monumental costs to rehouse and to repair and replace infrastructure for climate change. Governments cannot afford to maintain financing the historically unparalleled burden of NCDs. They cannot afford to continue to repair housing and public space vandalised by disenfranchised youth. Communities cannot continue to bear the social, environmental and economic costs of stress and depression. Administrators everywhere are looking for alternatives.

Abundant research, practical experience and post-occupancy evaluations have proven the efficacy of well designed green space within our urban areas. When appropriately designed, landscape-led interventions soften the built environment and improve health and well-being. Figure 13.3 shows an open access multi-generational natural play area adjacent to housing in Berlin, Germany. With diverse benefits accruing from healing gardens, funding can come from a wide variety of sectors. As places where people can come together to connect socially and with nature, healing gardens can be added across all settings, from car parks to shopping centres, schools to housing, public parks and playgrounds, commercial centres to heathcare centres. Healing gardens are changemakers, ideas that inspire action to change the world. They can effect transformation across health, employment, investment, education, welfare and crime prevention. Internationally, in Europe, the Americas, the Middle East, Oceania, Africa and Asia, governments are becoming aware of the benefits of a long term, holistic view of the links between environment, public health and the economy. They are lagging behind private investors, however, as they maintain disconnected silo thinking.

TOP LEFT: Figure 13.3
Low cost fun: simple timber boarding affords sand and water play.

TOP RIGHT: Figure 13.4
Sustainable playground in a nursery school in Kent, UK. Designed by Greenstone Design UK.

Source: Matt Dunkinson Photography.

To date, funding for the principle areas of urban gardens and green space has come from individual enlightened private benefactors, or city authorities. Amenity strips added to meet planning conditions of new developments are funded by the developers. Often they comprise uninspiring planting and offer little to engage either wildlife or passers-by, though for the same cost a health-giving garden could be developed. From a salutogenic design perspective as much as a prudent financial management perspective, it makes sense to spend money wisely, requiring minimum outlay for maximum benefit.

Funding on a cost–benefit basis

As we saw in Chapter 9, the cost–benefits of developing healing gardens are diverse and potentially profound. According to Dr Tony Johnson of Shanghai, developers have found that a simple, green visual upgrade attracts tourists and business, and helps people feel good. Sale times are decreased as value is increased:

> Investors are building monuments to their new-found wealth. They are not interested in sustainability but do recognise the influence of good fengshui on health and wealth. For example, the 'norm' for residential projects is to have a mountain or tall trees behind the buildings to make you feel secure and water in front. This can NOT be changed, residential buildings do NOT sell if there is a mountain in front and water behind, the plot needs to be rotated and forget the expense as this will improve sales dramatically.

Case study 34: Highfield and Brookham School, Hampshire, UK

The school is set in wooded countryside 90 minutes south of London. Catering for day and boarding students from 3 to 13 years, they have a strong tradition of allowing and encouraging children in their care to enjoy their childhood. I was asked to design the 3–5 year olds' play area as a sensory-rich natural play space, to reflect the ambition of the families who send their children there, but being mindful of needing to add value to a strictly controlled budget. Cost comparisons were made as part of the design development phase. In school playgrounds rubberised play surfaces are often the aspiration. We counselled the client against this option. Considered by many to be an essential in any play space, expensive impact attenuating surfaces (IAS) have been shown to increase risk-taking behaviours and offer little by way of reduced injury rates. With almost zero play value, except for wheeled activities, they offer a dead-feeling, indoor-like play space, as shown in the photo of the inner city Wapping Women's Centre before we redesigned their outdoor children's play space into a healing garden (Figure 13.5).

Natural play surfacing materials were costed for Highfield Brookham on a whole-of-life basis, including a sum assigned to their play value, or ability to be played with. Maintenance costs were included to cover the reseeding of grass, cleaning of sand and topping-up of bark. The client decided that natural play development is more cost effective, and often requires little specialist labour so can be installed by volunteers. In this way the salutogenic design approach offers a preventative healthcare option for the wider community, as it creates a social connection point around the development project, as well as a nature connection opportunity. Community involvement, volunteer labour, co-design and creative, living, biophilic spaces are easy to fund as people want to be involved, want to be associated with the feelgood vibe.

Figure 13.5 Impact-attenuating surfacing offers little play value.

Figure 13.6 Recycled tyres under a blossom tree create a simple play space in a school in Hampshire.

Developers are willing to fund and own developments for 7 to 10 years. Given that most countries have a short 3–5 year political election term, this length of private sector mid-term thinking is an improvement (Johnson, 2013).

1 Within the existing funding framework, to achieve everything a healing garden is capable of will require some changes to the funding criteria and the way funds are administered.

2   Private and public funders must be made to recognise that their money will be best spent when the client does not have to rush to spend their budget, when they can give due consideration to the design phase. Good things take time. Instant gratification is only possible through the manufactured economy. The green economy supports longer term thinking for sustainable, long term results.
3   Funders will also benefit from a collaborative approach. When the benefits of a development cross various interest groups and jurisdictions, additional funding can be brought to bear on a scheme.
4   Governments may wish to provide tax breaks for investors in healing garden schemes, where those schemes are shown to meet strict salutogenic design criteria.

Design for health and well-being is at the heart of how successful sustainable businesses operate and can grow the economy, adding positive environmental and social impact. Salutogenically responsible businesses are those that recognise that society's success is their success. As we have seen, without ecological health there can be no human health and well-being. As such the sustainable, resilient triple bottom line of social, economic and environmental gain is salutogenic. Environmentalist and author Paul Gilding says truly sustainable companies 'do good things in order to make money', whereas a greenwasher merely does good things after they've made money (Gilding, 2013).

Landscape and urban design for human health and well-being is ecologically robust, inclusive, accessible, child friendly, pet dog friendly, senior friendly and welcoming to persons living with disability. It promotes public health through positive mental health and an active lifestyle. With good mental health comes a positive social outcome across education, crime, relationships, workplace productivity and environmental stewardship. It creates attractive communities in which to live and do business. It is, in short, good for all; everyone benefits when we have healing garden spaces embedded within each suburb and each city quarter.

The sectors or areas of benefit (education, health, justice, etc.) are generally individually, centrally funded. Most countries have a separate court system for families and criminals, an education department funded independently of the health ministry. Behind the separation is one central treasury. Design for health and well-being is about thinking big, and thinking holistically. When we create the business case for a salutogenic design proposal we can draw on diverse funding streams, as the benefits are broad. Used to its fullest potential, salutogenic design can create liveable cities with sustainable economies; even the economists and accountants are happy and healthy, with high returns on investment for business owners and residents.

Social goods and public goods

Healing gardens have been shown to be useful to society generally and to communities and individuals in particular. In economic terms, they are a social utility. A social good is something deemed to benefit society, and therefore is worthy of investment. That level of investment varies, however, across cultures and economies.

In the Western world gardens have a history as a luxury item, affordable and accessible by the rich. This contrasts with traditional societies where a home garden is seen as a necessity.

As we have seen in previous chapters, across the developed world healing gardens are not restricted to healthcare settings. Nature is at her most therapeutic when incorporated into urban planning as an integral part of our everyday lives, at home, at work and at school. But too often we get caught up with the need for land to be commercially 'productive', so it is stripped bare and built on or farmed for timber, food or fuel.

The more disconnected from nature we have become, the less value we have placed on landscape. This is somewhat counter-intuitive, however, as at the same time as landscape and nature are devalued in the public realm, health spas and luxury residential developments push nature for its healing powers. The perception that nature is a luxury good has influenced urban design and development decisions.

Often the developing countries that do not have access to high tech solutions resort to tried and true traditional architectures and traditional family-based healthcare. Although seemingly 'worse off' that others in First World settings, in fact they can be better off as long term community mental and physical health and associated social and economic indicators improve.

In order to find funding, something first must be valued. In a business setting a commercial valuation involves testing future market values and depreciation.

Without a financial value being placed on a landscape feature it is hard for mainstream accountants to see the value. What we must first establish is *why* we are creating a garden or public green space. If the impetus has come from a desire to improve human health and well-being, we can cost out the development cost of the healing garden versus the maintenance cost to society of not having the garden. If the stimulus is purely aesthetic it is more difficult financially to justify.

Public funds

Funding for public gardens has traditionally come from local government, and from individual wealthy benefactors. For 200 years green space has been seen as a social good, necessary to make a place look attractive, but readily cut when budgets were tight. Municipalities in wealthy areas used their higher tax take to plant street trees and provide leafy playgrounds for the children. The benefits of the trees and associated green space was not quantified other than through aesthetics. People reported a feeling of well-being when in those areas but it was not quantified, until recently.

By proving the cost effectiveness of healing gardens, funding is more readily diverted from various budgets. Health budgets have traditionally been spent on treatment options, with a lesser amount spent on prevention through community education programmes.

Funding is often available for gardens that can prove their usefulness in terms of aiding biodiversity, adapting for climate change, and assisting the health and well-being of a community.

Government funding or grants for specific population groups are available, where that group forms a significant portion of a wider population.

Grant funding

With healing gardens funding often comes from a third party. Grant funding for a social good such as green space development may mean that various criteria need to be met to satisfy the funder. Where environmental-based grants are available it is easy to satisfy their requirements with a salutogenic design approach. Given the project's need for wildlife-attracting, bio-diverse planting, local food sources and the development of a community health asset, we can tick a lot of boxes! Environmental credentials and community benefit need to be demonstrated as part of the funding application.

Grant funding is often tagged to be used within a certain timeframe. While this may be convenient for the funder's balance sheet, a rushed design phase often leads to sub-optimal and unsustainable results. Where possible it can be useful to invoice the funder for the full amount, bank it and use the money slowly, in a sustainable, considered fashion. This option requires a high degree of ethics and of trust, with which some people may be uncomfortable and unfamiliar. When developing healing gardens, however, trust is a necessary feature of the relationship between stakeholders, designers and contractors. In a competitive world, old fashioned business ethics can provide a point of difference. With grant funding, as with other forms of finance, it is vital to the long term success of the project that everyone is fully informed, engaged and consulted.

Crowd funding

Crowd funding is a new online community funding option. The concept is simple. A large number of people (the crowd) each funds small amounts of money to accumulate into an investment large enough to finance a project. Crowd funding is a means to market your project to an interested audience. It is effective for large sums and small. US president Barack Obama financed his 2008 election campaign using crowd funding, and raised $137 million through online channels (Prive, 2012).

Described as the finance option of the future, crowd funding is an important funding innovation for green space. The idea of 'it's not what you do but why you do it' is essential to selling the idea to potential funders. Given the positive health and well-being message of healing gardens, crowd funding will be a significant funding agent. Where communities are engaged and value the environment they will be motivated to fund projects that make a difference to their community. Biophilic design makes a fundamental difference to the health and well-being of a community and so it is expected that crowd funding will be an effective means of financing healing garden projects.

Current landscape and urban regeneration projects being financed through crowd funding include the bid by Manchester, the UK's second largest city, to turn the urban square into a nature hub. It is a way for people to connect personally with projects that are interesting and important to them (LI, 2013)

Adding value through landscape

When applying for funding, it is important to be able to show how the project will add value, socially, economically and/or environmentally. Increasingly the community is impatient and leads the project without waiting for 'official' funding or recognition. Planting, maintenance and urban regeneration and ecological restoration projects have all been tackled by individuals coming together to make a difference. Each type of project has the capacity to become a healing garden space as it offers people a chance to connect with nature and their community. At times such community-led projects do not achieve all they might. They may lack professional input and landowner support. However, each landscape improvement project goes some way towards creating healthy, liveable towns and cities, and as such deserves recognition.

Guerrilla gardening

Guerrilla gardening heals communities at zero cost to developers. This type of community initiative is becoming increasingly common around the world.

Case study 35: the guerrilla gardening approach

'Guerrilla gardening' describes the unofficial greening of a city or environmental improvements made by an unfunded, self-selected group of people, sometimes under cover of darkness. In the bankrupt city of Detroit, Michigan, parks and playgrounds lie untended, quietly decaying as the City withdraws its services. Children and their families suffer as they have nowhere safe to play. As children are kept indoors, the inactive lifestyle spiral hits and community and well-being suffer. Not only does mental and physical health deteriorate, but educational outcomes decline, crime rates increase, residential values decline and local businesses fail, adding more stress to the community.

Fortunately, resilient individuals can be found in any community. Resilient individuals come together to form resilient communities, capable of adapting to adversity. The opportunity to play outdoors safely is a basic human right. The United Nations Convention on the Rights of the Child, Article 31 (leisure, play and culture), states that children have the right to relax and play, and to join in a wide range of cultural, artistic and other recreational activities (UNICEF, 2013). Led by Tom Nardone in Detroit, a group of individuals calling themselves the Mower Gang have come together to do something about provision for children's play within their decaying community. The group's founder says they are 'one-part biker rally and one-part clean-up' and that their group 'have fun while mowing the abandoned parks and playgrounds of Detroit'.

Their particular emphasis is on playgrounds because, as they say, '6 year olds can't mow their own park'. The group organise themselves through Facebook. Mowing and clean-up events are held every second Wednesday evening. In some locations it is suggested that members wear their Kevlar bullet-proof vests that have been supplied by a local manufacturer keen to sponsor the community initiative. Mowers and other garden tools are owned by the members, who also supply fuel. Events are made social with some people bringing food and drink to celebrate at the end of another park or playground clearance, or sometimes rehabilitation. The group also repaint or repair play equipment where possible or where necessary.

This guerrilla garden (Figure 13.7) stakes an unofficial claim on the street verge of Berlin. Fencing, amenity planting, a bird feeder, nest box and seat make this a very personal space. Such private incursions into public space are tolerated for the positive effect they have on the wider community. As attitudes change towards the value of landscape interventions as a cost-effective aid to health and well-being, we will see more initiatives such as Detroit's Mower Gang. As governments wake up to the benefits of a health-in-all-policies approach we will see funds diverted from one departmental budget to support another, with a salutogenic environment being the beneficiary. As corporates see the benefits to their staff in ensuring appropriate convenient green space is available, we will see pressure to supply additional parks, roof gardens and green walls throughout our cities. As researchers collaborate across multi-disciplinary teams we will see more evidence of the benefits of a salutogenic design approach. Soon landscapes for health and well-being will become part of mainstream budget allocations.

Figure 13.7 Berlin, Germany: an individual has created a street-side haven outside her apartment building, tolerated by city authorities as she maintains it and it benefits the local community.

References

Gilding, P. (2013, October). How to tell a sustainable business from a greenwashing one: interview with Paul Gilding. Retrieved from *Eco-Business.com*, www.eco-business.com/news/how-tell-sustainable-business-greenwashing-one-interview-paul-gilding/

Investpedia (2013). Social good definition. Retrieved from *Investopedia*: www.investopedia.com/terms/s/social_good.asp

Johnson, T. (2013, 4 November). Ph.D. Interviewed by the author.

LI (2013). Landscape Institute. Retrieved 2013, from *Landscape Institute*: www.landscapeinstitute.org/news/index.php/news_articles/view/manchester_launches_collaborative_crowd-funded_regeneration_project

Parkinson, Dr. (2013, 15 November). Interviewed by the author.

Prive, T. (2012, 27 November). What is crowd funding and how does it benefit the economy? Retrieved 28 December 2013, from *Forbes Magazine*, www.forbes.com/sites/tanyaprive/2012/11/27/what-is-crowdfunding-and-how-does-it-benefit-the-economy

UNICEF (2013, 1 February). Fact sheet: a summary of the rights under the convention. Retrieved from *Rights Overview*: www.unicef.org/crc/files/Rights_overview.pdf and http://ipaworld.org/general-comment-on-31/un-general-comment/un-stands-up-for-childrens-right-to-play-arts-and-leisure-in-a-landmark-moment-for-children

CHAPTER 14

How and where to develop community green space

With an understanding of *why* we need to take a salutogenic approach to urban and landscape design and hence find additional green space in and around our urban centres, and a feeling for *how* to fund healing landscape developments, we also need to understand *where* we can effect healing garden spaces.

Community place making is at the heart of green space planning and provision. The addition of green space to an urban area can help bring previously unused spaces to life. When we talk about bringing life to the town or city it is in both the literal and the figurative sense. Life literally comes from the people, plants and animals that colonise the space. As planners and designers it is easy to forget the importance of soil micro-organisms that support invertebrates, insects, birds and a wide variety of plant life. Although used to working with design elements above ground we must be mindful of what goes on below. Storm water filtration, slowing runoff, recycling energy and nutrients are all evident when we look. Nature is incredibly resilient. When creating resilient human communities it is helpful to remember our dependence on natural communities for our health and well-being. Life comes to a space literally when children fly their kites, families picnic under trees and old men snooze in the afternoon sunshine.

The Scottish charity Greenspace Scotland (2011) defines green spaces as

> the 'green lungs' of our towns and cities which contribute to improving people's physical and mental health by providing places for informal recreation – walking, cycling, sitting, socialising and children's play – and 'breathing spaces' to take time out from the stresses of modern life.

Such breathing spaces allow fresh air to replace the often polluted indoors air of modern, sealed buildings. It also allows a break from the sensory overload of digital information available to us when 'plugged in' indoors. Of course with portable devices we can take our phones and iPads outside with us. Outdoors, however, with so much raw beauty in front, above, below and around us, we are tempted to remove the earphones and take our eyes away from the screen, to savour the sights, sounds, smells and taste of the land. Greenspace Scotland goes further in their definition of the importance green spaces to say: 'they bring the countryside into our towns and cities, and make it accessible from our "backdoors". Greenspaces also create safe and attractive places where people want to live and businesses invest.'

Figure 14.1 Attractive pocket park.

Figure 14.2 Wide city street turned into healing public green space, encouraging active transport.

Green spaces are multi-functional; they are used in many different ways. They include not only areas to which the public have physical access, but also visual access, for example, in the way green spaces provide settings for buildings, communities and everyday activities (Greenspace Scotland, 2011).

Figure 14.3 Living walls combine with colourful personal plantings on apartment balconies to create an attractive, healthy green view.

First steps

The idea for a healing community greening initiative historically has come from an interest group within the community. An individual may have a dream of how local quality of life could be improved, and then gauges response and potential support from within the wider population. Over time they attract others who share the vision, the idea gains momentum, and with luck and a great deal of hard work may come to fruition.

As mentioned in Chapter 3, degraded urban areas are an international issue affecting public mental health and quality of life. Taking a salutogenic approach to urban renewal, we see gardens and green space for health and well-being rely on high quality place making, with pocket parks, community gardens, and playful spaces developed in close collaboration with local residents, the business community, landowners and policy makers. Community involvement, recognition and support are vital to the long term success of any green space development. Where urban space has become degraded it is generally because the community and policy makers have disconnected from the area.

Degraded urban areas are often viewed as blight on the landscape. However, out of the challenge comes opportunity. At Gyllin's Garden in Malmö, Sweden, community groups and landscape architects worked together to formalise community use of the derelict nursery site. The community took 'ownership' of the space when the legal owner moved out. Eventually the municipality decided to formalise the arrangement, protecting some of the land and developing other areas for housing and schools. During the process of reclaiming the green space for the city, what was abstract space became conventional. Landscape architects, using the metaphor of a room or enclosure, made a visual analysis of topography and vegetation. This then facilitated an interpretation of the potential of the outdoor environment in terms of rooms, and allowed spaces to be classified as open or enclosed. From there it was an easy step to create contrasts, sequences and rhythm and a sense of direction. The wild nature of the garden was retained where it was considered important, both from a regenerating planting point of view and for unstructured use. The community valued being able to create their own paths, pick seasonal fruit as it ripened on the trees and bushes, and tend certain plants for their own horticultural satisfaction. Being allowed to bring their secateurs into the garden and use them, in certain areas, as they saw fit was an important part of community ownership of the public green space project (Qvistrōm, 2012).

The project, from the city's point of view, paused in 2012 to consider the potential effects of proposed interventions; reclassification of open space as closed and formal paths replacing seasonal, self-determined routes could fundamentally alter the accessibility and desirability of the green space. In its current form it is valued by local residents and developers. Adjacent land prices have risen as the city has expanded out around the green space to envelop what was urban fringe.

Green space can be discovered once derelict machinery is removed from an old industrial site, when a building site is deemed uneconomic to rebuild after a storm,

Figure 14.4 New York, USA: trees planted along the old railway line add healing nature connections in the city.

Source: Jenny Brown.

flood, earthquake or other natural disaster; or as in New York when the elevated freight railway line was abandoned. In New York the community group Friends of the Highline was formed with a view to preserving the heritage of the freight line, and also as a unique opportunity to link areas of the city. It took eleven years and US$173 million for the vision to come to fruition, but as the group gained support and funding, momentum grew and with it the scope of the park expanded. Place making may not have been a stated aim or a term known to the 'Friends of' group but that is exactly what they set out to achieve. The 'park in the sky' has created public green space in an old industrial part of town. The 2.4-km (1.5-mile) old rail line on Manhattan's West Side was visited by 2 million people in its first year of opening. It is now a recognised part of New York's tourist attractions, as well as offering free health and well-being benefits to local residents who choose to access it in their lunch hour, on the way to work, with the family on the weekend or as an outdoor studio for their art. A place where anyone can get up above the shade of the buildings and feel the sun on their face, admire the view and bathe in the green space became the vision and the reality of the Friends community group. The 23rd Street Lawn is a favourite gathering space, with an open, green space for picnicking, sunbathing and marvelling at human individuality.

Figure 14.5 New York, USA: trees planted to provide shade over the seating area soften the effect of hard seating set in anti-social rows.

Source: Jenny Brown.

The idea of creating a ribbon of green space using disused railways is now being copied in other cities. In Rotterdam, the Netherlands, the Hofplein Viaduct is being rejuvenated to a (semi-) public recreational area. Designed by architects and community groups, it is hoped to be an essential influence on the quality of life of local residents. It will also be a leading contributor to the qualitative upgrading of the northern districts. Manchester, Singapore, Chile and numerous cities around the USA and Canada all have projects inspired by the Highline on the drawing board. As China and other newly industrialised countries seek to mitigate air pollution they will need to create more green space. Sometimes a bottom-up or community-led approach works well, but sometimes a municipality or local government agency can gift land to the people to develop as they see fit. In that instance 'Friends of' groups appear almost overnight as the community effects a locally appropriate response. Track building, habitat restoration, stream clean-ups, regeneration planting, community garden, play space projects, seating and viewing platforms are evident across the range of cities and sites.

Developing a sense of place through public green space is a powerful mental health tool. When a person identifies strongly with an area, feels attached to it and a valued part of the community, their mental health is stronger than for those who do not have such attachments (Jones, 2013).

A wide open, natural, prairie-style area; a living wall of creepers and climbers as shown in Figure 14.3 earlier; or cultivated gardens for local food growing can all be described as green space. Their key feature is that the land is not paved over or built on – other than the occasional small garden shed or kiosk.

City farms and urban agriculture

The Transition Towns movement is one example of a movement that developed within communities around the world as a positive response to peak oil and climate change. Tasking themselves with finding ways to lower their carbon footprint and adapt homes and lifestyles to climate change has led some community groups, such as in Totnes, England, to establish a local currency as well as local food growing initiatives. As happened in Cuba after the oil crisis following the Soviet Union's collapse in 1991, the people of Totnes aim to grow food, study and work locally. Spare land has been made available and accessible to people of the town as growing space. So-called bottom-up initiatives are a powerful way to bring a community closer together, socially and economically. Skills and experience are shared and cooperation is valued.

Urban agriculture developments are not restricted to Transition Towns. Communities in cities in North America, Europe and South America are benefiting from city farms and the experience of being around animals. When we talk about a disconnection from nature it is not just experience of butterflies in their natural habitat that we lack, but also knowledge of where our milk and meat come from. A 2013 study of 27,500 5–16 year old children in England found that 30 per cent of them thought cheese came from a plant and 10 per cent believed potatoes grew on a tree (BNF, 2013). Twenty-one per cent of the surveyed children under 12 years of age had never been on a farm. 'This may go part way to explaining why over a

Figure 14.6 City farm, Mauerplatz, Berlin, Germany.

Source: Karsten Wachholtz.

Figure 14.7 Berlin, Germany: currant bushes in public green space encourage people to pick and eat, providing fresh, free, healthy food. This passive public health promotion is cost effective for the city.

third (34 per cent) of 5–8 year olds and 17 per cent of 8–11 year olds believe that pasta comes from animals', says Roy Ballam, education programme manager at the British Nutrition Foundation. With childhood obesity rates increasing it is important that we make as many linkages as possible with living things in general, and to our food supply in particular.

At the same time as community groups are finding ways to improve the amount of green space around their towns, increasing numbers of municipalities are legislating for more green space. Biophilia is being recognised as an important influence in liveability ratings. As urban centres compete for commerce they are working harder to make themselves more attractive to prospective householders as well as investors. In cities like Wellington, New Zealand, Scottsdale, Arizona, New York City, Shanghai and Singapore, administrators are seeing the benefits of nature in the city with increased tourism and improved quality of life for residents. In Singapore most people live in high rise apartments, but enjoy a wealth of connected parks and gardens, at ground, wall and rooftop level. The city shifted from being a garden city to one that aspires to be a city in a garden (Beatley, 2011).

Top-down programmes require significant community engagement to succeed in the long term. Bottom-up, community-led initiatives such as the urban agriculture project in Berlin shown in Figure 14.9, have a much higher chance of success. We are called in to assist both types of greening projects. Regardless of whether it is a public or private project, it is important to engage the wider community, beyond the immediate interest group, to gauge their awareness, support and the resources they may be able to bring to the project. Community consultation and co-design are vital for the success of a community initiative. However, the process requires careful guidance to ensure the best result. 'Design by committee' has been a problem for many projects, both commercial and community-based. As with all design, it is important to achieve a balance between forcing your views on the group and educating them, if necessary, to the possibilities.

Urban forests and healthy active lifestyles

In areas affected by natural disasters, often the best way to achieve cost-effective healing of the people is through the landscape. In 2012, the New Zealand Forest Research Institute, SCION, approached me to design and develop an urban forest as an over-sized healing garden for the people of Christchurch. After the devastating earthquakes of 2010 and 2011, large areas of the city were found to be uneconomic or unsafe to rebuild on. Many people lost their homes and their livelihoods. The mental health of the community deteriorated as stress levels rose. Alongside growing levels of depression, poor lifestyle choices meant increasing incidences of alcohol and drug abuse, obesity and sexually transmitted diseases. With a necessary triage system in place, only the most pressing concerns are dealt with. The cost to society in terms of dysfunctional families, unproductive workplaces, delayed development

Figure 14.9 Urban agriculture projects, done well, form an oasis in the city and a healthy nature connection point, as well as providing a local food supply.

of children, delayed treatment for the elderly, and large areas of space inaccessible to disabled people, is growing. How will an urban forest help? The 'Residential Red Zone' incudes almost 150 hectares of previously occupied residential land, adjacent to the Avon River. It is to be demolished and redeveloped as healing green space. People want a memorial to the communities who once lived there, acknowledging their home gardens as part of the ecological legacy. They want somewhere beautiful to sit quietly and reflect. They want a place they feel a connection with, to walk the dog, cycle with the kids, make new friendships. They don't expect the new urban forest to give them back their past, but to offer a sense of hope and renewal.

The design of the urban forest incorporates open parkland, natural playgrounds, extensive walking and cycling trails, with connections to new and existing built areas of the city. The cost of the project is estimated to be $3 million. The total cost of the social impact has not been calculated, but health interventions alone are already in the tens of millions. As mentioned in Chapter 13, the social determinants of health and well-being are of critical importance. If we can create community green space that offers a healing function we must take that opportunity.

Figure 14.10 Brisbane, Australia: shade trees planted in the middle of this walkway take a hard, aggressive-feeling urban environment and make it attractive and welcoming.

Urban forests do not necessarily comprise just large blocks of trees. Street trees can be planted to create a continuous green swathe through a town or city. In Brisbane, Australia, street trees are planted to create an urban forest. They serve to cool the air, filter airborne pollutants, and shade pedestrians. Street trees also bring the opportunity to for local residents and shopkeepers to garden at their base, as we saw in Berlin in Chapter 13.

Community gardens

Community gardens are spaces developed for the community to grow food and flowers. They are run on a co-operative basis, unlike allotment gardens which are individually organised and managed. Community gardens are being developed on the roofs of office buildings, and on the top floor/open deck of unused car parking buildings, as well as on vacant land throughout towns and cities. Due to the nature of ownership of the land/space, lease agreements tend to be short term, which can lend a precarious feel to the development. For the long term success of community garden initiatives it is helpful for gardeners to be able to plan ahead at least through a full cycle of the seasons. As access arrangements are made, explanation of the growing seasons may be needed for the landowner to fully appreciate the situation.

Goals for a typical community garden include:

1 Provision of an attractive, functional space for multi-generational groups to come together, outdoors.
2 Provision of sheltered outdoor dining and cooking facilities, e.g. BBQ, pizza, tandoor oven, picnic tables and seating.
3 Provision of good quality, fresh local food.
4 Provision of safe, natural play opportunities.
5 Reduction or elimination of toxic and hazardous substances in the garden and surrounding environment, e.g. through composting, mulching and companion planting.
6 Increased use of renewable energy resources.
7 Using resources and materials efficiently.
8 Selecting materials and products to minimise safety hazard and life-cycle environmental impact (e.g. local materials and lowest 'embodied energy' materials).
9 Promotion of an active healthy lifestyle, thus locating gardens near public facilities such as schools and on skate, cycle and pedestrian routes.
10 Use of found, recycled and repurposed materials.
11 Salvage and recycling of construction waste and building materials during construction and demolition.
12 Implementing maintenance and operational practices that reduce or eliminate harmful effects on people and the natural environment.
13 Reuse of existing infrastructure, locating facilities near public transportation and housing.
14 Considering off-site impacts such as storm water discharge and water quality.
15 Bringing the community together through the design process.

Figure 14.11 Low-cost, edible garden interventions in a public park can be added as a temporary or permanent feature.

Figure 14.12 London: a calm, communal public space, with edible planting, in a therapeutic garden for people living with post-traumatic stress.

Figure 14.13 Playing with building materials in a preschool, Berlin, Germany.

Social and therapeutic horticulture

Social and therapeutic horticulture (shortened to 'horticultural therapy' or simply STH) is the process of using gardening to facilitate the individual's development at vulnerable stages in their lives, which includes those with physical disabilities, learning difficulties, mental health problems, social isolation and long term unemployed. Through carefully structured programmes, STH aims to:

- provide the work experience, skills and practical qualifications that can lead to permanent employment;
- bring individuals who are alienated – for whatever reason – back into a caring and sustaining community;
- help rehabilitate individuals by building confidence and social skills;
- restore strength, self-confidence and mobility after illness, trauma or accident;
- provide a peaceful, restorative haven for those recovering from illness and for those whose illness is terminal.

In Causeway Bay on Hong Kong Island, a therapeutic horticulture programme was established as part of a chinese medicine health centre. The design of the garden, called 'Serene Oasis', includes colourful flowers, vegetable gardens and a

ABOVE: **Figure 14.14** Wellington, New Zealand: teenage girls ride scooters and skateboards to school, encouraging active transport through salutogenic urban design principles.

RIGHT: **Figure 14.15** Garden tools for community gardens.

BELOW: **Figure 14.16** Concept sketch of plans for local food initiative gardens, showing growing areas, communal social space, and pond to attract beneficial wildlife to combat plant pests, orientated for maximum sunshine on south facing slope. Designed by Greenstone Design UK.

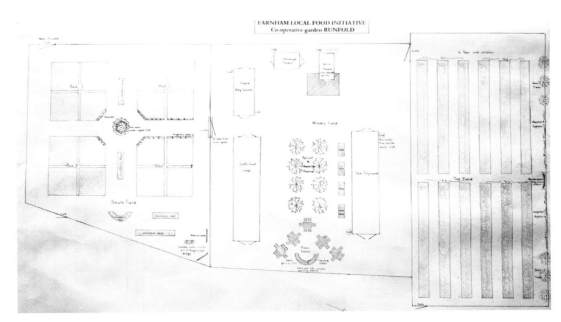

water wall, to help stimulate the senses of visitors. Green space in densely populated Hong Kong is highly valued and the role gardens play in health and well-being is equally acknowledged, so much so that the Hong Kong and Shanghai Banking Corporation Limited and the Community Chest of Hong Kong support the centre's programme.

The project integrated the concept of greenery and social services to set up the first horticultural therapy garden in the urban area of Hong Kong. 'Serene Oasis' is 7,000 square feet in size, and serves as a training venue for horticultural therapy expertise as well as providing horticultural therapy and related social services, in order to promote the application of the service.

Conclusion

We have seen the benefits of a broad-scale application of landscape-led interventions for health and well-being. Sensory, healing and therapeutic gardens can engage and encourage people of all backgrounds, ages and abilities to reconnect socially and with nature.

Figure 14.17 Auckland, New Zealand: rounded forms in city square create a soothing, welcoming respite from the busy outside streets.

As a value proposition, soft landscape treatments have been shown to be a cost-efficient health promotion tool. Numerous studies have been cross-referenced across multi-disciplinary research in support of the case for increased green space within our towns and cities. Where previously we only had anecdotal, qualitative data, now longitudinal studies are starting to come through showing clear correlations between time spent in nature and follow-on health effects. As the urban environment is softened with green space, economic and social benefits are also seen.

Disability, urban degradation and an ageing population provide an excellent opportunity to address contemporary issues through cost-effective environmental enhancements. Healing landscapes are not to be restricted to healthcare environments. Community health gains are maximised when gardens are introduced across parks, housing, schools and workplaces. City office rooftops afford additional space to green the urban centre.

Evidence of the benefit of a salutogenic approach is accepted by the World Health Organisation and the United Nations, amongst others. They asked for an innovative asset-based healthcare option. *Landscape and Urban Design for Health and Well-Being: Using healing, sensory and therapeutic gardens* provides that.

References

Beatley, P. T. (2011). *Biophilic cities: integrating nature into urban design*. Washington, DC: Island Press.

BNF (2013). *Cheese comes from plants and fish fingers are made of chicken*. London: British Nutrition Foundation.

Greenspace Scotland (2011). Definition greenspace. Retrieved 2 September 2013, from Greenspace Scotland: www.greenspacescotland.org.uk/definition.aspx

Jones, L. (2013, 24 February). Ph.D. Interviewed by the author.

Qviström, M. (2012). Taming the wild. In A. J. Keenan, *Urban wildscapes* (p. 195). New York: Routledge.

APPENDIX 1

Plants for natural play spaces

Plant name	Evergreen (E), deciduous (D), semi-evergreen (SE)	Use/benefit	Flowering, Y/N	Fruiting, Y/N	Attractive to wildlife, Y/N
Climbers					
Clematis	D or SE	Fast growing, covers fences and arbours with fragrant flowers, varieties available for year-round interest	Y	N	N
Honeysuckle	D	Fast growing, fragrant flowers, edible fruit, covers fences, will grow up fruit trees	Y	Y	Y
Passiflora	D	Attractive flower, edible fruit, glossy leaf, needs support to climb up walls	Y	Y	Y
Rosa 'Madam Alfred Carrier'	SE	Glossy leaves reflect light, fragrant repeat flowering, will cover ugly fences and scramble up small trees	Y	N	N
Shrubs					
Cotoneaster sp.	E	Good screening plant to hide boundaries	Y	Y	Y
Hebe sp.	E	Glossy leaf reflects light, dense foliage makes good shelter for hide and seek	Y	N	Y
Lavendula	E	Powerful natural oils released when crushed or brushed, edible	Y	N	Y
Rosemarinus sp.	E	Powerful natural oils released when crushed or brushed, edible	Y	N	Y

Plant name	Evergreen (E), deciduous (D), semi-evergreen (SE)	Use/benefit	Flowering, Y/N	Fruiting, Y/N	Attractive to wildlife, Y/N
Trees					
Betula sp.	D	Smooth bark feels great, plant immediately adjacent to paths. Casts light shade	N	N	N
Chitalpa	E	Fast growing drought tolerant	Y	N	Y
Ficus carica	E	Fast growing, casts deep shade in hot climates, edible fruit	Y	Y	Y
Malus sp. (apples)	D	Climbing – low branching habit is ideal. Dwarf root stock means trees grow to a maximum of 2–3 m (6–8ft), edible fruit. Casts dappled light shade	Y	Y	Y
Pittosporum sp.	E	Fast growing, attractive small leaf, pliable foliage won't break easily. Insignificant, fragrant flowers smell like vanilla	Y	Y	Y
Salix sp.	D	Grows readily from whips, can be woven into living willow bowers, tunnels, huts and hide-outs. Salix tortuosa creates a curtain of leaves in summer when mature, making an ideal private hide-out underneath the branches (do not allow maintenance to trim). Casts dappled shade, depending on variety	N	N	N

Accessible and inclusive design features for children

Benefit	Design element
Give protection from the elements, and vary sensory input	Shade and shelter whether planted or built
To promote mental health and well-being	Area/s where children can go if they wish to sit quietly or feel safe away from the rough and tumble of the main activity areas
Healthy eating, healthy living lifestyle message	Access to drinking water to be provided in the form of outdoor water fountains
Designed/manufactured features can limit imaginative use whereas a simple enclosed structure can become a magic carpet to go anywhere a child's imagination takes it.	Fixed elements and equipment should be versatile
Shade, scent, flowers and fruit at eye height, and easy picking height for healthy local urban food supply	A seating or walkway area framed by a simple pergola can have vines or fruit grown over it
Children and adults can stop, pause and 'smell the roses'	Seating – comfortable for elderly and disabled carers and young children, with backs for support and arms for ease of use
Sensory sound input	The addition of wind chimes will change the feeling of the area
Children and adults with disabilities require facilities adjacent to any public space where we want them to spend more than 20 minutes	Bathroom (toilet) and change facilities
Individuality can be expressed	Children's artwork, pathways designed and developed with children, local school or sports team' s colours used in planting

Source: With thanks to Richard Louv, *Last Child in the Woods: Saving Our Children from Nature-Deficit Disorder*, pp. 131–32.

Glossary of disability related terms

The following glossary of terms is reproduced by kind permission of Dr Kirby Alby at the Centre for Improvement of Child Caring (Alvy, 2013). It is a US-based resource but includes general terms used internationally that you may come across as clients present their brief for a healing garden.

The glossary, while devised by CICC parenting.org, has been edited for an international audience and to be broadly applicable to both adult and child disability. Advocacy groups for each condition you may encounter are in many countries around the world. An online search will find additional resources on specific features required by specific user groups. It is outside the scope of this book to detail them here.

Glossary

ADA (US)   Americans with Disabilities Act

Adaptive Development   Adaptive development is sometimes referred to as self-care or daily living skills. The child may use skills that they have already developed, or it may be necessary to acquire new skills.

Adjusted Age   The age of a child, less the number of weeks the child was born premature. For example, if a child was born 8 weeks premature, and currently is 20 weeks old, the adjusted age is 12 weeks.

Aetiology   The causes of a disease.

Affect   The observable emotion or feeling state of an individual. Examples include anger, sadness, hope, and joy.

Age Appropriate   The age, or level, that most children can accomplish the tasks being considered.

Anomaly   A significant difference or deviation from what is standard or common.

Asperger's Disorder or Asperger's Syndrome   The essential features are severe and sustained impairment in social interaction and the development of restricted, repetitive patterns of behaviour, interests, and activities. The disturbance must cause clinically significant impairment in social, occupational, or other important areas of functioning. In contrast to Autistic Disorder, there are no clinically significant delays or deviance in language acquisition (e.g., single non-echoed words are used communicatively by age 2 years, and spontaneous communicative phrases are used by age 3 years), although more subtle aspects of social communication (e.g. typical give-and-take in conversation) may be affected.

Assistive Technology   Devices, equipment, or services used to help assist a person with special needs. For example, a computer word program may be used for a child who has difficulty with fine motor skills and handwriting.

Attachment   A special relationship between a newborn child and its primary caregiver, usually the mother.

Attention-Deficit/Hyperactive Disorder   The essential feature is a persistent pattern of inattention and/or hyperactivity-impulsivity that is more frequently displayed and more severe than is typically observed in children at a comparable level of development.

Attuned Response   A form of reply to a person that reveals an understanding of what has been communicated.

Audiologist   A healthcare professional who specialises in the branch of science, especially the treatment of individuals with hearing loss or impairment

Autism   A developmental disorder that is present prior to the age of 3 that affects normal development of communication and social skills. Other behaviours that may be present include preoccupation with parts of objects, hand or finger flapping (self-stimulating behaviour), body rocking or self-injurious behaviour.

Autistic Spectrum Disorder   A developmental disorder that is present prior to the age of 3 that affects normal development of communication and social skills. Other behaviours that may be present include preoccupation with parts of objects, hand or finger flapping (self-stimulating behaviour), body rocking or self-injurious behaviour. Autism is usually considered on a spectrum ranging from the more severe autistic disorder usually detected early in a child's life, to high functioning autism which may not be identified until later.

Behavioural Difficulties   Problems in an individual's way of acting, behaving, or conducting him/herself. A child with behavioural difficulties may have difficulty following the rules of the classroom at school.

Birth Defect   A structural, functional, or metabolic abnormality present at birth that results in physical or mental disability or is fatal. There are more than 4,000 known birth defects, which may be caused by genetic or environmental factors. About 150,000 babies are born each year with birth defects.

Blindness   Refers to a condition in an individual of the inability to see, or the loss of normal or correctable vision. This is usually due to damage or disorders of the eyes, or of the area of the brain that is responsible for vision.

Brain Injury   Damage or trauma to the brain. The extent of the damage is often influenced by the age of the person at time of injury and the sections of the brain that are affected.

Breathing Tube   An endotracheal (breathing) tube is used to assist breathing. One end is connected to a ventilator (breathing machine), the other is passed through the vocal cords.

Cerebral Palsy   A condition caused by damage to the brain that results in problems with movement and posture. This damage usually occurs during the time the brain is developing before, during or soon after birth. The term cerebral involves the brain, and palsy refers to a problem with muscle control, movement or posture.

Childcare Providers   Professionals who provide care for children when parents or primary caregivers are not available. A mother may place her child in an infant daycare setting with a childcare provider, for example, while she is at work.

Chronological Age   The actual age of a person (e.g. 2 years and 4 months).

Cognitive   Refers to the process of thought, or thinking.

Cognitive Abilities   The various ways people become mentally aware of their surroundings. These mental processes include functions such as, learning, perception, memory, imagination, and use of language.

Cognitive Development   The development of the functions of the brain including perception, memory, imagination and use of language.

Communicate   Pass information from one person to another; to make something known. People communicate both verbally (through words) and non-verbally (through facial expressions, body movements, etc.).

Communication   The process of passing information from one person to another; to make something known. People communicate both verbally (through words) and non-verbally (through facial expressions, body movements, etc.).

Communication Development   The process of growth whereby a child acquires and masters the necessary skills to pass information to, and receive information from, another person.

Conduct Disorder   The essential feature is a repetitive and persistent pattern of behaviour in which the basic rights of others or major age-appropriate societal norms or rules are violated.

Congenital   Any trait or condition that exists from birth.

Daily Living Skills   The necessary tasks and functions required to function on a daily or regular basis. As children grow and develop, additional skills become necessary.

Deafness   Refers to a condition in an individual in which there is a total or partial loss of the sense of hearing in one or both ears, or in the area of the brain that is responsible for hearing.

Delivery (birth)   The process of giving birth.

Development   The process of growth whereby a child acquires and masters skills in the areas of motor, cognitive, language, social-emotional and adaptive functioning.

Developmental Assessment   A developmental assessment is a comprehensive examination of a child's skills, behaviours, and family situation, conducted by a highly trained professional like a licensed psychologist. This in-person examination usually includes testing the child, using a variety of professional instruments like language, intelligence and social adaptation tests, and the careful interviewing of the child's family members. The best types of developmental assessments also include observations of children in natural settings like the home, school, the playground, etc., as well as being done by a team of experts, including psychologists, pediatricians, neurologists, etc. These comprehensive assessments should conclude with detailed treatment plans on how best to help the child and family, with clear objectives and time lines for accomplishing the needed help.

Developmental Coordination Disorder   The essential feature is a marked impairment in the development of motor coordination. The diagnosis is made only if this impairment significantly interferes with academic achievement or activities of daily living and if the coordination difficulties are not due to a general medical condition (e.g. cerebral palsy, hemiplegia, or muscular dystrophy).

Developmental Delay   A term used to describe the development of children who have not reached various milestones in the time frame that is typical for children of his or her chronological age in one or more areas of functioning.

Developmental Disability   A mental or physical condition beginning in childhood manifesting the following: (1) the child acquires skills at a slower rate than his or her peers, (2) the condition is expected to go on indefinitely, and (3) the condition restricts the child's ability to function in society.

Developmental Milestones   An important achievement in a person's growth, such as a child's first words or steps.

Developmental Stage   An extended period of time during the growth process where the thoughts, behaviours, and feelings of an individual remain relatively the same.

Developmentally Disabled   A person who, in the course of their growth, becomes substantially impaired either physically or mentally. Their basic life activities such as hearing, seeing, speaking, walking, caring for oneself, learning, or working are significantly affected.

Diagnosis   Identification of a disease, disorder, or syndrome through a method of consistent analysis.

Diagnostic and Statistical Manual of Mental Disorders (US)   The fourth edition includes guidelines and criteria for diagnosing and classifying mental disorders.

Disability   A substantially limiting physical or mental impairment which affects basic life activities such as hearing, seeing, speaking, walking, caring for oneself, learning, or working.

Disabled   Individuals who display a substantially limiting physical or mental impairment which affects basic life activities such as hearing, seeing, speaking, walking, caring for oneself, learning or working.

Down's Syndrome   A genetic syndrome in which a child usually experiences development delays and often has concurrent medical conditions including mental retardation, a small mouth, and short height.

DSM IV (US)   The fourth edition of the *Diagnostic and Statistical Manual of Mental Disorders* includes guidelines and criteria for diagnosing and classifying mental disorders.

Early Development   The growth of children in the formative years often identified from birth to 5 years of age.

Early Head Start   Head Start is a preschool programme for the children of families with low income started by the US federal government in 1965. Early Head Start, established in 1994, serves infants and toddlers (birth to age 3) for qualifying low-income families.

Early Intervention   Specific services which are provided to infants and toddlers who show signs of, or are at risk of, having a developmental delay. These services are often tailored to the specific needs of each child with the goal of furthering development. Early intervention services are often provided at no cost to children who qualify and their families.

Early Start Program (US)   A federally funded early intervention programme administered in each state providing treatment and other support services for children aged from birth to 3 who either have a developmental delay in one or more areas, or are at risk for developmental delay.

Emotional Development   Emotional development involves the ways children understand, express and learn to regulate their emotions as they grow.

Emotional Disturbance   A qualifying term under the Individuals with Disabilities Education Act that refers to an individual who exhibits chronic difficulties in the emotional and behavioural areas.

Encopresis   The essential feature is repeated passage of faeces into inappropriate places (e.g. clothing or floor). Most often this is involuntary but occasionally may be intentional. The event must occur at least once a month for at least 3 months, and the chronological age of the child must be at least 4 years (or for children with developmental delays, a mental age of at least 4 years).

Enuresis   The essential feature is repeated voiding of urine during the day or at night into bed or clothes. Most often this is involuntary but occasionally may be intentional. To qualify for a diagnosis of enuresis, the voiding of urine must occur at least twice per week for at least 3 months or else must cause clinically significant distress or impairment in social, academic (occupational), or other important areas of functioning. The child must have reached an age at which continence is expected (i.e. the chronological age of the child must be at least 5 years, or, for children with developmental delays, a mental age of at least 5 years).

Epilepsy   A seizure disorder of the brain characterised by abnormal electrical discharge in the brain, sometimes accompanied by convulsions, or lack of consciousness. Epilepsy is the repeated pattern of seizures.

Established Risk   When a child has already been identified with a condition known to be related to as developmental delay or disability or other medical conditions impacting on the child's development.

Expressive Language   The verbal and non-verbal elements of communicating to others.

Expressive Language Disorder   The essential feature is an impairment in expressive language development as demonstrated by scores on standardised, individually administered measures of expressive language development which are substantially below the scores obtained from standardised measures of both non-verbal intellectual capacity and receptive language development.

Failure to Thrive   A condition in some children below the third percentile in weight and height (compared to other children of the same age) caused by problems with feeding and/or caregiving.

Feeding Disorder of Infancy or Early Childhood   The essential feature is the persistent failure to eat adequately, as reflected in significant failure to gain weight or significant weight loss over at least 1 month.

Fine Motor Skills   Abilities that require coordination of the small muscles of the body such as picking up a small block with a thumb and finger.

Functional Development   Children grow, develop, and function in various areas called domains. These domains include cognitive, communication, motor, adaptive, social/emotional and sensory.

Functional Developmental Approach   One of the ways a person is defined as having a special need. A child is assessed in the functional areas of child development, including such domains as cognitive, communication, motor, adaptive, social/emotional and sensory.

Gait   The movement and style of the feet and legs as a person walks. Adults have symmetrical gait where both legs move at the same time, creating the appearance of one moving forward and one moving backwards in relation to the body. Toddlers often have unsymmetrical gait where this movement does not occur.

Genetic Condition   Traits or a disorder that have been passed through the genes by one or both parents to the child.

Genetic Disorder   Biological traits are transmitted from one generation to the next through genes. Problems occur when diseases are passed to the next generation. Common genetic diseases include cystic fibrosis and sickle-cell anaemia.

Genetics   The study of the transmission of biological traits from one generation to the next.

Gestation   The period of time during which an unborn baby develops in the mother's uterus with the average being 38–42 weeks.

Gross Motor Skills   Abilities that require coordination of the large muscles of the body such as arms and legs. Examples include jumping or climbing.

Head Start Program (US)   A preschool programme for the children of families with low income started by the federal government in 1965. Ten per cent or more of the children served are children with special needs. The programme's goal is to help children attain their potential before beginning school.

ICD-9   A standardised coding resource used by physicians and other healthcare professionals to identify various diseases and conditions. Categorised into seventeen different areas, the coding system ranges from 001 to 999. The *International Classification of Disorders* is in its ninth edition.

IEP, Individualised Education Plan (US)   Every child receiving special education must have a written. Individualised Education Program (IEP). This written programme plan states the individual goals for the child, and the accommodations and services the school district agrees to provide for the child receiving special education.

IFSP, The Individual Family Service Plan (US)   IFSP stands for Individual Family Service Plan. By federal and state laws this plan is intended to document the delivery of community-based, interagency services for families with young children who have disabilities.

Inclusion   For children with special needs or disabilities, inclusion means full participation in programmes designed for typically developing children.

Intervention   Treatment or assistance given to improve a deficit or a lag in mental or physical functioning.

Language   There are two different parts of language, the type we receive (receptive language) and the part we send (expressive language). Receptive language involves the understanding of thoughts, feelings, desires and the needs of others. Expressive language involves the verbal and non-verbal elements of communicating to others.

Language Development Skills   The process through which an infant and young child acquires the capacity to communicate their wants, needs, feelings, and thoughts with another. Language development includes both receptive and expressive language development. Receptive language is the ability to receive and understand language. Expressive language is the ability to speak and use language to communicate with others.

Learning   The process of gaining knowledge and skills.

Learning Difficulties   A disorder involving difficulties in listening, speaking, reading, writing, spelling, or performing maths, where academic skills appear significantly below what would be expected given the person's intellectual capability.

Learning Disabilities   A disorder that impacts a person's ability to interpret what they see and hear and/or link information from different parts of the brain. These difficulties are not caused by mental retardation or known physical problems. Areas affected can include, but are not limited to, difficulty with language, reading, or writing, and attention.

Learning Disorders   are diagnosed when a child's achievement on individually administered, standardised tests in reading, mathematics or writen expression is substantially below that expected of the child's age, schooling and level of intelligence. The learning problems significantly interfere with academic achievement or activities of daily living that require reading, mathematical or writing skills.

Local Community Health Centres   Local medical clinics and facilities often dedicated to provide comprehensive medical services to all people

Mastered Skills   Children gain or acquire abilities at different stages of their growth. These abilities are gained in different areas or domains, such as movement (e.g. walking), thinking (e.g. the ability to solve certain problems), and language (e.g. speaking three-word sentences).

Mathematical Disorder   The essential feature is mathematic ability (as measured by individually administered standardised tests of mathematical calculation or reasoning) that falls substantially below that expected of the child's chronological age, measured intelligence, and age-appropriate education

Medi-Cal (US)   Government-supported medical services for qualifying California residents. Known in other states as Medicaid.

Medical Risk Factors   A factor is a condition that brings about a result. A risk is a chance that something may occur. Therefore a medical risk factor involves the possibility that certain conditions may create or lead to a significant health problem or concern.

Memory   The mental process of retaining information that is learned and recalling it at a later point in time.

Mental Retardation   Intellectual functioning that is significantly below average, usually indicated by IQ scores below 70 coupled with significantly below average adaptive functioning.

Mentally Retarded   Sub-average intelligence (usually below 70 IQ) combined with difficulties in two or more areas required to function in the day-to-day world.

Motor   Movement of the body carried out by a combination of the brain, nervous system and muscles.

Motor Development   The process of growth whereby a child acquires and masters skills to be able to move their body. These are carried out by a combination of the brain, nervous system, and muscles.

Motor Skill   A person's capacity to move their body depends upon the development of motor abililties. These abilities, or skills, involve the use of large body movements (gross motor skills) and those that require small movements (fine motor skills).

Multiple Births   Referring to one mother carrying and delivering more than one infant during a particular pregnancy.

Multiple Disabilities   Having more than one disability.

Neonatal Intensive Care Unit (NICU)   A unit of a hospital where seriously ill or significantly premature newborns needing special care are tested. Typically those infants who are premature, born with a low birth weight, or who are seriously ill will be placed in the NICU.

Neonatologist   A medical doctor specialising in the care of newborn babies.

Neurobiological   An understanding of human functioning through two branches of medicine, neurology and biology. Neurology deals with the nervous system, including the brain and all the nerves in the body. Biology is the scientific study of the natural processes of living things.

Neurological Disorder   Various disorders or significant problems of the central nervous system.

Non-verbal   There are two types of interpersonal communication, verbal and non-verbal. Non-verbal communication includes information that is transmitted without words, through body language, gestures, facial expressions or the use of symbols.

Normal Development   The typical or usual development of children. Development norms are based on years of research and observations of the usual pattern of children's development, noting when most children of a chronological age have mastered specific skills.

Nurse–Family Partnership Program (US)   A programme dedicated to families at risk. Goals often include improvement of the outcome of pregnancy, support of the child's health, and increasing self-sufficiency for the young family.

Occupational Therapy   A type of healthcare treatment to improve self-help skills and adaptive behaviour for people with development delays, illnesses, or injuries that impede their ability to function independently. New skills are taught as well as assistance in the areas of motor and sensory development.

Ongoing Medical Condition   A chronic illness or disease that continues over a significant period of time.

Operational Stage   In cognitive or mental development, performing operations involves the ability to reason about events that have occurred (e.g., replaying in the mind the event of pouring water from one beaker to the next). Piaget's theory of cognitive development involves the Preoperational Stage (approx.

2–7), Concrete Operational Stage (approx. 7–11) and the Formal Operational Stage (approx. 11 and older).

Oppositional Defiant Disorder   The essential feature is a recurrent pattern of negativistic, defiant, disobedient, and hostile behaviour towards authority figures that persists for at least 6 months and is characterised by the frequent occurrence of at least four of the following behaviours: losing temper, arguing with adults, actively defying or refusing to comply with the requests or rules of adults, deliberately doing things that will annoy other people, blaming others for his or her own mistakes or misbehaviour, being touchy or easily annoyed by others, being angry and resentful, or being spiteful or vindictive.

Orthopedic Impairment   A condition of the skeletal system of the body that may result in restricted movement and with development delays, illnesses, or injuries that impede their ability to function.

Other Health Impairment (US)   A qualifying term under the Individuals with Disabilities Education Act that refers to an individual who exhibits chronic difficulties in the emotional and behavioural areas.

Parroting   A type of communication that involves repeating back to the sender almost the identical message that has been received. Some children with an autistic disorder parrot phrases heard from earlier conversations or television programmes.

Pediatrician   A medical doctor who specialises in the treatment and care of infants, children and adolescents.

Pervasive Developmental Disorder   Characterised by severe and pervasive impairment in several areas of development: reciprocal social interaction skills, communication skills, or the presence of stereotyped behaviour, interests, and activities.

Phonological Disorder   The essential feature is a failure to use developmentally expected speech sounds that are appropriate for the child's age and dialect. This may involve errors in sound production, use, representation, or organisation such as, but not limited to, substitutions of one sound for another (use of /t/ for target /k/ sound) or omissions of sounds (e.g. final consonants).

Physical Development   A healthy body grows and changes over time in every area, such as height, weight, muscle growth and bone thickness. Physical development encompasses the growth of the entire human body.

Physical Therapy   A type of treatment or therapy designed to help an individual who has difficulty with physical movement. The physical therapist uses heat, exercise, water and other treatments to help improve muscle strength, range of motion and motor skills.

Pica   The essential feature is the eating of one or more non-nutritive substances on a persistent basis for a period of at least 1 month. The typical substances ingested tend to vary with age. Infants and younger children typically eat paint, plaster, string, hair, or cloth. Older children may eat animal droppings, sand, insects, leaves, or pebbles.

Premature   A baby born before 37 weeks gestation (the time from conception to birth) is considered premature; when born before 32 weeks, a child is considered significantly premature.

Prenatal Development   The growth of an embryo and foetus from conception to birth. There are many factors, such as genetics and the mother's health, that influence the health of the child.

Problem Behaviour   A behaviour is a way a person acts, reacts, or functions. In the development of a child, certain behaviours may become a problem when they interfere with everyday functioning. Causes of these behaviours may include physical, emotional, or intellectual factors.

Problem Solving   The skill of trying different approaches to resolve a difficulty or problem. Children (and people of all ages) learn from this trial-and-error process helping them to resolve similar problems in a more efficient way.

Psychologist   A specialist in one or more areas of psychology, a field of science that studies the mind and behaviours. Areas of speciality can include psychological testing and practitioners of therapy or counselling.

Reading Disorder   The essential feature is reading achievement (i.e. reading accuracy, speed or comprehension as measured by individually administered standardised tests) that falls substantially below that expected given the child's chronological age, measured intelligence, and age-appropriate education.

Reasoning   Using systematic logical thinking to solve problems or come to a conclusion.

Receptive and Expressive Language Development   The process of growth whereby a child acquires and masters skills in the two different parts of language. Receptive language is the type we receive and expressive language is the part we send. Receptive language involves the understanding of thoughts, feelings, desires and the needs of others. Expressive language involves the verbal and non-verbal elements of communicating to others.

Receptive Language   Understanding the thoughts, feelings, desires, and needs communicated by others through verbal and non-verbal elements.

Regress   When a person retreats to a form of behaviour common to a younger person (e.g., a 13 year old wetting the bed). This can occur when a person is dealing with significant stress.

Respite Care   A short period of rest or relief. Parents of a child with a disability may qualify for respite services when a child is cared for by a third party, allowing the parent(s) to take care of other needs away from the child, like the needs of themselves or other children in the family.

Risk Factors   A factor is a condition that brings about a result. A risk is a chance that something may occur. With health concerns, and specifically **Special Needs**, certain conditions, such as genetics, may increase the possibility of diseases or disabilities developing.

Author's note: 'at risk' individuals describes children and adults likely to require intervention or care if lifestyle or environmental conditions persist.

Rumination Disorder   The essential feature is the repeated regurgitation and re-chewing of food occurring after feeding that develops in an infant or child after a period of normal functioning and lasts for at least 1 month. Partially digested food is brought up into the mouth without apparent nausea, retching, disgust, or associated gastrointestinal disorder. The food is then either ejected from the mouth or, more frequently, chewed and reswallowed.

Seizure   A condition when the brain fires electrical impulses at a rate up to four times higher than normal. Patterns of repeated seizures are referred to as epilepsy or

Seizure Disorder   A seizure disorder includes any condition of the brain in which there are repeated seizures. A seizure can be mild and brief, such as in many petit mal seizures where an individual may appear to have been daydreaming momentarily. Or they can be more dramatic, as in the violent uncontrollable contraction of a group of muscles and unconsciousness.

Selective Mutism   The essential feature is the persistent failure to speak in specific social situations (e.g. at school, with playmates) where speaking is expected, despite speaking in other situations. The disturbance must last for at least 1 month and is not limited to the first month of school (during which many children may be shy and reluctant to speak).

Self-Care   A person's ability to use certain skills and resources to attend to their own needs. At each age in life a society has certain expectations about what their members are to accomplish.

Self-Esteem   An overall evaluation of the self regarding a sense of worth. A person with a positive self-concept generally likes and feels good about who they are.

Self-Injurious Behaviour   Self-inflicted bodily harm. Harm done to the self by an individual. Individuals with an autistic spectrum disorder are often prone to self-injurious behaviour.

Sensorimotor Stage   The first stage of mental development according to theorist Jean Piaget. During the first 2 years of life children learn about the world through their five senses: touch, taste, hearing, vision and smell.

Sensory Integration   Information is received from both internal and external environments through the five senses of touch, taste, hearing, vision and smell. Our senses are integrated when the nervous system directs this information to the appropriate parts of the brain that enables an individual to attain skills.

Separation Anxiety Disorder   The essential feature is excessive anxiety concerning separation from the home or from those to whom the child is attached. This anxiety is beyond that which is expected for the child's developmental level. The disturbance must last for a period of at least 4 weeks, begin before age 18 years, and cause clinically significant distress or impairment in social, academic (occupational), or other important areas of functioning.

Service Eligibility   Conditions that must be met to qualify for particular resources and help.

Sign Language   A method of communicating using hand gestures. Individuals with a hearing loss or impairment often use this form of language.

Social Development   The process of development in which a child learns the skills, rules and values that will enable him or her to form connections and function among family members, peers and members of society.

Special Needs   The special or unique, out-of-the-ordinary concerns created by a person's medical, physical, mental, or developmental condition or disability. Additional services are usually needed to help a person in one or more of the following areas, among others: thinking, communication, movement, getting along with others, and taking care of oneself.

Specific Learning Disability   A disorder that affects a person's ability to interpret what they see and hear and/or link information from different parts of the brain in learning tasks. These difficulties are not caused by mental retardation or known physical problems. Specific areas can include, but are not limited to, such areas as reading, writing, or maths.

Speech   The act of talking, often involving a verbal interaction and communication with another person.

Speech and Language Therapy   Therapeutic treatment to address the concerns of speech and language impairments or deficits.

Speech or Language Impairment   Communication problems that have to do with speech disorders include not speaking at all, speaking at a later time in life than peers, substituting sounds, or difficulties with coordination of tongue, lips, and mouth to perform certain sounds.

Stuttering   The essential feature is a disturbance in the normal fluency and time patterning of speech that is inappropriate for the child's age. This disturbance is characterised by frequent repetitions or prolongations of sounds or syllables.

Syndrome   A group of signs or symptoms that are usually clustered together and characterise a disease or a condition. Down Syndrome is an example of a syndrome resulting from an extra chromosome that affects both the physical and intellectual development of the child.

Toddler   A child between the approximate ages of 1 and 3. Prior to age 1, children are referred to as infants, and at approximately age 3, they become preschoolers. The name toddler is used because of the way a young child toddles around when first learning to walk.

Tourette's Disorder   The essential features are multiple motor ticks and one or more vocal tics. These may appear simultaneously or at different periods during the illness. The tics occur many times a day, recurrently throughout a period of more than 1 year. During this period, there is never a tic-free period of more than three consecutive months. The onset of the disorder is before age 18 years.

Traumatic Brain Injury   Harm or damage to the brain causing different problems including loss or lack of cognitive abilities, seizures, and difficulties with movement and speaking.

Typical   Traits that are common to a specific group of people. Walking is typical for 2 year old children.

Ventilator   Also known as a respirator. A medical device with an attached tube inserted into the lungs that helps a person breathe when they cannot breathe on their own. The ventilator pumps oxygen into the lungs.

Visual Impairment   An individual with a visual impairment has a reduction in their ability to see, ranging from partial sight to total loss of vision.

Written Expression Disorder   The essential feature is writing skills (as measured by an individually administered standardised test or functional assessment of writing skills) that fall substantially below those expected given the child's chronological age, measured intelligence, and age-appropriate education.

Reference

Alvy, D. K. (2013). Glossary. Retrieved from *CICC*: www.ciccparenting.org/Glossary1.aspx

Index